W9-AUR-479

THE SOCIOLOGY AND PSYCHOLOGY OF TERRORISM: WHO BECOMES A TERRORIST AND WHY?

*A Report Prepared under an Interagency Agreement
by the Federal Research Division,
Library of Congress*

Author: Rex A. Hudson
Editor: Marilyn Majeska
Project Managers: Andrea M. Savada
                          Helen C. Metz

**University Press of the Pacific
Honolulu, Hawaii**

The Sociology and Psychology of Terrorism:
Who Becomes a Terrorist and Why?

by
Rex A. Hudson

for
Federal Research Division
Library of Congress

ISBN: 1-4102-1277-7

Copyright © 2005 by University Press of the Pacific

Reprinted from the 1999 edition

University Press of the Pacific
Honolulu, Hawaii
http://www.universitypressofthepacific.com

All rights reserved, including the right to reproduce
this book, or portions thereof, in any form.

PREFACE

The purpose of this study is to focus attention on the types of individuals and groups that are prone to terrorism (see Glossary) in an effort to help improve U.S. counterterrorist methods and policies.

The emergence of amorphous and largely unknown terrorist individuals and groups operating independently (freelancers) and the new recruitment patterns of some groups, such as recruiting suicide commandos, female and child terrorists, and scientists capable of developing weapons of mass destruction, provide a measure of urgency to increasing our understanding of the psychological and sociological dynamics of terrorist groups and individuals. The approach used in this study is twofold. First, the study examines the relevant literature and assesses the current knowledge of the subject. Second, the study seeks to develop psychological and sociological profiles of foreign terrorist individuals and selected groups to use as case studies in assessing trends, motivations, likely behavior, and actions that might deter such behavior, as well as reveal vulnerabilities that would aid in combating terrorist groups and individuals.

Because this survey is concerned not only with assessing the extensive literature on sociopsychological aspects of terrorism but also providing case studies of about a dozen terrorist groups, it is limited by time constraints and data availability in the amount of attention that it can give to the individual groups, let alone individual leaders or other members. Thus, analysis of the groups and leaders will necessarily be incomplete. A longer study, for example, would allow for the collection and study of the literature produced by each group in the form of autobiographies of former members, group communiqués and manifestos, news media interviews, and other resources. Much information about the terrorist mindset (see Glossary) and decision-making process can be gleaned from such sources. Moreover, there is a language barrier to an examination of the untranslated literature of most of the groups included as case studies herein.

Terrorism databases that profile groups and leaders quickly become outdated, and this report is no exception to that rule. In order to remain current, a terrorism database ideally should be updated periodically. New groups or terrorist leaders may suddenly emerge, and if an established group perpetrates a major terrorist incident, new information on the group is likely to be reported in news media. Even if a group appears to be quiescent, new information may become available about the group from scholarly publications.

There are many variations in the transliteration for both Arabic and Persian. The academic versions tend to be more complex than the popular forms used in the news media and by the Foreign Broadcast Information Service (FBIS). Thus, the latter usages are used in this study. For example, although Ussamah bin Ladin is the proper transliteration, the more commonly used Osama bin Laden is used in this study.

TABLE OF CONTENTS

EXECUTIVE SUMMARY: MINDSETS OF MASS DESTRUCTION

New Types of Post-Cold War Terrorists

In the 1970s and 1980s, it was commonly assumed that terrorist use of weapons of mass destruction (WMD) would be counterproductive because such an act would be widely condemned. "Terrorists want a lot of people watching, not a lot of people dead," Brian Jenkins (1975:15) opined. Jenkins's premise was based on the assumption that terrorist behavior is normative, and that if they exceeded certain constraints and employed WMD they would completely alienate themselves from the public and possibly provoke swift and harsh retaliation. This assumption does seem to apply to certain secular terrorist groups. If a separatist organization such as the Provisional Irish Republic Army (PIRA) or the Basque Fatherland and Liberty (Euzkadi Ta Askatasuna—ETA), for example, were to use WMD, these groups would likely isolate their constituency and undermine sources of funding and political support. When the assumptions about terrorist groups not using WMD were made in the 1970s and 1980s, most of the terrorist groups making headlines were groups with political or nationalist-separatist agenda. Those groups, with some exceptions, such as the Japanese Red Army (JRA—Rengo Sekigun), had reason not to sabotage their ethnic bases of popular support or other domestic or foreign sympathizers of their cause by using WMD.

Trends in terrorism over the past three decades, however, have contradicted the conventional thinking that terrorists are averse to using WMD. It has become increasingly evident that the assumption does not apply to religious terrorist groups or millenarian cults (see Glossary). Indeed, since at least the early 1970s analysts, including (somewhat contradictorily) Jenkins, have predicted that the first groups to employ a weapon of mass destruction would be religious sects with a millenarian, messianic, or apocalyptic mindset.

When the conventional terrorist groups and individuals of the early 1970s are compared with terrorists of the early 1990s, a trend can be seen: the emergence of religious fundamentalist and new religious groups espousing the rhetoric of mass-destruction terrorism. In the 1990s, groups motivated by religious imperatives, such as Aum Shinrikyo, Hizballah, and al-Qaida, have grown and proliferated. These groups have a different attitude toward violence—one that is extranormative and seeks to maximize violence against the perceived enemy, essentially anyone who is not a fundamentalist Muslim or an Aum Shinrikyo member. Their outlook is one that divides the world simplistically into "them" and "us." With its sarin attack on the Tokyo subway system on March 20, 1995, the doomsday cult Aum Shinrikyo turned the prediction of terrorists using WMD into reality.

Beginning in the early 1990s, Aum Shinrikyo engaged in a systematic program to develop and use WMD. It used chemical or biological WMD in about a dozen largely unreported instances in the first half of the 1990s, although they proved to be no more effective—actually less effective—than conventional weapons because of the terrorists' ineptitude. Nevertheless, it was Aum Shinrikyo's sarin attack on the Tokyo subway on March 20, 1995, that showed the world how dangerous the mindset of a religious terrorist group could be. The attack provided convincing evidence that Aum Shinrikyo probably would not hesitate to use WMD in a U.S. city, if it had an opportunity to do so. These religiously motivated groups would have no reason to take "credit" for such an act of mass destruction, just as Aum Shinrikyo did not take credit for its attack on the Tokyo subway, and just as Osama bin Laden did not take credit for various acts of high-casualty terrorism against U.S. targets in the 1990s. Taking credit means asking for retaliation. Instead, it is enough for these groups to simply take private satisfaction in knowing that they have dealt a harsh blow to what they perceive to be the "Great Satan." Groups unlikely to be deterred by fear of public disapproval, such as Aum Shinrikyo, are the ones who seek chaos as an end in itself.

The contrast between key members of religious extremist groups such as Hizballah, al-Qaida, and Aum Shinrikyo and conventional terrorists reveals some general trends relating to the personal attributes of terrorists likely to use WMD in coming years. According to psychologist Jerrold M. Post (1997), the most dangerous terrorist is likely to be the religious terrorist. Post has explained that, unlike the average political or social terrorist, who has a defined mission that is somewhat measurable in terms of media attention or government reaction, the religious terrorist can justify the most heinous acts "in the name of Allah," for example. One could add, "in the name of Aum Shinrikyo's Shoko Asahara."

Psychologist B.J. Berkowitz (1972) describes six psychological types who would be most likely to threaten or try to use WMD: paranoids, paranoid schizophrenics, borderline mental defectives, schizophrenic types, passive-aggressive personality (see Glossary) types, and sociopath (see Glossary) personalities. He considers sociopaths the most likely actually to use WMD. Nuclear terrorism expert Jessica

Stern (1999: 77) disagrees. She believes that "Schizophrenics and sociopaths, for example, may *want* to commit acts of mass destruction, but they are less likely than others to succeed." She points out that large-scale dissemination of chemical, biological, or radiological agents requires a group effort, but that "Schizophrenics, in particular, often have difficulty functioning in groups...."

Stern's understanding of the WMD terrorist appears to be much more relevant than Berkowitz's earlier stereotype of the insane terrorist. It is clear from the appended case study of Shoko Asahara that he is a paranoid. Whether he is schizophrenic or sociopathic is best left to psychologists to determine. The appended case study of Ahmed Ramzi Yousef, mastermind of the World Trade Center (WTC) bombing on February 26, 1993, reported here does not suggest that he is schizophrenic or sociopathic. On the contrary, he appears to be a well-educated, highly intelligent Islamic terrorist. In 1972 Berkowitz could not have been expected to foresee that religiously motivated terrorists would be prone to using WMD as a way of emulating God or for millenarian reasons. This examination of about a dozen groups that have engaged in significant acts of terrorism suggests that the groups most likely to use WMD are indeed religious groups, whether they be wealthy cults like Aum Shinrikyo or well-funded Islamic terrorist groups like al-Qaida or Hizballah.

The fall of the Berlin Wall in 1989 and the collapse of the Soviet Union in 1991 fundamentally changed the operating structures of European terrorist groups. Whereas groups like the Red Army Faction (Rote Armee Faktion—RAF; see Glossary) were able to use East Germany as a refuge and a source of logistical and financial resources during the Cold War decades, terrorist groups in the post Cold War period no longer enjoy the support of communist countries. Moreover, state sponsors of international terrorism (see Glossary) toned down their support of terrorist groups. In this new environment where terrorist groups can no longer depend on state support or any significant popular support, they have been restructuring in order to learn how to operate independently.

New breeds of increasingly dangerous religious terrorists emerged in the 1990s. The most dangerous type is the Islamic fundamentalist. A case in point is Ramzi Yousef, who brought together a loosely organized, ad hoc group, the so-called Liberation Army, apparently for the sole purpose of carrying out the WTC operation on February 26, 1993. Moreover, by acting independently the small self-contained cell led by Yousef prevented authorities from linking it to an established terrorist organization, such as its suspected coordinating group,

Osama bin Laden's al-Qaida, or a possible state sponsor.

Aum Shinrikyo is representative of the other type of religious terrorist group, in this case a cult. Shoko Asahara adopted a different approach to terrorism by modeling his organization on the structure of the Japanese government rather than an ad hoc terrorist group. Accordingly, Aum Shinrikyo "ministers" undertook a program to develop WMD by bringing together a core group of bright scientists skilled in the modern technologies of the computer, telecommunications equipment, information databases, and financial networks. They proved themselves capable of developing rudimentary WMD in a relatively short time and demonstrated a willingness to use them in the most lethal ways possible. Aum Shinrikyo's sarin gas attack in the Tokyo subway system in 1995 marked the official debut of terrorism involving WMD. Had a more lethal batch of sarin been used, or had the dissemination procedure been improved slightly, the attack might have killed thousands of people, instead of only a few. Both of these incidents—the WTC bombing and the Tokyo subway sarin attack—had similar casualty totals but could have had massive casualties. Ramzi Yousef's plot to blow up the WTC might have killed an estimated 50,000 people had his team not made a minor error in the placement of the bomb. In any case, these two acts in Manhattan and Tokyo seem an ominous foretaste of the WMD terrorism to come in the first decade of the new millennium.

(www.GreatBuildings.com/buildings/ World_Trade_Center.html)

Increasingly, terrorist groups are recruiting members with expertise in fields such as communications, computer programming, engineering, finance, and the sciences. Ramzi Yousef graduated from Britain's Swansea University with a degree in engineering. Aum Shinrikyo's Shoko Asahara recruited a scientific team with all the expertise needed to develop WMD. Osama bin Laden also recruits highly skilled professionals in the fields of engineering, medicine, chemistry, physics, computer programming, communications, and so forth. Whereas the skills of the elite terrorist commandos of the 1960s and 1970s were often limited to what they learned in training camp, the terrorists of the 1990s who have carried out major operations have included biologists, chemists, computer specialists, engineers, and physicists.

New Forms of Terrorist-Threat Scenarios

The number of international terrorist incidents has declined in the 1990s, but the potential threat posed by terrorists has increased. The increased threat level, in the form of terrorist actions aimed at achieving a larger scale of destruction than the conventional attacks of the previous three decades of terrorism, was dramatically demonstrated with the bombing of the WTC. The WTC bombing illustrated how terrorists with technological sophistication are increasingly being recruited to carry out lethal terrorist bombing attacks. The WTC bombing may also have been a harbinger of more destructive attacks of international terrorism in the United States.

Although there are not too many examples, if any, of guerrilla (see Glossary) groups dispatching commandos to carry out a terrorist operation in the United States, the mindsets of four groups discussed herein—two guerrilla/terrorist groups, a terrorist group, and a terrorist cult—are such that these groups pose particularly dangerous actual or potential terrorist threats to U.S. security interests. The two guerrilla/terrorist groups are the Liberation Tigers of Tamil Ealam (LTTE) and Hizballah, the terrorist group is al-Qaida, and the terrorist cult is Aum Shinrikyo.

The LTTE is not known to have engaged in anti-U.S. terrorism to date, but its suicide commandos have already assassinated a prime minister of India, a president of Sri Lanka, and a former prime minister of Sri Lanka. In August 1999, the LTTE reportedly deployed a 10-member suicide squad in Colombo to assassinate Prime Minister Chandrika Kumaratunga and others. It cannot be safely assumed, however, that the LTTE will restrict its terrorism to the South Asian subcontinent. Prabhakaran has repeatedly warned the Western nations providing military support to Sri Lanka that they are exposing their citizens to possible attacks. The LTTE, which has an extensive international network, should not be underestimated in the terrorist threat that it could potentially pose to the United States, should it perceive this country as actively aiding the Sri Lankan government's counterinsurgency campaign. Prabhakaran is a megalomaniac whose record of ordering the assassinations of heads of state or former presidents, his meticulous planning of such actions, his compulsion to have the acts photographed and chronicled by LTTE members, and the limitless supply of female suicide commandos at his disposal add a dangerous new dimension to potential assassination threats. His highly trained and disciplined Black Tiger commandos are far more deadly than Aum Shinrikyo's inept cultists. There is little protection against the LTTE's trademark weapon: a belt-bomb suicide commando.

Hizballah is likewise quite dangerous. Except for its ongoing terrorist war against Israel, however, it appears to be reactive, often carrying out terrorist attacks for what it perceives to be Western military, cultural, or political threats to the establishment of an Iranian-style Islamic republic in Lebanon.

The threat to U.S. interests posed by Islamic fundamentalist terrorists in particular was underscored by al-Qaida's bombings of the U.S. Embassies in Kenya and Tanzania in August 1998. With those two devastating bombings, Osama bin Laden resurfaced as a potent terrorist threat to U.S. interests worldwide. Bin Laden is the prototype of a new breed of terrorist—the private entrepreneur who puts modern enterprise at the service of a global terrorist network.

With its sarin attack against the Tokyo subway system in March 1995, Aum Shinrikyo has already used WMD, and very likely has not abandoned its quest to use such weapons to greater effect. The activities of Aum's large membership in Russia should be of particular concern because Aum Shinrikyo has used its Russian organization to try to obtain WMD, or at least WMD technologies.

The leaders of any of these groups—Prabhakaran, bin Laden, and Asahara—could become paranoid, desperate, or simply vengeful enough to order their suicide devotees to employ the belt-bomb technique against the leader of the Western World. Iranian intelligence leaders could order Hizballah to attack the U.S. leadership in retaliation for some future U.S. or Israeli action, although Iran may now be distancing itself from Hizballah. Whether or not a U.S. president would be a logical target of Asahara, Prabhakaran, or bin Laden is not a particularly useful guideline to assess the probability of such an attack. Indian Prime Minister Rajiv Gandhi was not a logical target for the LTTE, and his assassination had very negative consequences for the LTTE. In Prabhakaran's "psycho-logic," to use Post's term, he may conclude that his cause needs greater international attention, and targeting a country's top leaders is his way of getting attention. Nor does bin Laden need a logical reason, for he believes that he has a mandate from Allah to punish the "Great Satan." Instead of thinking logically, Asahara thinks in terms of a megalomaniac with an apocalyptic outlook. Aum Shinrikyo is a group whose delusional leader is genuinely paranoid about the United States and is known to have plotted to assassinate Japan's emperor. Shoko Asahara's cult is already on record for having made an assassination threat against President Clinton.

If Iran's mullahs or Iraq's Saddam Hussein decide to use terrorists to attack the continental United States, they would likely turn to bin Laden's al-Qaida. Al-Qaida *wk 2* is among the Islamic groups recruiting increasingly skilled professionals, such as computer and communications technicians, engineers, pharmacists, and physicists, as well as Ukrainian chemists and biologists, Iraqi chemical weapons experts, and others capable of helping to develop WMD. Al-Qaida poses the most serious terrorist threat to U.S. security interests, for al-Qaida's well-trained terrorists are actively engaged in a terrorist jihad against U.S. interests worldwide.

These four groups in particular are each capable of perpetrating a horrific act of terrorism in the United States, particularly on the occasion of the new millennium. Aum Shinrikyo has already threatened to use WMD in downtown Manhattan or in Washington, D.C., where it could attack the Congress, the Pentagon's Concourse, the White House, or President Clinton. The cult has threatened New York City with WMD, threatened to assassinate President Clinton, unsuccessfully attacked a U.S. naval base in Japan with biological weapons, and plotted in 1994 to attack the White House and the Pentagon with sarin and VX. If the LTTE's serial assassin of heads of state were to become angered by President Clinton, Prabhakaran could react by dispatching a Tamil "belt-bomb girl" to detonate a powerful semtex bomb after approaching the President in a crowd with a garland of flowers or after jumping next to his car.

Al-Qaida's expected retaliation for the U.S. cruise missile attack against al-Qaida's training facilities in Afghanistan on August 20, 1998, could take several forms of terrorist attack in the nation's capital. Al-Qaida could detonate a Chechen-type building-buster bomb at a federal building. Suicide bomber(s) belonging to al-Qaida's Martyrdom Battalion could crash-land an aircraft packed with high explosives (C-4 and semtex) into the Pentagon, the headquarters of the Central Intelligence Agency (CIA), or the White House. Ramzi Yousef had planned to do this against the CIA headquarters. In addition, both al-Qaida and Yousef were linked to a plot to assassinate President Clinton during his visit to the Philippines in early 1995. Following the August 1998 cruise missile attack, at least one Islamic religious leader called for Clinton's assassination, and another stated that "the time is not far off" for when the White House will be destroyed by a nuclear bomb. A horrendous scenario consonant with al-Qaida's mindset would be its use of a nuclear suitcase bomb against any number of targets in the nation's capital. Bin Laden allegedly has already purchased a number of nuclear suitcase bombs from the Chechen Mafia. Al-Qaida's retaliation, however, is more likely to take the lower-risk form of bombing one or more U.S. airliners with time-bombs. Yousef was planning simultaneous bombings of 11 U.S. airliners prior to his capture. Whatever form an attack may take, bin Laden will most likely retaliate in a spectacular way for the cruise missile attack against his Afghan camp in August 1998.

While nothing is easier than to denounce the evildoer,
nothing is more difficult than to understand him.

– Fyodor Mikhailovich Dostoevsky

INTRODUCTION

Why do some individuals decide to break with society and embark on a career in terrorism? Do terrorists share common traits or characteristics? Is there a terrorist personality or profile? Can a terrorist profile be developed that could reliably help security personnel to identify potential terrorists, whether they be would-be airplane hijackers, assassins, or suicide bombers? Do some terrorists have a psychotic (see Glossary) personality? Psychological factors relating to terrorism are of particular interest to psychologists, political scientists, and government officials, who would like to be able to predict and prevent the emergence of terrorist groups or to thwart the realization of terrorist actions. This study focuses on individual psychological and sociological characteristics of terrorists of different generations as well as their groups in an effort to determine how the terrorist profile may have changed in recent decades, or whether they share any common sociological attributes.

The assumption underlying much of the terrorist-profile research in recent decades has been that most terrorists have some common characteristics that can be determined through psychometric analysis of large quantities of biographical data on terrorists. One of the earliest attempts to single out a terrorist personality was done by Charles A. Russell and Bowman H. Miller (1977) (see Attributes of Terrorists).

Ideally, a researcher attempting to profile terrorists in the 1990s would have access to extensive biographical data on several hundred terrorists arrested in various parts of the world and to data on terrorists operating in a specific country. If such data were at hand, the researcher could prepare a psychometric study analyzing attributes of the terrorist: educational, occupational, and socioeconomic background; general traits; ideology; marital status; method and place of recruitment; physical appearance; and sex. Researchers have used this approach to study West German and Italian terrorist groups (see Females). Such detailed information would provide more accurate sociological profiles of terrorist groups. Although there appears to be no single terrorist personality, members of a terrorist group(s) may share numerous common sociological traits.

Practically speaking, however, biographical databases on large numbers of terrorists are not readily available. Indeed, such data would be quite difficult to obtain unless one had special access to police files on terrorists around the world. Furthermore, developing an open-source biographical database on enough terrorists to have some scientific validity would require a substantial investment of time. The small number of profiles contained in this study is hardly sufficient to qualify as scientifically representative of terrorists in general, or even of a particular category of terrorists, such as religious fundamentalists or ethnic separatists. Published terrorism databases, such as Edward F. Mickolus's series of chronologies of incidents of international terrorism and the Rand-St. Andrews University Chronology of International Terrorism, are highly informative and contain some useful biographical information on terrorists involved in major incidents, but are largely incident-oriented.

This study is not about terrorism per se. Rather, it is concerned with the perpetrators of terrorism. Prepared from a social sciences perspective, it attempts to synthesize the results of psychological and sociological findings of studies on terrorists published in recent decades and provide a general assessment of what is presently known about the terrorist mind and mindset.

Because of time constraints and a lack of terrorism-related biographical databases, the methodology, but not the scope, of this research has necessarily been modified. In the absence of a database of terrorist biographies, this study is based on the broader database of knowledge contained in academic studies on the psychology and sociology of terrorism published over the past three decades. Using this extensive database of open-source literature available in the Library of Congress and other information drawn from Websites, such as the Foreign Broadcast Information Service (FBIS), this paper assesses the level of current knowledge of the subject and presents case studies that include sociopsychological profiles of about a dozen selected terrorist groups and more than two dozen terrorist leaders or other individuals implicated in acts of terrorism. Three profiles of noteworthy terrorists of the early 1970s who belonged to other groups are included in order to provide a better basis of contrast with terrorists of the late 1990s. This paper does not presume to have any scientific validity in terms of general sampling representation of terrorists, but it does provide a preliminary theoretical, analytical, and biographical framework for further research on the general subject or on particular groups or individuals.

By examining the relatively overlooked behaviorist literature on sociopsychological aspects of terrorism, this study attempts to gain psychological and sociological insights into international terrorist groups and individuals. Of particular interest is whether members of at least a dozen terrorist organizations in diverse regions of the world have any psychological or sociological characteristics in common that might be useful in profiling terrorists, if profiling is at all feasible, and in understanding somewhat better the motivations of individuals who become terrorists.

Because this study includes profiles of diverse groups from Western Europe, Asia, the Middle East, and Latin America, care has been taken when making cross-national, cross-cultural, and cross-ideological comparisons. This paper examines such topics as the age, economic and social background, education and occupation, gender, geographical origin, marital status, motivation, recruitment, and religion or ideology of the members of these designated groups as well as others on which relevant data are available.

It is hoped that an examination of the extensive body of behaviorist literature on political and religious terrorism authored by psychologists and sociologists as well as political scientists and other social scientists will provide some answers to questions such as: Who are terrorists? How do individuals become terrorists? Do political or religious terrorists have anything in common in their sociopsychological development? How are they recruited? Is there a terrorist mindset, or are terrorist groups too diverse to have a single mindset or common psychological traits? Are there instead different terrorist mindsets?

TERMS OF ANALYSIS

Defining Terrorism and Terrorists

Unable to achieve their unrealistic goals by conventional means, international terrorists attempt to send an ideological or religious message by terrorizing the general public. Through the choice of their targets, which are often symbolic or representative of the targeted nation, terrorists attempt to create a high-profile impact on the public of their targeted enemy or enemies with their act of violence, despite the limited material resources that are usually at their disposal. In doing so, they hope to demonstrate various points, such as that the targeted government(s) cannot protect its (their) own citizens, or that by assassinating a specific victim they can teach the general public a lesson about espousing viewpoints or policies antithetical to their own. For example, by assassinating Egyptian President Anwar Sadat on October 6, 1981, a year after his historic trip to Jerusalem, the al-Jihad terrorists hoped to convey to the world, and especially to Muslims, the error that he represented.

This tactic is not new. Beginning in 48 A.D., a Jewish sect called the Zealots carried out terrorist campaigns to force insurrection against the Romans in Judea. These campaigns included the use of assassins (*sicarii*, or dagger-men), who would infiltrate Roman-controlled cities and stab Jewish collaborators or Roman legionnaires with a *sica* (dagger), kidnap members of the Staff of the Temple Guard to hold for ransom, or use poison on a large scale. The Zealots' justification for their killing of other Jews was that these killings demonstrated the consequences of the immorality of collaborating with the Roman invaders, and that the Romans could not protect their Jewish collaborators.

Definitions of terrorism vary widely and are usually inadequate. Even terrorism researchers often neglect to define the term other than by citing the basic U.S. Department of State (1998) definition of terrorism as "premeditated, politically motivated violence perpetrated against noncombatant targets by subnational groups or clandestine agents, usually intended to influence an audience." Although an act of violence that is generally regarded in the United States as an act of terrorism may not be viewed so in another country, the type of violence that distinguishes terrorism from other types of violence, such as ordinary crime or a wartime military action, can still be defined in terms that might qualify as reasonably objective.

This social sciences researcher defines a terrorist *action* as the calculated use of unexpected, shocking, and unlawful violence against noncombatants (including, in addition to civilians, off-duty military and security personnel in peaceful situations) and other symbolic targets perpetrated by a clandestine member(s) of a subnational group or a clandestine agent(s) for the psychological purpose of publicizing a political or religious cause and/or intimidating or coercing a government(s) or civilian population into accepting demands on behalf of the cause.

In this study, the nouns "terrorist" or "terrorists" do not necessarily refer to everyone within a terrorist organization. Large organizations, such as the Revolutionary Armed Forces of Colombia (FARC), the Irish Republic Army (IRA), or the Kurdistan Workers' Party (PKK), have many members—for example, accountants, cooks, fund-raisers, logistics specialists, medical doctors, or recruiters—who may play only a passive support role. We are not particularly concerned here with the passive support membership of terrorist organizations.

Rather, we are primarily concerned in this study with the leader(s) of terrorist groups and the activists or operators who personally carry out a group's terrorism strategy. The top leaders are of particular interest because there may be significant differences between them and terrorist activists or operatives. In contrast to the top leader(s), the individuals who carry out orders to perpetrate an act of political violence (which they would not necessarily regard as a terrorist act) have generally been recruited into the organization. Thus, their motives for joining may be different. New recruits are often isolated and alienated young people who want to join not only because they identify with the cause and idolize the group's leader, but also because they want to belong to a group for a sense of self-importance and companionship.

The top leaders of several of the groups profiled in this report can be subdivided into contractors or freelancers. The distinction actually highlights an important difference between the old generation of terrorist leaders and the new breed of international terrorists. Contractors are those terrorist leaders whose services are hired by rogue states, or a particular government entity of a rogue regime, such as an intelligence agency. Notable examples of terrorist contractors include Abu Nidal, George Habash of the Popular Front for the Liberation of Palestine (PFLP), and Abu Abbas of the Palestine Liberation Front (PLF). Freelancers are terrorist leaders who are completely independent of a state, but who may collude with a rogue regime on a short-term basis. Prominent examples of freelancers include Sheikh Omar Abdul Rahman, Ahmed Ramzi Yousef, and Osama bin Laden. Contractors like Abu Nidal, George Habash, and Abu Abbas are representative of the old style of high-risk international terrorism. In the 1990s, rogue states, more mindful of the consequences of Western diplomatic, economic, military, and political retaliation were less inclined to risk contracting terrorist organizations. Instead, freelancers operating independently of any state carried out many of the most significant acts of terrorism in the decade.

This study discusses groups that have been officially designated as terrorist groups by the U.S. Department of State. A few of the groups on the official list, however, are guerrilla organizations. These include the FARC, the LTTE, and the PKK. To be sure, the FARC, the LTTE, and the PKK engage in terrorism as well as guerrilla warfare, but categorizing them as terrorist groups and formulating policies to combat them on that basis would be simplistic and a prescription for failure. The FARC, for example, has the official status in Colombia of a political insurgent movement, as a result of a May 1999 accord between the FARC and the Colombian government. To dismiss a guerrilla group, especially one like the FARC which has been fighting for four decades, as only a terrorist group is to misunderstand its political and sociological context.

It is also important to keep in mind that perceptions of what constitutes terrorism will differ from country to country, as well as among various sectors of a country's population. For example, the Nicaraguan elite regarded the Sandinista National Liberation Front (FSLN) as a terrorist group, while much of the rest of the country regarded the FSLN as freedom fighters. A foreign extremist group labeled as terrorist by the Department of State may be regarded in heroic terms by some sectors of the population in another country. Likewise, an action that would be regarded as indisputably terrorist in the United States might not be regarded as a terrorist act in another country's law courts. For example, India's Supreme Court ruled in May 1999 that the assassination of Prime Minister Rajiv Gandhi by a LTTE "belt-bomb girl" was not an act of terrorism because there was no evidence that the four co-conspirators (who received the death penalty) had any desire to strike terror in the country. In addition, the Department of State's labeling of a guerrilla group as a terrorist group may be viewed by the particular group as a hostile act. For example, the LTTE has disputed, unsuccessfully, its designation on October 8, 1997, by the Department of State as a terrorist organization. By labeling the LTTE a terrorist group, the United States compromises its potential role as neutral mediator in Sri Lanka's civil war and waves a red flag at one of the world's deadliest groups, whose leader appears to be a psychopathic (see Glossary) serial killer of heads of state. To be sure, some terrorists are so committed to their cause that they freely acknowledge being terrorists. On hearing that he had been sentenced to 240 years in prison, Ramzi Yousef, mastermind of the WTC bombing, defiantly proclaimed, "I am a terrorist, and I am proud of it."

Terrorist Group Typologies

This study categorizes foreign terrorist groups under one of the following four designated, somewhat arbitrary typologies: nationalist-separatist, religious fundamentalist, new religious, and social revolutionary. This group classification is based on the assumption that terrorist groups can be categorized by their political background or ideology. The social revolutionary category has also been labeled "idealist." Idealistic terrorists fight for a radical cause, a religious belief, or a political ideology, including anarchism. Although some groups do not fit neatly into any one category, the general typologies are important because all terrorist campaigns are different, and the mindsets of groups within the same general category tend to have more in common than those in different categories. For example, the Irish Republic Army (IRA), Basque Fatherland and Freedom (Euzkadi

Ta Askatasuna—ETA), the Palestinian terrorist groups, and the LTTE all have strong nationalistic motivations, whereas the Islamic fundamentalist and the Aum Shinrikyo groups are motivated by religious beliefs. To be at all effective, counterterrorist policies necessarily would vary depending on the typology of the group.

A fifth typology, for right-wing terrorists, is not listed because right-wing terrorists were not specifically designated as being a subject of this study. In any case, there does not appear to be any significant right-wing group on the U.S. Department of State's list of foreign terrorist organizations. Right-wing terrorists are discussed only briefly in this paper (see Attributes of Terrorists). This is not to minimize the threat of right-wing extremists in the United States, who clearly pose a significant terrorist threat to U.S. security, as demonstrated by the Oklahoma City bombing on April 19, 1995.

APPROACHES TO TERRORISM ANALYSIS

The Multicausal Approach

Terrorism usually results from multiple causal factors—not only psychological but also economic, political, religious, and sociological factors, among others. There is even an hypothesis that it is caused by physiological factors, as discussed below. Because terrorism is a multicausal phenomenon, it would be simplistic and erroneous to explain an act of terrorism by a single cause, such as the psychological need of the terrorist to perpetrate an act of violence.

For Paul Wilkinson (1977), the causes of revolution and political violence in general are also the causes of terrorism. These include ethnic conflicts, religious and ideological conflicts, poverty, modernization stresses, political inequities, lack of peaceful communications channels, traditions of violence, the existence of a revolutionary group, governmental weakness and ineptness, erosions of confidence in a regime, and deep divisions within governing elites and leadership groups.

The Political Approach

The alternative to the hypothesis that a terrorist is born with certain personality traits that destine him or her to become a terrorist is that the root causes of terrorism can be found in influences emanating from environmental factors. Environments conducive to the rise of terrorism include international and national environments, as well as subnational ones such as universities, where many terrorists first become familiar with Marxist-Leninist ideology or other revolutionary ideas and get involved with radical groups. Russell and Miller identify universities as the major recruiting ground for terrorists.

Having identified one or more of these or other environments, analysts may distinguish between precipitants that started the outbreak of violence, on the one hand, and preconditions that allowed the precipitants to instigate the action, on the other hand. Political scientists Chalmers Johnson (1978) and Martha Crenshaw (1981) have further subdivided preconditions into permissive factors, which engender a terrorist strategy and make it attractive to political dissidents, and direct situational factors, which motivate terrorists. Permissive causes include urbanization, the transportation system (for example, by allowing a terrorist to quickly escape to another country by taking a flight), communications media, weapons availability, and the absence of security measures. An example of a situational factor for Palestinians would be the loss of their homeland of Palestine.

Various examples of international and national or subnational theories of terrorism can be cited. An example of an international environment hypothesis is the view proposed by Brian M. Jenkins (1979) that the failure of rural guerrilla movements in Latin America pushed the rebels into the cities. (This hypothesis, however, overlooks the national causes of Latin American terrorism and fails to explain why rural guerrilla movements continue to thrive in Colombia.) Jenkins also notes that the defeat of Arab armies in the 1967 Six-Day War caused the Palestinians to abandon hope for a conventional military solution to their problem and to turn to terrorist attacks.

The Organizational Approach

Some analysts, such as Crenshaw (1990: 250), take an organization approach to terrorism and see terrorism as a rational strategic course of action decided on by a group. In her view, terrorism is not committed by an individual. Rather, she contends that "Acts of terrorism are committed by groups who reach collective decisions based on commonly held beliefs, although the level of individual commitment to the group and its beliefs varies."

Crenshaw has not actually substantiated her contention with case studies that show how decisions are supposedly reached collectively in terrorist groups. That kind of inside information, to be sure, would be quite difficult to obtain without a former decision-maker within a terrorist group providing it in the form of a published autobiography or an interview, or even as a paid police informer. Crenshaw may be partly right, but her organizational approach would seem to be more relevant to guerrilla organizations that are organized along traditional Marxist-Leninist lines, with a general secretariat headed by a secretary general, than to terrorist groups per se. The FARC, for example, is a guerrilla organization, albeit one that is not averse to using terrorism as a tactic. The six members of the FARC's General Secretariat participate in its decision-making under the overall leadership of Secretary General Manuel Marulanda Vélez. The hard-line military leaders, however, often exert disproportionate influence over decision-making.

Bona fide terrorist groups, like cults, are often totally dominated by a single individual leader, be it Abu Nidal, Ahmed Jibril, Osama bin Laden, or Shoko Asahara. It seems quite improbable that the terrorist groups of such dominating leaders make their decisions collectively. By most accounts, the established terrorist leaders give instructions to their lieutenants to hijack a jetliner, assassinate a particular person, bomb a U.S. Embassy, and so forth, while leaving operational details to their lieutenants to work out. The top leader may listen to his lieutenants' advice, but the top leader makes the final decision and gives the orders.

The Physiological Approach

The physiological approach to terrorism suggests that the role of the media in promoting the spread of terrorism cannot be ignored in any discussion of the causes of terrorism. Thanks to media coverage, the methods, demands, and goals of terrorists are quickly made known to potential terrorists, who may be inspired to imitate them upon becoming stimulated by media accounts of terrorist acts.

The diffusion of terrorism from one place to another received scholarly attention in the early 1980s. David G. Hubbard (1983) takes a physiological approach to analyzing the causes of terrorism. He discusses three substances produced in the body under stress: norepinephrine, a compound produced by the adrenal gland and sympathetic nerve endings and associated with the "fight or flight" (see Glossary) physiological response of individuals in stressful situations; acetylcholine, which is produced by the parasympathetic nerve endings and acts to dampen the accelerated norepinephrine response; and endorphins, which develop in the brain as a response to stress and "narcotize" the brain, being 100 times more powerful than morphine. Because these substances occur in the terrorist, Hubbard concludes that much terrorist violence is rooted not in the psychology but in the physiology of the terrorist, partly the result of "stereotyped, agitated tissue response" to stress. Hubbard's conclusion suggests a possible explanation for the spread of terrorism, the so-called contagion effect.

Kent Layne Oots and Thomas C. Wiegele (1985) have also proposed a model of terrorist contagion based on physiology. Their model demonstrates that the psychological state of the potential terrorist has important implications for the stability of society. In their analysis, because potential terrorists become aroused in a violence-accepting way by media presentations of terrorism, "Terrorists must, by the nature of their actions, have an attitude which allows violence." One of these attitudes, they suspect, may be Machiavellianism because terrorists are disposed to manipulating their victims as well as the press, the public, and the authorities. They note that the potential terrorist "need only see that terrorism has worked for others in order to become aggressively aroused."

According to Oots and Wiegele, an individual moves from being a potential terrorist to being an actual terrorist through a process that is psychological, physiological, and political. "If the neurophysiological model of aggression is realistic," Oots and Wiegele assert, "there is no basis for the argument that terrorism could be eliminated if its sociopolitical causes were eliminated." They characterize the potential terrorist as "a frustrated individual who has become aroused and has repeatedly experienced the fight or flight syndrome. Moreover, after these repeated arousals, the potential terrorist seeks relief through an aggressive act and also seeks, in part, to remove the initial cause of his frustration by achieving the political goal which he has hitherto been denied."

D. Guttman (1979) also sees terrorist actions as being aimed more at the audience than at the immediate victims. It is, after all, the audience that may have to meet the terrorist's demands. Moreover, in Guttman's analysis, the terrorist requires a liberal rather than a right-wing audience for success. Liberals make the terrorist respectable by accepting the ideology that the terrorist alleges informs his or her acts. The terrorist also requires liberal control of the media for the transmission of his or her ideology.

The Psychological Approach

In contrast with political scientists and sociologists, who are interested in the political and social contexts of terrorist groups, the relatively few psychologists who study terrorism are primarily interested in the micro-level of the individual terrorist or terrorist group. The psychological approach is concerned with the study of terrorists per se, their recruitment and induction into terrorist groups, their personalities, beliefs, attitudes, motivations, and careers as terrorists.

GENERAL HYPOTHESES OF TERRORISM

If one accepts the proposition that political terrorists are made, not born, then the question is what makes a terrorist. Although the scholarly literature on the psychology of terrorism is lacking in full-scale, quantitative studies from which to ascertain trends and develop general theories of terrorism, it does appear to focus on several theories. One, the Olson hypothesis, suggests that participants in revolutionary violence predicate their behavior on a rational cost-benefit calculus and the conclusion that violence is the best available course of action given the social conditions. The notion that a group rationally chooses a terrorism strategy is questionable, however. Indeed, a group's decision to resort to terrorism is often divisive, sometimes resulting in factionalization of the group.

Frustration-Aggression Hypothesis

The frustration-aggression hypothesis (see Glossary) of violence is prominent in the literature. This hypothesis is based mostly on the relative-deprivation hypothesis (see Glossary), as proposed by Ted Robert Gurr (1970), an expert on violent behaviors and movements, and reformulated by J.C. Davies (1973) to include a gap between rising expectations and need satisfaction. Another proponent of this hypothesis, Joseph Margolin (1977: 273-4), argues that "much terrorist behavior is a response to the frustration of various political, economic, and personal needs or objectives." Other scholars, however have dismissed the frustration-aggression hypothesis as simplistic, based as it is on the erroneous assumption that aggression is always a consequence of frustration.

According to Franco Ferracuti (1982), a University of Rome professor, a better approach than these and other hypotheses, including the Marxist theory, would be a subcultural theory, which takes into account that terrorists live in their own subculture, with their own value systems. Similarly, political scientist Paul Wilkinson (1974: 127) faults the frustration-aggression hypothesis for having "very little to say about the social psychology of prejudice and hatred..." and fanaticisms that "play a major role in encouraging extreme violence." He believes that "Political terrorism cannot be understood outside the context of the development of terroristic, or potentially terroristic, ideologies, beliefs and life-styles (133)."

Negative Identity Hypothesis

Using Erikson's theory of identity formation, particularly his concept of negative identity, the late political psychologist Jeanne N. Knutson (1981) suggests that the political terrorist consciously assumes a negative identity. One of her examples is a Croatian terrorist who, as a member of an oppressed ethnic minority, was disappointed by the failure of his aspiration to attain a university education, and as a result assumed a negative identity by becoming a terrorist. Negative identity involves a vindictive rejection of the role regarded as desirable and proper by an individual's family and community. In Knutson's view, terrorists engage in terrorism as a result of feelings of rage and helplessness over the lack of alternatives. Her political science-oriented viewpoint seems to coincide with the frustration-aggression hypothesis.

Narcissistic Rage Hypothesis

The advocates of the narcissism-aggression hypothesis include psychologists Jerrold M. Post, John W. Crayton, and Richard M. Pearlstein. Taking the-terrorists-as-mentally-ill approach, this hypothesis concerns the early development of the terrorist. Basically, if primary narcissism in the form of the "grandiose self" is not neutralized by reality testing, the grandiose self produces individuals who are sociopathic, arrogant, and lacking in regard for others. Similarly, if the psychological form of the "idealized parental ego" is not neutralized by reality testing, it can produce a condition of helpless defeatism, and narcissistic defeat can lead to reactions of rage and a wish to destroy the source of narcissistic injury. "As a specific manifestation of narcissistic rage, terrorism occurs in the context of narcissistic injury," writes Crayton (1983:37-8). For Crayton, terrorism is an attempt to acquire or maintain power or control by intimidation. He suggests that the "meaningful high ideals" of the political terrorist group "protect the group members from experiencing shame."

In Post's view, a particularly striking personality trait of people who are drawn to terrorism "is the reliance placed on the psychological mechanisms of "externalization" and 'splitting'." These are psychological mechanisms, he explains, that are found in "individuals with narcissistic and borderline personality disturbances." "Splitting," he explains, is a mechanism characteristic of people whose personality development is shaped by a particular type of psychological damage (narcissistic injury) during childhood. Those individuals with a damaged self-concept have failed to integrate the good and bad parts of the self, which are instead split into the "me" and the "not me." These individuals, who have included Hitler, need an outside enemy to blame for their own inadequacies and weaknesses. The data examined by Post, including a 1982 West German study, indicate that many terrorists have not been successful in their personal, educational, and vocational lives. Thus, they are drawn to terrorist groups, which have an us-versus-them outlook. This hypothesis, however, appears to be contradicted by the increasing number of terrorists who are well-educated professionals, such as chemists, engineers, and physicists.

The psychology of the self is clearly very important in understanding and dealing with terrorist behavior, as in incidents of hostage-barricade terrorism (see Glossary). Crayton points out that humiliating the terrorists in such situations by withholding food, for example, would be counterproductive because "the very basis for their activity stems from their sense of low self-esteem and humiliation."

Using a Freudian analysis of the self and the narcissistic personality, Pearlstein (1991) eruditely applies the psychological concept of narcissism to terrorists. He observes that the political terrorist circumvents the psychopolitical liabilities of accepting himself or herself as a terrorist with a negative identity through a process of rhetorical self-justification that is reinforced by the group's group-think. His hypothesis, however, seems too speculative a construct to be used to analyze terrorist motivation independently of numerous other factors. For example, politically motivated hijackers have rarely acted for self-centered reasons, but rather in the name of the political goals of their groups. It also seems questionable that terrorist suicide-bombers, who deliberately sacrificed themselves in the act, had a narcissistic personality.

THE PSYCHOLOGY OF THE TERRORIST

Terrorist Motivation

In addition to drawing on political science and sociology, this study draws on the discipline of psychology, in an attempt to explain terrorist motivation and to answer questions such as who become terrorists and what kind of individuals join terrorist groups and commit public acts of shocking violence. Although there have been numerous attempts to explain terrorism from a psychiatric or psychological perspective, Wilkinson notes that the psychology and beliefs of terrorists have been inadequately explored. Most psychological analyses of terrorists and terrorism, according to psychologist Maxwell Taylor (1988), have attempted to address what motivates terrorists or to describe personal characteristics of terrorists, on the assumption that terrorists can be identified by these attributes. However, although an understanding of the terrorist mindset would be the key to understanding how and why an individual becomes a terrorist, numerous psychologists have been unable to adequately define it. Indeed, there appears to be a general agreement among psychologists who have studied the subject that there is no one terrorist mindset. This view, however, itself needs to be clarified.

The topic of the terrorist mindset was discussed at a Rand conference on terrorism coordinated by Brian M. Jenkins in September 1980. The observations made about terrorist mindsets at that conference considered individuals, groups, and individuals as part of a group. The discussion revealed how little was known about the nature of terrorist mindsets, their causes and consequences, and their significance for recruitment, ideology, leader-follower relations, organization, decision making about targets and tactics, escalation of violence, and attempts made by disillusioned terrorists to exit from the terrorist group. Although the current study has examined these aspects of the terrorist mindset, it has done so within the framework of a more general tasking requirement. Additional research and analysis would be needed to focus more closely on the concept of the terrorist mindset and to develop it into a more useful method for profiling terrorist groups and leaders on a more systematic and accurate basis.

Within this field of psychology, the personality dynamics of individual terrorists, including the causes and motivations behind the decision to join a terrorist group and to commit violent acts, have also received attention. Other small-group dynamics that have been of particular interest to researchers include the terrorists' decision-making patterns, problems of leadership and authority, target selection, and group mindset as a pressure tool on the individual.

Attempts to explain terrorism in purely psychological terms ignore the very real economic, political, and social factors that have always motivated radical activists, as well as the possibility that biological or physiological variables may play a role in bringing an individual to the point of perpetrating terrorism. Although this study provides some interdisciplinary context to the study of terrorists and terrorism, it is concerned primarily with the sociopsychological approach. Knutson (1984), Executive Director of the International Society of Political Psychology until her death in 1982, carried out an extensive international research project on the psychology of political terrorism. The basic premise of terrorists whom she evaluated in depth was "that their violent acts stem from feelings of rage and hopelessness engendered by the belief that society permits no other access to information-dissemination and policy-formation processes."

The social psychology of political terrorism has received extensive analysis in studies of terrorism, but the individual psychology of political and religious terrorism has been largely ignored. Relatively little is known about the terrorist as an individual, and the psychology of terrorists remains poorly understood, despite the fact that there have been a number of individual biographical accounts, as well as sweeping sociopolitical or psychiatric generalizations.

A lack of data and an apparent ambivalence among many academic researchers about the academic value of terrorism research have contributed to the relatively little systematic social and psychological research on terrorism. This is unfortunate because psychology, concerned as it is with behavior and the factors that influence and control behavior, can provide practical as opposed to conceptual knowledge of terrorists and terrorism.

A principal reason for the lack of psychometric studies of terrorism is that researchers have little, if any, direct access to terrorists, even imprisoned ones. Occasionally, a researcher has gained special access to a terrorist group, but usually at the cost of compromising the credibility of her/his research. Even if a researcher obtains permission to interview an incarcerated terrorist, such an interview would be of limited value and reliability for the purpose of making generalizations. Most terrorists, including imprisoned ones, would be loath to reveal their group's operational secrets to their interrogators, let alone to journalists or academic researchers, whom the terrorists are likely to view as representatives of the "system" or perhaps even as intelligence agents in disguise. Even if terrorists agree to be interviewed in such circumstances, they may be less than candid in answering questions. For example, most imprisoned Red Army Faction members reportedly declined to be interviewed by West German social scientists. Few researchers or former terrorists write exposés of terrorist groups. Those who do could face retaliation. For example, the LTTE shot to death an anti-LTTE activist, Sabaratnam Sabalingam, in Paris on May 1, 1994, to prevent him from publishing an anti-LTTE book. The LTTE also murdered Dr. Rajani Thiranagama, a Tamil, and one of the four Sri Lankan authors of *The Broken Palmyrah*, which sought to examine the "martyr" cult.

The Process of Joining a Terrorist Group

Individuals who become terrorists often are unemployed, socially alienated individuals who have dropped out of society. Those with little education, such as youths in Algerian ghettos or the Gaza Strip, may try to join a terrorist group out of boredom and a desire to have an action-packed adventure in pursuit of a cause they regard as just. Some individuals may be motivated mainly by a desire to use their special skills, such as bomb-making. The more educated youths may be motivated more by genuine political or religious convictions. The person who becomes a terrorist in Western countries is generally both intellectual and idealistic. Usually, these disenchanted youths, both educated or uneducated, engage in occasional protest and dissidence. Potential terrorist group members often start out as sympathizers of the group. Recruits often come from support organizations, such as prisoner support groups or student activist groups. From sympathizer, one moves to passive supporter. Often, violent encounters with police or other security forces motivate an already socially alienated individual to join a terrorist group. Although the circumstances vary, the end result of this gradual process is that the individual, often with the help of a family member or friend with terrorist contacts, turns to terrorism. Membership in a terrorist group, however, is highly selective. Over a period as long as a year or more, a recruit generally moves in a slow, gradual fashion toward full membership in a terrorist group.

An individual who drops out of society can just as well become a monk or a hermit instead of a terrorist. For an individual to choose to become a terrorist, he or she would have to be motivated to do so. Having the proper motivation, however, is still not enough. The would-be terrorist would need to have the opportunity to join a terrorist group. And like most job seekers, he or she would have to be acceptable to the terrorist group, which is a highly exclusive group. Thus, recruits would not only need to have a personality that would allow them to fit into the group, but ideally a certain skill needed by the group, such as weapons or communications skills.

The psychology of joining a terrorist group differs depending on the typology of the group. Someone joining an anarchistic or a Marxist-Leninist terrorist group would not likely be able to count on any social support, only social opprobrium, whereas someone joining an ethnic separatist group like ETA or the IRA would enjoy considerable social support and even respect within ethnic enclaves.

Psychologist Eric D. Shaw (1986:365) provides a strong case for what he calls "The Personal Pathway Model," by which terrorists enter their new profession. The components of this pathway include early socialization processes; narcissistic injuries; escalatory events, particularly confrontation with police; and personal connections to terrorist group members, as follows:

> The personal pathway model suggests that terrorists came from a selected, at risk population, who have suffered from early damage to their self-esteem. Their subsequent political activities may be consistent with the liberal social philosophies of their families, but go beyond their perception of the contradiction in their family's beliefs and lack of social action. Family political philosophies may also serve to sensitize these persons to the economic and political tensions inherent throughout modern society. As a group, they appear to have been unsuccessful in obtaining a desired traditional place in society, which has contributed to their frustration. The underlying need to belong to a terrorist group is symptomatic of an incomplete or fragmented psychosocial identity. (In Kohut's terms—a defective or fragmented "group self"). Interestingly, the acts of security forces or police are cited as provoking more violent political activity by these individuals and it is often a personal connection to other terrorists which leads to membership in a violent group (shared external targets?).

Increasingly, terrorist organizations in the developing world are recruiting younger members. The only role models for these young people to identify with are often terrorists and guerrillas. Abu Nidal, for example, was able to recruit alienated, poor, and uneducated youths thrilled to be able to identify themselves with a group led by a well-known but mysterious figure.

During the 1980s and early 1990s, thousands of foreign Muslim volunteers (14,000, according to *Jane's Intelligence Review*)—angry, young, and zealous and from many countries, including the United States—flocked to training camps in Afghanistan or the Pakistan-Afghan border region to learn the art of combat. They ranged in age from 17 to 35. Some had university educations, but most were uneducated, unemployed youths without any prospects.

Deborah M. Galvin (1983) notes that a common route of entry into terrorism for female terrorists is through political involvement and belief in a political cause. The Intifada (see Glossary), for example, radicalized many young Palestinians, who later joined terrorist organizations. At least half of the Intifada protesters were young girls. Some women are recruited into terrorist organizations by boyfriends. A significant feature that Galvin feels may characterize the involvement of the female terrorist is the "male or female lover/female accomplice ... scenario." The lover, a member of the terrorist group, recruits the female into the group. One ETA female member, "Begona," told Eileen MacDonald (1992) that was how she joined at age 25: "I got involved [in ETA] because a man I knew was a member."

A woman who is recruited into a terrorist organization on the basis of her qualifications and motivation is likely to be treated more professionally by her comrades than one who is perceived as lacking in this regard. Two of the PFLP hijackers of Sabena Flight 517 from Brussels to Tel Aviv on May 8, 1972, Therese Halsa, 19, and Rima Tannous, 21, had completely different characters. Therese, the daughter of a middle-class Arab family, was a nursing student when she was recruited into Fatah by a fellow student and was well regarded in the organization. Rima, an orphan of average intelligence, became the mistress of a doctor who introduced her to drugs and recruited her into Fatah. She became totally dependent on some Fatah members, who subjected her to physical and psychological abuse.

Various terrorist groups recruit both female and male members from organizations that are lawful. For example, ETA personnel may be members of Egizan ("Act Woman!"), a feminist movement affiliated with ETA's political wing; the Henri Batasuna (Popular Unity) party; or an amnesty group seeking release for ETA members. While working with the amnesty group, a number of women reportedly tended to become frustrated over mistreatment of prisoners and concluded that the only solution was to strike back, which they did by joining the ETA. "Women seemed to become far more emotionally involved than men with the suffering of prisoners," an ETA member, "Txikia," who joined at age 20, told MacDonald, "and when they made the transition from supporter to guerrilla, appeared to carry their deeper sense of commitment with them into battle."

The Terrorist as Mentally Ill

A common stereotype is that someone who commits such abhorrent acts as planting a bomb on an airliner, detonating a vehicle bomb on a city street, or tossing a grenade into a crowded sidewalk café is abnormal. The psychopathological (see Glossary) orientation has dominated the psychological approach to the terrorist's personality. As noted by Taylor, two basic psychological approaches to understanding terrorists have been commonly used: the terrorist is viewed either as mentally ill or as a fanatic. For Walter Laqueur (1977:125), "Terrorists are fanatics and fanaticism frequently makes for cruelty and sadism."

This study is not concerned with the lone terrorist, such as the Unabomber in the United States, who did not belong to any terrorist group. Criminologist Franco Ferracuti has noted that there is "no such thing as an isolated terrorist—that's a mental case." Mentally unbalanced individuals have been especially attracted to airplane hijacking. David G. Hubbard (1971) conducted a psychiatric study of airplane hijackers in 1971 and concluded that skyjacking is used by psychiatrically ill patients as an expression of illness. His study revealed that skyjackers shared several common traits: a violent father, often an alcoholic; a deeply religious mother, often a religious zealot; a sexually shy, timid, and passive personality; younger sisters toward whom the skyjackers acted protectively; and poor achievement, financial failure, and limited earning potential.

Those traits, however, are shared by many people who do not hijack airplanes. Thus, profiles of mentally unstable hijackers would seem to be of little, if any, use in detecting a potential hijacker in advance. A useful profile would probably have to identify physical or behavioral traits that might alert authorities to a potential terrorist before a suspect is allowed to board an aircraft, that is, if hijackers have identifiable personality qualities. In the meantime, weapons detection, passenger identification, and onboard security guards may be the only preventive measures. Even then, an individual wanting to hijack an airplane can often find a way. Japan's Haneda Airport screening procedures failed to detect a large knife that a 28-year-old man carried aboard an All Nippon Airways jumbo jet on July 23, 1999, and used to stab the pilot (who died) and take the plane's controls until overpowered by others. Although police have suggested that the man may have psychiatric problems, the fact that he attempted to divert the plane to the U.S. Yokota Air Base north of Tokyo, at a time when the airbase was a subject of controversy because the newly elected governor of Tokyo had demanded its closure, suggests that he may have had a political or religious motive.

There have been cases of certifiably mentally ill terrorists. Klaus Jünschke, a mental patient, was one of the most ardent members of the Socialist Patients'

Collective (SPK), a German terrorist group working with the Baader-Meinhof Gang (see Glossary). In some instances, political terrorists have clearly exhibited psychopathy (see Glossary). For example, in April 1986 Nezar Hindawi, a freelance Syrian-funded Jordanian terrorist and would-be agent of Syrian intelligence, sent his pregnant Irish girlfriend on an El Al flight to Israel, promising to meet her there to be married. Unknown to her, however, Hindawi had hidden a bomb (provided by the Abu Nidal Organization (ANO)) in a false bottom to her hand luggage. His attempt to bomb the airliner in midair by duping his pregnant girlfriend was thwarted when the bomb was discovered by Heathrow security personnel. Taylor regards Hindawi's behavior in this incident as psychopathic because of Hindawi's willingness to sacrifice his fiancé and unborn child.

Jerrold Post (1990), a leading advocate of the terrorists-as-mentally ill approach, has his own psychological hypothesis of terrorism. Although he does not take issue with the proposition that terrorists reason logically, Post argues that terrorists' reasoning process is characterized by what he terms "terrorist psycho-logic." In his analysis, terrorists do not willingly resort to terrorism as an intentional choice. Rather, he argues that "political terrorists are driven to commit acts of violence as a consequence of psychological forces, and that their special psycho-logic is constructed to rationalize acts they are psychologically compelled to commit"(1990:25). Post's hypothesis that terrorists are motivated by psychological forces is not convincing and seems to ignore the numerous factors that motivate terrorists, including their ideological convictions.

Post (1997) believes that the most potent form of terrorism stems from those individuals who are bred to hate, from generation to generation, as in Northern Ireland and the Basque country. For these terrorists, in his view, rehabilitation in nearly impossible because ethnic animosity or hatred is "in their blood" and passed from father to son. Post also draws an interesting distinction between "anarchic-ideologues"such as the Italian Red Brigades (Brigate Rosse) and the German RAF (aka the Baader-Meinhof Gang), and the "nationalist-separatist" groups such as the ETA, or the IRA, stating that:

> There would seem to be a profound difference between terrorists bent on destroying their own society, the "world of their fathers," and those whose terrorist activities carry on the mission of their fathers. To put it in other words, for some, becoming terrorists is an act of retaliation for real and imagined hurts *against the society of their parents*; for others, it is an act of retaliation against society *for the hurt done to their parents*.... This would suggest more

conflict, more psychopathology, among those committed to anarchy and destruction of society.... (1984:243)

Indeed, author Julian Becker (1984) describes the German terrorists of the Baader-Meinhof Gang as "children without fathers." They were sons and daughters of fathers who had either been killed by Nazis or survived Nazism. Their children despised and rebelled against them because of the shame of Nazism and a defeated Germany. One former RAF female member told MacDonald: "We hated our parents because they were former Nazis, who had never come clean about their past." Similarly, Gunther Wagenlehner (1978:201) concludes that the motives of RAF terrorists were unpolitical and belonged "more to the area of psychopathological disturbances." Wagenlehner found that German terrorists blamed the government for failing to solve their personal problems. Not only was becoming a terrorist "an individual form of liberation" for radical young people with personal problems, but "These students became terrorists because they suffered from acute fear and from aggression and the masochistic desire to be pursued." In short, according to Wagenlehner, the West German anarchists stand out as a major exception to the generally nonpathological characteristics of most terrorists. Psychologist Konrad Kellen (1990:43) arrives at a similar conclusion, noting that most of the West German terrorists "suffer from a deep psychological trauma" that "makes them see the world, including their own actions and the expected effects of those actions, in a grossly unrealistic light" and that motivates them to kill people. Sociologist J. Bowyer Bell (1985) also has noted that European anarchists, unlike other terrorists, belong more to the "province of psychologists than political analysts...."

Post's distinction between anarchic-ideologues and ethnic separatists appears to be supported by Rona M. Fields's (1978) psychometric assessment of children in Northern Ireland. Fields found that exposure to terrorism as a child can lead to a proclivity for terrorism as an adult. Thus, a child growing up in violence-plagued West Belfast is more likely to develop into a terrorist as an adult than is a child growing up in peaceful Oslo, Norway, for example. Maxwell Taylor, noting correctly that there are numerous other factors in the development of a terrorist, faults Fields's conclusions for, among other things, a lack of validation with adults. Maxwell Taylor overlooks, however, that Field's study was conducted over an eight-year period. Taylor's point is that Field's conclusions do not take into account that relatively very few children exposed to violence, even in Northern Ireland, grow up to become terrorists.

A number of other psychologists would take issue with another of Post's contentions—that the West German anarchists were more pathological than Irish terrorists. For example, psychiatrist W. Rasch (1979), who interviewed a number of West German terrorists, determined that "no conclusive evidence has been found for the assumption that a significant number of them are disturbed or abnormal." For Rasch the argument that terrorism is pathological behavior only serves to minimize the political or social issues that motivated the terrorists into action. And psychologist Ken Heskin (1984), who has studied the psychology of terrorism in Northern Ireland, notes that "In fact, there is no psychological evidence that terrorists are diagnosably psychopathic or otherwise clinically disturbed."

Although there may have been instances in which a mentally ill individual led a terrorist group, this has generally not been the case in international terrorism. Some specialists point out, in fact, that there is little reliable evidence to support the notion that terrorists in general are psychologically disturbed individuals. The careful, detailed planning and well-timed execution that have characterized many terrorist operations are hardly typical of mentally disturbed individuals.

There is considerable evidence, on the contrary, that international terrorists are generally quite sane. Crenshaw (1981) has concluded from her studies that "the outstanding common characteristic of terrorists is their normality." This view is shared by a number of psychologists. For example, C.R. McCauley and M.E. Segal (1987) conclude in a review of the social psychology of terrorist groups that "the best documented generalization is negative; terrorists do not show any striking psychopathology." Heskin (1984) did not find members of the IRA to be emotionally disturbed. It seems clear that terrorists are extremely alienated from society, but alienation does not necessarily mean being mentally ill.

Maxwell Taylor (1984) found that the notion of mental illness has little utility with respect to most terrorist actions. Placing the terrorist within the ranks of the mentally ill, he points out, makes assumptions about terrorist motivations and places terrorist behavior outside the realms of both the normal rules of behavior and the normal process of law. He points out several differences that separate the psychopath from the political terrorist, although the two may not be mutually exclusive, as in the case of Hindawi. One difference is the psychopath's inability to profit from experience. Another important difference is that, in contrast to the terrorist, the purposefulness, if any, of a psychopath's actions is personal. In addition, psychopaths are too unreliable and incapable of being controlled to be of use to terrorist groups. Taylor notes that terrorist groups need discreet activists who do not draw attention to themselves and who can merge back into the crowd after executing an operation. For these reasons, he believes that "it may be inappropriate to think of the terrorist as mentally ill in conventional terms" (1994:92). Taylor and Ethel Quayle (1994:197) conclude that "the active terrorist is not discernibly different in psychological terms from the non-terrorist." In other words, terrorists are recruited from a population that describes most of us. Taylor and Quayle also assert that "in psychological terms, there are no special qualities that characterize the terrorist." Just as there is no necessary reason why people sharing the same career in normal life necessarily have psychological characteristics in common, the fact that terrorists have the same career does not necessarily mean that they have anything in common psychologically.

The selectivity with which terrorist groups recruit new members helps to explain why so few pathologically ill individuals are found within their ranks. Candidates who appear to be potentially dangerous to the terrorist group's survival are screened out. Candidates with unpredictable or uncontrolled behavior lack the personal attributes that the terrorist recruiter is looking for.

Many observers have noted that the personality of the terrorist has a depressive aspect to it, as reflected in the terrorist's death-seeking or death-confronting behavior. The terrorist has often been described by psychologists as incapable of enjoying anything (anhedonic) or forming meaningful interpersonal relationships on a reciprocal level. According to psychologist Risto Fried, the terrorist's interpersonal world is characterized by three categories of people: the terrorist's idealized heroes; the terrorist's enemies; and people one encounters in everyday life, whom the terrorist regards as shadow figures of no consequence. However, Fried (1982:123) notes that some psychologists with extensive experience with some of the most dangerous terrorists "emphasize that the terrorist may be perfectly normal from a clinical point of view, that he may have a psychopathology of a different order, or that his personality may be only a minor factor in his becoming a terrorist if he was recruited into a terrorist group rather than having volunteered for one."

The Terrorist as Suicidal Fanatic

Fanatics

The other of the two approaches that have predominated, the terrorist as fanatic, emphasizes the terrorist's rational qualities and views the terrorist as a cool, logical planning individual whose rewards are ideological and political, rather than financial. This approach takes into account that terrorists are often well educated and capable of sophisticated, albeit highly biased, rhetoric and political analysis.

Notwithstanding the religious origins of the word, the term "fanaticism" in modern usage, has broadened out of the religious context to refer to more generally held extreme beliefs. The terrorist is often labeled as a fanatic, especially in actions that lead to self-destruction. Although fanaticism is not unique to terrorism, it is, like "terrorism," a pejorative term. In psychological terms, the concept of fanaticism carries some implications of mental illness, but, Taylor (1988:97) points out, it "is not a diagnostic category in mental illness." Thus, he believes that "Commonly held assumptions about the relationship between fanaticism and mental illness...seem to be inappropriate." The fanatic often seems to view the world from a particular perspective lying at the extreme of a continuum.

Two related processes, Taylor points out, are prejudice and authoritarianism, with which fanaticism has a number of cognitive processes in common, such as an unwillingness to compromise, a disdain for other alternative views, the tendency to see things in black-and-white, a rigidity of belief, and a perception of the world that reflects a closed mind. Understanding the nature of fanaticism, he explains, requires recognizing the role of the cultural (religious and social) context. Fanaticism, in Taylor's view, may indeed "...be part of the cluster of attributes of the terrorist." However, Taylor emphasizes that the particular cultural context in which the terrorist is operating needs to be taken into account in understanding whether the term might be appropriate.

Suicide Terrorists

Deliberate self-destruction, when the terrorist's death is necessary in order to detonate a bomb or avoid capture, is not a common feature of terrorism in most countries, although it happens occasionally with Islamic fundamentalist terrorists in the Middle East and Tamil terrorists in Sri Lanka and southern India. It is also a feature of North Korean terrorism. The two North Korean agents who blew up Korean Air Flight 858 on November 28, 1987, popped cyanide capsules when confronted by police investigators. Only one of the terrorists succeeded in killing himself, however.

Prior to mid-1985, there were 11 suicide attacks against international targets in the Middle East using vehicle bombs. Three well-known cases were the bombing of the U.S. Embassy in Beirut on April 18, 1983, which killed 63 people, and the separate bombings of the U.S. Marine barracks and the French military headquarters in Lebanon on October 23, 1983, which killed 241 U.S. Marines and 58 French paratroopers, respectively. The first instance, however, was the bombing of Israel's military headquarters in Tyre, in which 141 people were killed. Inspired by these suicide attacks in Lebanon and his closer ties with Iran and Hizballah, Abu Nidal launched "suicide squads" in his attacks against the Rome and Vienna airports in late December 1985, in which an escape route was not planned.

The world leaders in terrorist suicide attacks are not the Islamic fundamentalists, but the Tamils of Sri Lanka. The LTTE's track record for suicide attacks is unrivaled. Its suicide commandos have blown up the prime ministers of two countries (India and Sri Lanka), celebrities, at least one naval battleship, and have regularly used suicide to avoid capture as well as simply a means of protest. LTTE terrorists do not dare not to carry out their irrevocable orders to use their cyanide capsules if captured. No fewer than 35 LTTE operatives committed suicide to simply avoid being questioned by investigators in the wake of the Gandhi assassination. Attempting to be circumspect, investigators disguised themselves as doctors in order to question LTTE patients undergoing medical treatment, but, Vijay Karan (1997:46) writes about the LTTE patients, "Their reflexes indoctrinated to react even to the slightest suspicion, all of them instantly popped cyanide capsules." Two were saved only because the investigators forcibly removed the capsules from their mouths, but one investigator suffered a severe bite wound on his hand and had to be hospitalized for some time.

To Western observers, the acts of suicide terrorism by adherents of Islam and Hinduism may be attributable to fanaticism or mental illness or both. From the perspective of the Islamic movement, however, such acts of self-destruction have a cultural and religious context, the historical origins of which can be seen in the behavior of religious sects associated with the Shi'ite movement, notably the Assassins (see Glossary). Similarly, the suicide campaign of the Islamic Resistance Movement (Hamas) in the 1993-94 period involved young Palestinian terrorists, who, acting on individual initiative, attacked Israelis in crowded places, using home-made improvised weapons such as knives and axes. Such attacks were suicidal because escape was not part of the attacker's plan. These attacks were, at least in part, motivated by revenge.

According to scholars of Muslim culture, so-called suicide bombings, however, are seen by Islamists and Tamils alike as instances of martyrdom, and should be understood as such. The Arabic term used is *istishad*, a religious term meaning to give one's life in the name of Allah, as opposed to *intihar*, which refers to suicide resulting from personal distress. The latter form of suicide is not condoned in Islamic teachings.

There is a clear correlation between suicide attacks and concurrent events and developments in the Middle Eastern area. For example, suicide attacks increased in frequency after the October 1990 clashes between Israeli security forces and Muslim worshipers on Temple Mount, in the Old City of Jerusalem, in which 18 Muslims were killed. The suicide attacks carried out by Hamas in Afula and Hadera in April 1994 coincided with the talks that preceded the signing by Israel and the PLO of the Cairo agreement. They were also claimed to revenge the massacre of 39 and the wounding of 200 Muslim worshipers in a Hebron mosque by an Israeli settler on February 25, 1994. Attacks perpetrated in Ramat-Gan and in Jerusalem in July and August 1995, respectively, coincided with the discussions concerning the conduct of elections in the Territories, which were concluded in the Oslo II agreement. The primary reason for Hamas's suicide attacks was that they exacted a heavy price in Israeli casualties. Most of the suicide attackers came from the Gaza Strip. Most were bachelors aged 18 to 25, with high school education, and some with university education. Hamas or Islamic Jihad operatives sent the attackers on their missions believing they would enter eternal Paradise.

Terrorist Group Dynamics

Unable to study terrorist group dynamics first-hand, social scientists have applied their understanding of small-group behavior to terrorist groups. Some features of terrorist groups, such as pressures toward conformity and consensus, are characteristic of all small groups. For whatever reason individuals assume the role of terrorists, their transformation into terrorists with a political or religious agenda takes places within the structure of the terrorist group. This group provides a sense of belonging, a feeling of self-importance, and a new belief system that defines the terrorist act as morally acceptable and the group's goals as of paramount importance. As Shaw (1988:366) explains:

> Apparently membership in a terrorist group often provides a solution to the pressing personal needs of which the inability to achieve a desired niche in traditional society is the coup de grace. The terrorist identity offers the individual a role in society, albeit a negative one, which is commensurate with his or her prior expectations and sufficient to compensate for past losses. Group membership

provides a sense of potency, an intense and close interpersonal environment, social status, potential access to wealth and a share in what may be a grandiose but noble social design. The powerful psychological forces of conversion in the group are sufficient to offset traditional social sanctions against violence....To the terrorists their acts may have the moral status of religious warfare or political liberation.

Terrorist groups are similar to religious sects or cults. They require total commitment by members; they often prohibit relations with outsiders, although this may not be the case with ethnic or separatist terrorist groups whose members are well integrated into the community; they regulate and sometimes ban sexual relations; they impose conformity; they seek cohesiveness through interdependence and mutual trust; and they attempt to brainwash individual members with their particular ideology. According to Harry C. Holloway, M.D., and Ann E. Norwood, M.D. (1997:417), the joining process for taking on the beliefs, codes, and cult of the terrorist group "involves an interaction between the psychological structure of the terrorist's personality and the ideological factors, group process, structural organization of the terrorist group and cell, and the sociocultural milieu of the group."

Citing Knutson, Ehud Sprinzak (1990:79), an American-educated Israeli political scientist, notes: "It appears that, as radicalization deepens, the collective group identity takes over much of the individual identity of the members; and, at the terrorist stage, the group identity reaches its peak." This group identity becomes of paramount importance. As Post (1990:38) explains: "Terrorists whose only sense of significance comes from being terrorists cannot be forced to give up terrorism, for to do so would be to lose their very reason for being." The terrorist group displays the characteristics of Groupthink (see Glossary), as described by I. Janis (1972). Among the characteristics that Janis ascribes to groups demonstrating Groupthink are illusions of invulnerability leading to excessive optimism and excessive risk taking, presumptions of the group's morality, one-dimensional perceptions of the enemy as evil, and intolerance of challenges by a group member to shared key beliefs.

Some important principles of group dynamics among legally operating groups can also be usefully applied to the analysis of terrorist group dynamics. One generally accepted principle, as demonstrated by W. Bion (1961), is that individual judgment and behavior are strongly influenced by the powerful forces of group dynamics. Every group, according to Bion, has two opposing forces—a rare tendency to act in a fully cooperative, goal-directed, conflict-free manner to accomplish its stated purposes, and a stronger tendency to sabotage the stated goals. The latter tendency results in a group that defines itself in relation to the outside world and acts as if the only way it can survive is by fighting against or fleeing from the perceived enemy; a group that looks for direction to an omnipotent leader, to whom they subordinate their own independent judgment and act as if they do not have minds of their own; and a group that acts as if the group will bring forth a messiah who will rescue them and create a better world. Post believes that the terrorist group is the apotheosis of the sabotage tendency, regularly exhibiting all three of these symptoms.

Both structure and social origin need to be examined in any assessment of terrorist group dynamics. In Post's (1987) view, structural analysis in particular requires identification of the locus of power. In the autonomous terrorist action cell, the cell leader is within the cell, a situation that tends to promote tension. In contrast, the action cells of a terrorist group with a well-differentiated structure are organized within columns, thereby allowing policy decisions to be developed outside the cells.

Post found that group psychology provides more insights into the ways of terrorists than individual psychology does. After concluding, unconvincingly, that there is no terrorist mindset, he turned his attention to studying the family backgrounds of terrorists. He found that the group dynamics of nationalist-separatist groups and anarchic-ideological groups differ significantly. Members of nationalist-separatist groups are often known in their communities and maintain relationships with friends and family outside the terrorist group, moving into and out of the community with relative ease. In contrast, members of anarchic-ideological groups have irrevocably severed ties with family and community and lack their support. As a result, the terrorist group is the only source of information and security, a situation that produces pressure to conform and to commit acts of terrorism.

Pressures to Conform

Peer pressure, group solidarity, and the psychology of group dynamics help to pressure an individual member to remain in the terrorist group. According to Post (1986), terrorists tend to submerge their own identities into the group, resulting in a kind of "group mind" and group moral code that requires unquestioned obedience to the group. As Crenshaw (1985) has observed, "The group, as selector and interpreter of ideology, is central." Group cohesion increases or decreases depending on the degree of outside danger facing the group.

The need to belong to a group motivates most terrorists who are followers to join a terrorist group. Behavior among terrorists is similar, in Post's analysis, because of this need by alienated individuals to belong. For the new recruit, the terrorist group becomes a substitute family, and the group's leaders become substitute parents. An implied corollary of Post's observation that a key motivation for membership in a terrorist group is the sense of belonging and the fraternity of like-minded individuals is the assumption that there must be considerable apprehension among members that the group could be disbanded. As the group comes under attack from security forces, the tendency would be for the group to become more cohesive.

A member with wavering commitment who attempts to question group decisions or ideology or to quit under outside pressure against the group would likely face very serious sanctions. Terrorist groups are known to retaliate violently against members who seek to drop out. In 1972, when half of the 30-member Rengo Sekigun (Red Army) terrorist group, which became known as the JRA, objected to the group's strategy, the dissenters, who included a pregnant woman who was thought to be "too bourgeois," were tied to stakes in the northern mountains of Japan, whipped with wires, and left to die of exposure. By most accounts, the decision to join a terrorist group or, for that matter, a terrorist cult like Aum Shinrikyo, is often an irrevocable one.

Pressures to Commit Acts of Violence

Post (1990:35) argues that "individuals become terrorists in order to join terrorist groups and commit acts of terrorism." Joining a terrorist group gives them a sense of "revolutionary heroism" and self-importance that they previously lacked as individuals. Consequently, a leader who is action-oriented is likely to have a stronger position within the group than one who advocates prudence and moderation. Thomas Strentz (1981:89) has pointed out that terrorist groups that operate against democracies often have a field commander who he calls an "opportunist," that is, an activist, usually a male, whose criminal activity predates his political involvement. Strentz applies the psychological classification of the antisocial personality, also known as a sociopath or psychopath, to the life-style of this type of action-oriented individual. His examples of this personality type include Andreas Baader and Hans Joachim Klein of the Baader-Meinhof Gang and Akira Nihei of the JRA. Although the opportunist is not mentally ill, Strentz explains, he "is oblivious to the needs of others and unencumbered by the capacity to feel guilt or empathy." By most accounts, Baader was unpleasant, constantly abusive toward other members of the group, ill-read, and an action-oriented individual with a criminal past. Often recruited by the group's leader, the opportunist may eventually seek to take over the group, giving rise to increasing tensions between him and the leader. Often the leader will manipulate the opportunist by allowing him the fantasy of leading the group.

On the basis of his observation of underground resistance groups during World War II, J.K. Zawodny (1978) concluded that the primary determinant of underground group decision making is not the external reality but the psychological climate within the group. For action-oriented terrorists, inaction is extremely stressful. For action-oriented members, if the group is not taking action then there is no justification for the group. Action relieves stress by reaffirming to these members that they have a purpose. Thus, in Zawodny's analysis, a terrorist group needs to commit acts of terrorism in order to justify its existence.

Other terrorists may feel that their personal honor depends on the degree of violence that they carry out against the enemy. In 1970 Black September's Salah Khalef ("Abu Iyad") was captured by the Jordanians and then released after he appealed to his comrades to stop fighting and to lay down their arms. Dobson (1975:52) reports that, according to the Jordanians, Abu Iyad "was subjected to such ridicule by the guerrillas who had fought on that he reacted by turning from moderation to the utmost violence."

Pearlstein points out that other examples of the political terrorist's self-justification of his or her terrorist actions include the terrorist's taking credit for a given terrorist act and forewarning of terrorist acts to come. By taking credit for an act of terrorism, the terrorist or terrorist group not only advertises the group's cause but also communicates a rhetorical self-justification of the terrorist act and the cause for which it was perpetrated. By threatening future terrorism, the terrorist or terrorist group in effect absolves itself of responsibility for any casualties that may result.

Terrorist Rationalization of Violence

Living underground, terrorists gradually become divorced from reality, engaging in what Ferracuti (1982) has described as a "fantasy war." The stresses that accompany their underground, covert lives as terrorists may also have adverse social and psychological consequences for them. Thus, as Taylor (1988:93) points out, although "mental illness may not be a particularly helpful way of conceptualizing terrorism, the acts of terrorism and membership in a terrorist organization may well have implications for the terrorist's mental health."

Albert Bandura (1990) has described four techniques of moral disengagement that a terrorist group can use to insulate itself from the human consequences of its actions. First, by using moral justification terrorists may imagine themselves as the saviors of a constituency threatened by a great evil. For example, Donatella della Porta (1992:286), who interviewed members of left-wing militant groups in Italy and Germany, observed that the militants "began to perceive themselves as members of a heroic community of generous people fighting a war against 'evil.'"

Second, through the technique of displacement of responsibility onto the leader or other members of the group, terrorists portray themselves as functionaries who are merely following their leader's orders. Conversely, the terrorist may blame other members of the group. Groups that are organized into cells and columns may be more capable of carrying out ruthless operations because of the potential for displacement of responsibility. Della Porta's interviews with left-wing militants suggest that the more compartmentalized a group is the more it begins to lose touch with reality, including the actual impact of its own actions. Other manifestations of this displacement technique include accusations made by Asahara, the leader of Aum Shinrikyo, that the Central Intelligence Agency (CIA) used chemical agents against him and the Japanese population.

A third technique is to minimize or ignore the actual suffering of the victims. As Bonnie Cordes (1987) points out, terrorists are able to insulate themselves from moral anxieties provoked by the results of their hit-and-run attacks, such as the use of time bombs, by usually not having to witness first-hand the carnage resulting from them, and by concerning themselves with the reactions of the authorities rather than with civilian casualties. Nevertheless, she notes that "Debates over the justification of violence, the types of targets, and the issue of indiscriminate versus discriminate killing are endemic to a terrorist group." Often, these internal debates result in schisms.

The fourth technique of moral disengagement described by Bandura is to dehumanize victims or, in the case of Islamist groups, to refer to them as "the infidel." Italian and German militants justified violence by depersonalizing their victims as "tools of the system," "pigs," or "watch dogs." Psychologist Frederick Hacker (1996:162) points out that terrorists transform their victims into mere objects, for "terroristic thinking and practices reduce individuals to the status of puppets." Cordes, too, notes the role reversal played by terrorists in characterizing the enemy as the conspirator and oppressor and accusing it of state terrorism, while referring to themselves as "freedom fighters" or "revolutionaries." As Cordes explains, "Renaming themselves, their actions, their victims and their enemies accords the terrorist respectability."

By using semantics to rationalize their terrorist violence, however, terrorists may create their own self-destructive psychological tensions. As David C. Rapoport (1971:42) explains:

> All terrorists must deny the relevance of guilt and innocence, but in doing so they create an unbearable tension in their own souls, for they are in effect saying that a person is not a person. It is no accident that left-wing terrorists constantly speak of a "pig-society," by convincing *themselves* that they are confronting animals they hope to stay the remorse which the slaughter of the innocent necessarily generates.

Expanding on this rationalization of guilt, D. Guttman (1979:525) argues that "The terrorist asserts that he loves only the socially redeeming qualities of his murderous act, not the act itself." By this logic, the conscience of the terrorist is turned against those who oppose his violent ways, not against himself. Thus, in Guttman's analysis, the terrorist has projected his guilt outward. In order to absolve his own guilt, the terrorist must claim that under the circumstances he has no choice but to do what he must do. Although other options actually are open to the terrorist, Guttman believes that the liberal audience legitimizes the terrorist by accepting this rationalization of murder.

Some terrorists, however, have been trained or brainwashed enough not to feel any remorse, until confronted with the consequences of their actions. When journalist Eileen MacDonald asked a female ETA commando, "Amaia," how she felt when she heard that her bombs had been successful, she replied, after first denying being responsible for killing anyone: "Satisfaction. The bastards, they deserved it. Yes, I planted bombs that killed people." However, MacDonald felt that Amaia, who had joined the military wing at age 18, had never before questioned the consequences of her actions, and MacDonald's intuition was confirmed as Amaia's mood shifted from bravado to despondency, as she buried her head in her arms, and then groaned: "Oh, God, this is getting hard," and lamented that she had not prepared herself for the interview.

When Kim Hyun Hee (1993:104), the bomber of Korean Air Flight 858, activated the bomb, she had no moral qualms. "At that moment," she writes, "I felt no guilt or remorse at what I was doing; I thought only of completing the mission and not letting my country down." It was not until her 1988 trial, which resulted in a death sentence—she was pardoned a year later because she had been brainwashed—that she felt any remorse. "But being made to confront the victims' grieving families here in this courtroom," she writes, "I finally began to feel, deep down, the sheer horror of the atrocity I'd committed." One related characteristic of Kim, as told by one of her South Korean minders to McDonald, is that she had not shown any emotion whatsoever to anyone in the two years she (the minder) had known her.

The Terrorist's Ideological or Religious Perception

Terrorists do not perceive the world as members of governments or civil society do. Their belief systems help to determine their strategies and how they react to government policies. As Martha Crenshaw (1988:12) has observed, "The actions of terrorist organizations are based on a subjective interpretation of the world rather than objective reality."The variables from which their belief systems are formed include their political and social environments, cultural traditions, and the internal dynamics of their clandestine groups. Their convictions may seem irrational or delusional to society in general, but the terrorists may nevertheless act rationally in their commitment to acting on their convictions.

According to cognitive theory, an individual's mental activities (perception, memory, and reasoning) are important determinants of behavior. Cognition is an important concept in psychology, for it is the general process by which individuals come to know about and make sense of the world. Terrorists view the world within the narrow lens of their own ideology, whether it be Marxism-Leninism, anarchism, nationalism, Islamic fundamentalism (see Glossary), or some other ideology. Most researchers agree that terrorists generally do not regard themselves as terrorists but rather as soldiers, liberators, martyrs, and legitimate fighters for noble social causes. Those terrorists who recognize that their actions are terroristic are so committed to their cause that they do not really care how they are viewed in the outside world. Others may be just as committed, but loathe to be identified as terrorists as opposed to freedom fighters or national liberators.

Kristen Renwick Monroe and Lina Haddad Kreidie (1997) have found *perspective*—the idea that we all have a view of the world, a view of ourselves, a view of others, and a view of ourselves in relation to others—to be a very useful tool in understanding fundamentalism, for example. Their underlying hypothesis is that the perspectives of fundamentalists resemble one another and that they differ in significant and consistent ways from the perspectives of nonfundamentalists. Monroe and Kreidie conclude that "fundamentalists see themselves not as individuals but rather as symbols of Islam." They argue that it is a mistake for Western policymakers to treat Islamic fundamentalists as rational actors and dismiss them as irrational when they do not act as predicted by traditional cost/benefit models. "Islamic fundamentalism should not be dealt with simply as another set of political values that can be compromised or negotiated, or even as a system of beliefs or ideology—such as socialism or communism—in which traditional liberal democratic modes of political discourse and interaction are recognized." They point out that "Islamic fundamentalism taps into a quite different political consciousness, one in which religious identity sets and determines the range of options open to the fundamentalist. It extends to all areas of life and respects no separation between the private and the political."

Existing works that attempt to explain religious fundamentalism often rely on modernization theory and point to a crisis of identity, explaining religious fundamentalism as an antidote to the dislocations resulting from rapid change, or modernization. Islamic fundamentalism in particular is often explained as a defense against threats posed by modernization to a religious group's traditional identity. Rejecting the idea of fundamentalism as pathology, rational choice theorists point to unequal socioeconomic development as the basic reason for the discontent and alienation these individuals experience. Caught between an Islamic culture that provides moral values and spiritual satisfaction and a modernizing Western culture that provides access to material improvement, many Muslims find an answer to resulting anxiety, alienation, and disorientation through an absolute dedication to an Islamic way of life. Accordingly, the Islamic fundamentalist is commonly depicted as an acutely alienated individual, with dogmatic and rigid beliefs and an inferiority complex, and as idealistic and devoted to an austere lifestyle filled with struggle and sacrifice.

In the 1990s, however, empirical studies of Islamic groups have questioned this view. V. J. Hoffman-Ladd, for example, suggests that fundamentalists are not necessarily ignorant and downtrodden, according to the stereotype, but frequently students and university graduates in the physical sciences, although often students with rural or traditionally religious backgrounds. In his view, fundamentalism is more of a revolt of young people caught between a traditional past and a secular Western education. R. Euben and Bernard Lewis argue separately that there is a cognitive collision between Western and fundamentalist worldviews. Focusing on Sunni fundamentalists, Euben argues that their goals are perceived not as self-interests but rather as moral imperatives, and that their worldviews differ in critical ways from Western worldviews.

By having moral imperatives as their goals, the fundamentalist groups perceive the world through the distorting lens of their religious beliefs. Although the perceptions of the secular Arab terrorist groups are not so clouded by religious beliefs, these groups have their own ideological imperatives that distort their ability to see the world with a reasonable amount of objectivity. As a result, their perception of the world is as distorted as that of the fundamentalists. Consequently, the secular groups are just as likely to misjudge political, economic, and social realities as are the fundamentalist groups. For example, Harold M. Cubert argues that the Popular Front for the Liberation of Palestine (PFLP), guided by Marxist economic ideology, has misjudged the reasons for popular hostility in the Middle East against the West, "for such hostility, where it exists, is generally in response to the threat which Western culture is said to pose to Islamic values in the region rather than the alleged economic exploitation of the region's inhabitants." This trend has made the PFLP's appeals for class warfare irrelevant, whereas calls by Islamist groups for preserving the region's cultural and religious identity have been well received, at least among the nonsecular sectors of the population.

TERRORIST PROFILING

Hazards of Terrorist Profiling

The isolation of attributes or traits shared by terrorists is a formidable task because there are probably as many variations among terrorists as there may be similarities. Efforts by scholars to create a profile of a "typical" terrorist have had mixed success, if any, and the assumption that there is such a profile has not been proven. Post (1985:103) note that "behavioral scientists attempting to understand the psychology of individuals drawn to this violent political behavior have not succeeded in identifying a unique "terrorist mindset." People who have joined terrorist groups have come from a wide range of cultures, nationalities, and ideological causes, all strata of society, and diverse professions. Their personalities and characteristics are as diverse as those of people in the general population. There seems to be general agreement among psychologists that there is no particular psychological attribute that can be used to describe the terrorist or any "personality" that is distinctive of terrorists.

Some terrorism experts are skeptical about terrorist profiling. For example,

Laqueur (1997:129) holds that the search for a "terrorist personality" is a fruitless one. Paul Wilkinson (1997:193) maintains that "We already know enough about terrorist behavior to discount the crude hypothesis of a 'terrorist personality' or 'phenotype.'

The U.S. Secret Service once watched for people who fit the popular profile of dangerousness—the lunatic, the loner, the threatener, the hater. That profile, however, was shattered by the assassins themselves. In interviews with assassins in prisons, hospitals, and homes, the Secret Service learned an important lesson—to discard stereotypes. Killers are not necessarily mentally ill, socially isolated, or even male. Now the Secret Service looks for patterns of motive and behavior in potential presidential assassins. The same research methodology applies to potential terrorists. Assassins, like terrorists in general, use common techniques. For example, the terrorist would not necessarily threaten to assassinate a politician in advance, for to do so would make it more difficult to carry out the deed. In its detailed study of 83 people who tried to kill a public official or a celebrity in the United States in the past 50 years, the Secret Service found that not one assassin had made a threat. Imprisoned assassins told the Secret Service that a threat would keep them from succeeding, so why would they threaten? This was the second important lesson learned from the study.

The diversity of terrorist groups, each with members of widely divergent national and sociocultural backgrounds, contexts, and goals, underscores the hazards of making generalizations and developing a profile of members of individual groups or of terrorists in general. Post cautions that efforts to provide an overall "terrorist profile" are misleading: "There are nearly as many variants of personality who become involved in terrorist pursuits as there are variants of personality."

Many theories are based on the assumption that the terrorist has an "abnormal" personality with clearly identifiable character traits that can be explained adequately with insights from psychology and psychiatry. Based on his work with various West German terrorists, one German psychologist, L. Sullwold (1981), divided terrorist leaders into two broad classes of personality traits: the extrovert and the hostile neurotic, or one having the syndrome of neurotic hostility. Extroverts are unstable, uninhibited, inconsiderate, self-interested, and unemotional—thrill seekers with little regard for the consequences of their actions. Hostile neurotics share many features of the paranoid personality—they are intolerant of criticism, suspicious, aggressive, and defensive, as well as extremely sensitive to external hostility. Sullwold also distinguishes between leaders and followers, in that leaders are more likely to be people who combine a lack of scruples with extreme self-assurance; they often lead by frightening or pressuring their followers.

Some researchers have created psychological profiles of terrorists by using data provided by former terrorists who became informants, changed their political allegiance, or were captured. Franco Ferracuti conducted one such study of the Red Brigade terrorists in Italy. He analyzed the career and personalities of arrested terrorists by collecting information on demographic variables and by applying psychological tests to construct a typology of terrorists. Like Post, Ferracuti also found, for the most part, the absence of psychopathology (see Glossary), and he observed similar personality characteristics, that is, a basic division between extroverts and hostile neurotics. By reading and studying terrorist literature, such as group communiqués, news media interviews, and memoirs of former members, it would also be possible to ascertain certain vulnerabilities within the group by pinpointing its sensitivities, internal disagreements, and moral weaknesses. This kind of information would assist in developing a psychological profile of the group.

Post points out that the social dynamics of the "anarchic-ideologues," such as the RAF, differ strikingly from the "nationalist-separatists," such as ETA or the Armenian Secret Army for the Liberation of Armenia (ASALA). From studies of terrorists, Post (1990) has observed indications that terrorists, such as those of the ETA, who pursue a conservative goal, such as freedom for the Basque people, have been reared in more traditional, intact, conservative families, whereas anarchistic and left-wing terrorists (such as members of the Meinhof Gang/RAF) come from less conventional, nonintact families. In developing this dichotomy between separatists and anarchists, Post draws on Robert Clark's studies of the social backgrounds of the separatist terrorists of the ETA. Clark also found that ETA terrorists are not alienated and psychologically distressed. Rather, they are psychologically healthy people who are strongly supported by their families and ethnic community.

Post bases his observations of anarchists on a broad-cased investigation of the social background and psychology of 250 terrorists (227 left-wing and 23 right-wing) conducted by a consortium of West German social scientists under the sponsorship of the Ministry of Interior and published in four volumes in 1981-84. According to these West German analyses of RAF and June Second Movement terrorists, some 25 percent of the leftist terrorists had lost one or both parents by the age of fourteen and 79 percent reported severe conflict with other people, especially with parents (33 percent). The German authors conclude in general that the 250 terrorist lives demonstrated a pattern of failure both educationally and vocationally. Post concludes that "nationalist-separatist" terrorists such as the ETA are loyal to parents who are disloyal to their regime, whereas "anarchic-ideologues" are disloyal to their parents' generation, which is identified with the establishment.

Sociological Characteristics of Terrorists in the Cold War Period

A Basic Profile

Profiles of terrorists have included a profile constructed by Charles A. Russell and Bowman H. Miller (1977), which has been widely mentioned in terrorism-related studies, despite its limitations, and another study that involved systematically analyzing biographical and social data on about 250 German terrorists, both left-wing and right-right. Russell and Bowman attempt to draw a sociological portrait or profile of the modern urban terrorist based on a compilation and analysis of more than 350 individual terrorist cadres and leaders from Argentinian, Brazilian, German, Iranian, Irish, Italian, Japanese, Palestinian, Spanish, Turkish, and Uruguayan terrorist groups active during the 1966-76 period, the first decade of the contemporary terrorist era. Russell and Bowman (1977:31) conclude:

> In summation, one can draw a general composite picture into which fit the great majority of those terrorists from the eighteen urban guerrilla groups examined here. To this point, they have been largely single males aged 22 to 24...who have some university education, if not a college degree. The female terrorists, except for the West German groups and an occasional leading figure in the JRA and PFLP, are preoccupied with support rather than operational roles....Whether having turned to terrorism as a university student or only later, most were provided an anarchist or Marxist world view, as well as recruited into terrorist operations while in the university.

Russell and Miller's profile tends to substantiate some widely reported sociological characteristics of terrorists in the 1970s, such as the youth of most terrorists. Of particular interest is their finding that urban terrorists have largely urban origins and that many terrorist cadres have predominantly middle-class or even upper-class backgrounds and are well educated, with many having university degrees. However, like most such profiles that are based largely on secondary sources, such as newspaper articles and academic studies, the Russell and Miller profile cannot be regarded as definitive. Furthermore, their methodological approach lacks validity. It is fallacious to assume that one can compare characteristics of members of numerous terrorist groups in various regions of the world and then make generalizations about these traits. For example, the authors' conclusion that terrorists are largely single young males from urban, middle-class or upper-middle-class backgrounds with some university education would not accurately describe many members of terrorist groups operating in the 1990s. The rank and file of Latin American groups such as the FARC and Shining Path, Middle Eastern groups such as the Armed Islamic Group (Group Islamique Armé—GIA), Hamas, and Hizballah, Asian groups such as the LTTE, and Irish groups such as the IRA are poorly educated. Although the Russell and Miller profile is dated, it can still be used as a basic guide for making some generalizations about typical personal attributes of terrorists, in combination with other information.

Edgar O'Ballance (1979) suggests the following essential characteristics of the "successful" terrorist: dedication, including absolute obedience to the leader of the movement; personal bravery; a lack of feelings of pity or remorse even though victims are likely to include innocent men, women, and children; a fairly high standard of intelligence, for a terrorist must collect and analyze information, devise and implement complex plans, and evade police and security forces; a fairly high degree of sophistication, in order to be able to blend into the first-class section on airliners, stay at first-class hotels, and mix inconspicuously with the international executive set; and be a reasonably good educational background and possession of a fair share of general knowledge (a university degree is almost mandatory), including being able to speak English as well as one other major language.

Increasingly, terrorist groups are recruiting members who possess a high degree of intellectualism and idealism, are highly educated, and are well trained in a legitimate profession. However, this may not necessarily be the case with the younger, lower ranks of large guerrilla/terrorist organizations in less-developed countries, such as the FARC, the PKK, the LTTE, and Arab groups, as well as with some of the leaders of these groups.

Age

Russell and Miller found that the average age of an active terrorist member (as opposed to a leader) was between 22 and 25, except for Palestinian, German, and Japanese terrorists, who were between 20 and 25 years old. Another source explains that the first generation of RAF terrorists went underground at approximately 22 to 23 years of age, and that the average age shifted to 28 to 30 years for second-generation terrorists (June Second Movement). In summarizing the literature about international terrorists in the 1980s, Taylor (1988) characterizes their demography as being in their early twenties and unmarried, but he notes that there is considerable variability from group to group. Age trends for members of many terrorist groups were dropping in the 1980s, with various groups, such as the LTTE, having many members in the 16- to 17 year-old age level and even members who were preteens. Laqueur notes that Arab and Iranian groups tend to use boys aged 14 to 15 for dangerous missions, in part because they are less likely to question instructions and in part because they are less likely to attract attention.

In many countries wracked by ethnic, political, or religious violence in the developing world, such as Algeria, Colombia, and Sri Lanka, new members of terrorist organizations are recruited at younger and younger ages. Adolescents and preteens in these countries are often receptive to terrorist recruitment because they have witnessed killings first-hand and thus see violence as the only way to deal with grievances and problems.

In general, terrorist leaders tend to be much older. Brazil's Carlos Marighella, considered to be the leading theoretician of urban terrorism, was 58 at the time of his violent death on November 6, 1969. Mario Santucho, leader of Argentina's People's Revolutionary Army (ERP), was 40 at the time of his violent death in July 1976. Raúl Sendic, leader of the Uruguayan Tupamaros, was 42 when his group began operating in the late 1960s. Renato Curcio, leader of the Italian Red Brigades, was 35 at the time of his arrest in early 1976. Leaders of the Baader-Meinhof Gang were in their 30s or 40s. Palestinian terrorist leaders are often in their 40s or 50s.

Educational, Occupational, and Socioeconomic Background

Terrorists in general have more than average education, and very few Western terrorists are uneducated or illiterate. Russell and Miller found that about two-thirds of terrorist group members had some form of university training. The occupations of terrorist recruits have varied widely, and there does not appear to be any occupation in particular that produces terrorists, other than the ranks of the unemployed and students. Between 50 and 70 percent of the younger members of Latin American urban terrorist groups were students. The Free University of Berlin was a particularly fertile recruiting ground for Germany's June Second Movement and Baader-Meinhof Gang.

Highly educated recruits were normally given leadership positions, whether at the cell level or national level. The occupations of terrorist leaders have likewise varied. Older members and leaders frequently were professionals such as doctors, bankers, lawyers, engineers, journalists, university professors, and mid-level government executives. Marighella was a politician and former congressman. The PFLP's George Habash was a medical doctor. The PLO's Yasir Arafat was a graduate engineer. Mario Santucho was an economist. Raúl Sendic and the Baader-Meinhof's Horst Mahler were lawyers. Urika Meinhof was a journalist. The RAF and Red Brigades were composed almost exclusively of disenchanted intellectuals.

It may be somewhat misleading to regard terrorists in general as former professionals. Many terrorists who have been able to remain anonymous probably continue to practice their legitimate professions and moonlight as terrorists only when they receive instructions to carry out a mission. This may be more true about separatist organizations, such as the ETA and IRA, whose members are integrated into their communities, than about members of anarchist groups, such as the former Baader-Meinhof Gang, who are more likely to be on wanted posters, on the run, and too stressed to be able to function in a normal day-time job. In response to police infiltration, the ETA, for example, instituted a system of "sleeping commandos." These passive ETA members, both men and women, lead seemingly normal lives, with regular jobs, but after work they are trained for specific ETA missions. Usually unaware of each others' real identities, they receive coded instructions from an anonymous source. After carrying out their assigned actions, they resume their normal lives. Whereas terrorism for anarchistic groups such as the RAF and Red Brigades was a full-time profession, young ETA members serve an average of only three years before they are rotated back into the mainstream of society.

Russell and Miller found that more than two-thirds of the terrorists surveyed came from middle-class or even upper-class backgrounds. With the main exception of large guerrilla/terrorist organizations such as the FARC, the PKK, the LTTE, and the Palestinian or Islamic fundamentalist terrorist organizations, terrorists come from middle-class families. European and Japanese terrorists are more likely the products of affluence and higher education than of poverty. For example, the RAF and Red Brigades were composed almost exclusively of middle-class dropouts, and most JRA members were from middle-class families and were university dropouts. Well-off young people, particularly in the United States, West Europe, and Japan, have been attracted to political radicalism out of a profound sense of guilt over the plight of the world's largely poor population.

The backgrounds of the Baader-Meinhof Gang's members illustrate this in particular: Suzanne Albrecht, daughter of a wealthy maritime lawyer; Baader, the son of an historian; Meinhof, the daughter of an art historian; Horst Mahler, the son of a dentist; Holger Meins, the son of a business executive. According to Russell and Miller, about 80 percent of the Baader-Meinhof Gang had university experience.

Major exceptions to the middle- and upper-class origins of terrorist groups in general include three large organizations examined in this study—the FARC, the LTTE, and the PKK—as well as the paramilitary groups in Northern Ireland. Both the memberships of the Protestant groups, such as the Ulster Volunteer Force, and the Catholic groups, such as the Official IRA, the Provisional IRA, and the Irish National Liberation Army (INLA), are almost all drawn from the working class. These paramilitary groups are also different in that their members normally do not have any university education. Although Latin America has been an exception, terrorists in much of the developing world tend to be drawn from the lower sections of society. The rank and file of Arab terrorist organizations include substantial numbers of poor people, many of them homeless refugees. Arab terrorist leaders are almost all from the middle and upper classes.

General Traits

Terrorists are generally people who feel alienated from society and have a grievance or regard themselves as victims of an injustice. Many are dropouts. They are devoted to their political or religious cause and do not regard their violent actions as criminal. They are loyal to each other but will deal with a disloyal member more harshly than with the enemy. They are people with cunning, skill, and initiative, as well as ruthlessness. In order to be initiated into the group, the new recruit may be expected to perform an armed robbery or murder. They show no fear, pity, or remorse. The sophistication of the terrorist will vary depending on the significance and context of the terrorist action. The Colombian hostage-takers who infiltrated an embassy party and the Palace of Justice, for example, were far more sophisticated than would be, for example, Punjab terrorists who gun down bus passengers. Terrorists have the ability to use a variety of weapons, vehicles, and communications equipment and are familiar with their physical environment, whether it be a 747 jumbo jet or a national courthouse. A terrorist will rarely operate by himself/herself or in large groups, unless the operation requires taking over a large building, for example.

Members of Right-wing terrorist groups in France and Germany, as elsewhere, generally tend to be young, relatively uneducated members of the lower classes (see Table 1, Appendix). Ferracuti and F. Bruno (1981:209) list nine psychological traits common to right-wing terrorists: ambivalence toward authority; poor and defective insight; adherence to conventional behavioral patterns; emotional detachment from the consequences of their actions; disturbances in sexual identity with role uncertainties; superstition, magic, and stereotyped thinking; etero- and auto-destructiveness; low-level educational reference patterns; and perception of weapons as fetishes and adherence to violent subcultural norms. These traits make up what Ferracuti and Bruno call an "authoritarian-extremist personality." They conclude that right-wing terrorism may be more dangerous than left-wing terrorism because "in right-wing terrorism, the individuals are frequently psychopathological and the ideology is empty: ideology is outside reality, and the terrorists are both more normal and more fanatical."

Marital Status

In the past, most terrorists have been unmarried. Russell and Miller found that, according to arrest statistics, more than 75 to 80 percent of terrorists in the various regions in the late 1970s were single. Encumbering family responsibilities are generally precluded by requirements for mobility, flexibility, initiative, security, and total dedication to a revolutionary cause. Roughly 20 percent of foreign terrorist group memberships apparently consisted of married couples, if Russell and Miller's figure on single terrorists was accurate.

Physical Appearance

Terrorists are healthy and strong but generally undistinguished in appearance and manner. The physical fitness of some may be enhanced by having had extensive commando training. They tend to be of medium height and build to blend easily into crowds. They tend not to have abnormal physiognomy and peculiar features, genetic or acquired, that would facilitate their identification. Their dress and hair styles are inconspicuous. In addition to their normal appearance, they talk and behave like normal people. They may even be well dressed if, for example, they need to be in the first-class section of an airliner targeted for hijacking. They may resort to disguise or plastic surgery depending on whether they are on police wanted posters.

If a terrorist's face is not known, it is doubtful that a suspected terrorist can be singled out of a crowd only on the basis of physical features. Unlike the *yakuza* (mobsters) in Japan, terrorists generally do not have distinguishing physical features such as colorful tatoos. For example, author Christopher Dobson (1975) describes the Black September's Salah Khalef ("Abu Iyad") as "of medium height and sturdy build, undistinguished in a crowd." When Dobson, hoping for an interview, was introduced to him in Cairo in the early 1970s Abu Iyad made "so little an impression" during the brief encounter that Dobson did not realize until later that he had already met Israel's most-wanted terrorist. Another example is Imad Mughniyah, head of Hizballah's special operations, who is described by Hala Jaber (1997:120), as "someone you would pass in the street without even noticing or giving a second glance."

Origin: Rural or Urban

Guerrilla/terrorist organizations have tended to recruit members from the areas where they are expected to operate because knowing the area of operation is a basic principle of urban terrorism and guerrilla warfare. According to Russell and Miller, about 90 percent of the Argentine ERP and Montoneros came from the Greater Buenos Aires area. Most of Marighella's followers came from Recife, Rio de Janeiro, Santos, and São Paulo. More than 70 percent of the Tupamaros were natives of Montevideo. Most German and Italian terrorists were from urban areas: the Germans from Hamburg and West Berlin; the Italians from Genoa, Milan, and Rome.

Gender
Males

Most terrorists are male. Well over 80 percent of terrorist operations in the 1966-76 period were directed, led, and executed by males. The number of arrested female terrorists in Latin America suggested that female membership was less than 16 percent. The role of women in Latin American groups such as the Tupamaros was limited to intelligence collection, serving as couriers or nurses, maintaining safehouses, and so forth.

Females

Various terrorism specialists have noted that the number of women involved in terrorism has greatly exceeded the number of women involved in crime. However, no statistics have been offered to substantiate this assertion. Considering that the number of terrorist actions perpetrated worldwide in any given year is probably minuscule in comparison with the common crimes committed in the same period, it is not clear if the assertion is correct.

Nevertheless, it indeed seems as if more women are involved in terrorism than actually are, perhaps because they tend to get more attention than women involved in common crime.

Although Russell and Miller's profile is more of a sociological than a psychological profile, some of their conclusions raise psychological issues, such as why women played a more prominent role in left-wing terrorism in the 1966-76 period than in violent crime in general. Russell and Miller's data suggest that the terrorists examined were largely males, but the authors also note the secondary support role played by women in most terrorist organizations, particularly the Uruguayan Tupamaros and several European groups. For example, they point out that women constituted one-third of the personnel of the RAF and June Second Movement, and that nearly 60 percent of the RAF and June Second Movement who were at large in August 1976 were women.

Russell and Miller's contention that "urban terrorism remains a predominantly male phenomenon," with women functioning mainly in a secondary support role, may underestimate the active, operational role played by women in Latin American and West European terrorist organizations in the 1970s and 1980s. Insurgent groups in Latin America in the 1970s and 1980s reportedly included large percentages of female combatants: 30 percent of the Sandinista National Liberation Front (FSLN) combatants in Nicaragua by the late 1970s; one-third of the combined forces of the Farabundo Martí National Liberation Front (FMLN) in El Salvador; and one-half of the Shining Path terrorists in Peru. However, because these percentages may have been inflated by the insurgent groups to impress foreign feminist sympathizers, no firm conclusions can be drawn in the absence of reliable statistical data.

Nevertheless, women have played prominent roles in numerous urban terrorist operations in Latin America. For example, the second in command of the Sandinista takeover of Nicaragua's National Palace in Managua, Nicaragua, in late August 1979 was Dora María Téllez Argüello. Several female terrorists participated in the takeover of the Dominican Embassy in Bogotá, Colombia, by the 19th of April Movement (M-19) in 1980, and one of them played a major role in the hostage negotiations. The late Mélida Anaya Montes ("Ana María") served as second in command of the People's Liberation Forces (Fuerzas Populares de Liberación—FPL) prior to her murder at age 54 by FPL rivals in 1983. Half of the 35 M-19 terrorists who raided Colombia's Palace of Justice on November 6, 1985, were women, and they were among the fiercest fighters.

Leftist terrorist groups or operations in general have frequently been led by women. Many women joined German terrorist groups. Germany's Red Zora, a terrorist group active between the late 1970s and 1987, recruited only women and perpetrated many terrorist actions. In 1985 the RAF's 22 core activists included 13 women. In 1991 women formed about 50 percent of the RAF membership and about 80 percent of the group's supporters, according to MacDonald. Of the eight individuals on Germany's "Wanted Terrorists" list in 1991, five were women. Of the 22 terrorists being hunted by German police that year, 13 were women. Infamous German female terrorist leaders have included Susanne Albrecht, Gudrun Ensselin\Esslin, and Ulrike Meinhof of the Baader-Meinhof Gang. There are various theories as to why German women have been so drawn to violent groups. One is that they are more emancipated and liberated than women in other European countries. Another, as suggested to Eileen MacDonald by Astrid Proll, an early member of the Baader-Meinhof Gang, is that the anger of German women is part of a national guilt complex, the feeling that if their mothers had had a voice in Hitler's time many of Hitler's atrocities would not have happened.

Other noted foreign female terrorists have included Fusako Shigenobu of the JRA (Shigenobu, 53, was reported in April 1997 to be with 14 other JRA members—two other women and 12 men—training FARC guerrillas in terror tactics in the Urabá Region of Colombia); Norma Ester Arostito, who cofounded the Argentine Montoneros and served as its chief ideologist until her violent death in 1976; Margherita Cagol and Susana Ronconi of the Red Brigades; Ellen Mary Margaret McKearney of the IRA; Norma Ester Arostito of the Montoneros; and Geneveve Forest Tarat of the ETA, who played a key role in the spectacular ETA-V bomb assassination of Premier Admiral Carrero Blanco on December 20, 1973, as well as in the bombing of the Café Rolando in Madrid in which 11 people were killed and more than 70 wounded on September 13, 1974. ETA members told journalist Eileen MacDonald that ETA has always had female commandos and operators. Women make up about 10 percent of imprisoned ETA members, so that may be roughly the percentage of women in ETA ranks.

Infamous female commandos have included Leila Khaled, a beautiful PFLP commando who hijacked a TWA passenger plane on August 29, 1969, and then blew it up after evacuating the passengers, without causing any casualties (see Leila Khaled, Appendix). One of the first female terrorists of modern international terrorism, she probably inspired hundreds of other angry young women around the world who admired the thrilling pictures of her in newspapers and magazines worldwide showing her cradling a weapon, with her head demurely covered.

Another PFLP female hijacker, reportedly a Christian Iraqi, was sipping champagne in the cocktail bar of a Japan Air Lines Jumbo jet on July 20, 1973, when the grenade that she was carrying strapped to her waist exploded, killing her.

Women have also played a significant role in Italian terrorist groups. Leonard Weinberg and William Lee Eubank (1987: 248-53) have been able to quantify that role by developing a data file containing information on about 2,512 individuals who were arrested or wanted by police for terrorism from January 1970 through June 1984. Of those people, 451, or 18 percent, were female. Of those females, fewer than 10 percent were affiliated with neofascist groups (see Table 2, Appendix). The rest belonged to leftist terrorist groups, particularly the Red Brigades (Brigate Rosse—BR), which had 215 female members. Weinberg and Eubank found that the Italian women surveyed were represented at all levels of terrorist groups: 33 (7 percent) played leadership roles and 298 (66 percent) were active "regulars" who took part in terrorist actions. (see Table 3, Appendix). Weinberg and Eubank found that before the women became involved in terrorism they tended to move from small and medium-sized communities to big cities (see Table 4, Appendix). The largest group of the women (35 percent) had been students before becoming terrorists, 20 percent had been teachers, and 23 percent had held white-collar jobs as clerks, secretaries, technicians, and nurses (see Table 5, Appendix). Only a few of the women belonged to political parties or trade union organizations, whereas 80 (17 percent) belonged to leftist extraparliamentary movements. Also noteworthy is the fact that 121 (27 percent) were related by family to other terrorists. These researchers concluded that for many women joining a terrorist group resulted from a small group or family decision.

Characteristics of Female Terrorists

Practicality, Coolness

German intelligence officials told Eileen MacDonald that "absolute practicality...was particularly noticeable with women revolutionaries." By this apparently was meant coolness under pressure. However, Germany's female terrorists, such as those in the Baader-Meinhof Gang, have been described by a former member as "all pretty male-dominated; I mean they had male characteristics." These included interests in technical things, such as repairing cars, driving, accounting, and organizing. For example, the RAF's Astrid Proll was a first-rate mechanic, Gudrun Ensslin was in charge of the RAF's finances, and Ulrike Meinhof sought out apartments for the group.

According to Christian Lochte, the Hamburg director of the Office for the Protection of the Constitution, the most important qualities that a female member could bring to terrorist groups, which are fairly unstable, were practicality and pragmatism: "In wartime women are much more capable of keeping things together," Lochte told MacDonald. "This is very important for a group of terrorists, for their dynamics. Especially a group like the RAF, where there are a lot of quarrels about strategy, about daily life. Women come to the forefront in such a group, because they are practical."

Galvin points out the tactical value of women in a terrorist group. An attack by a female terrorist is normally less expected than one by a man. "A woman, trading on the impression of being a mother, nonviolent, fragile, even victim like, can more easily pass scrutiny by security forces...." There are numerous examples illustrating the tactical surprise factor that can be achieved by female terrorists. A LTTE female suicide commando was able to get close enough to Indian Prime Minister Rajiv Gandhi on May 21, 1991, to garland him with flowers and then set off her body bomb, killing him, herself, and 17 others. Nobody suspected the attractive Miss Kim of carrying a bomb aboard a Korean Air Flight 858. And Leila Khaled, dressed in elegant clothes and strapped with grenades, was able to pass through various El Al security checks without arousing suspicion. Female terrorists have also been used to draw male targets into a situation in which they could be kidnapped or assassinated.

Dedication, Inner Strength, Ruthlessness

Lochte also considered female terrorists to be stronger, more dedicated, faster, and more ruthless than male terrorists, as well as more capable of withstanding suffering because "They have better nerves than men, and they can be both passive and active at the same time." The head of the German counterterrorist squad told MacDonald that the difference between the RAF men and women who had been caught after the fall of the Berlin Wall was that the women had been far more reticent about giving information than the men, and when the women did talk it was for reasons of guilt as opposed to getting a reduced prison sentence, as in the case of their male comrades.

According to MacDonald, since the late 1960s, when women began replacing imprisoned or interned male IRA members as active participants, IRA women have played an increasingly important role in "frontline" actions against British troops and Protestant paramilitary units, as well as in terrorist actions against the British public. As a result, in the late 1960s the IRA merged its separate women's sections within the movement into one IRA. MacDonald cites several notorious IRA women terrorists. They include Marion Price, 19, and her sister (dubbed "the Sisters of Death"), who were part of the IRA's 1973 bombing campaign in London. In the early 1970s, Dr. Rose Dugdale, daughter of a wealthy English family, hijacked a helicopter and used it to try to bomb a police barracks. In 1983 Anna Moore was sentenced to life imprisonment for her role in bombing a Northern Ireland pub in which 17 were killed. Ella O'Dwyer and Martina Anderson, 23, a former local beauty queen, received life sentences in 1986 for their part in the plot to bomb London and 16 seaside resorts. Another such terrorist was Mairead Farrell, who was shot dead by the SAS in Gibraltar in 1988. A year before her death, Farrell, who was known for her strong feminist views, said in an interview that she was attracted to the IRA because she was treated the same as "the lads." As of 1992, Evelyn Glenholmes was a fugitive for her role in a series of London bombings.

MacDonald interviewed a few of these and a number of other female IRA terrorists, whom she described as all ordinary, some more friendly than others. Most were unmarried teenagers or in their early twenties when they became involved in IRA terrorism. None had been recruited by a boyfriend. When asked why they joined, all responded with "How could we not?" replies. They all shared a hatred for the British troops (particularly their foul language and manners) and a total conviction that violence was justified. One female IRA volunteer told MacDonald that "Everyone is treated the same. During training, men and women are equally taught the use of explosives and weapons."

Single-Mindedness

Female terrorists can be far more dangerous than male terrorists because of their ability to focus single-mindedly on the cause and the goal. Lochte noted that the case of Susanne Albrecht demonstrated this total dedication to a cause, to the exclusion of all else, even family ties and upbringing. The RAF's Suzanne Albrecht, daughter of a wealthy maritime lawyer, set up a close family friend, Jurgen Ponto, one of West Germany's richest and most powerful men and chairman of the Dresden Bank, for assassination in his home, even though she later admitted to having experienced nothing but kindness and generosity from him. Lochte told MacDonald that if Albrecht had been a man, she would have tried to convince her RAF comrade to pick another target to kidnap. "Her attitude was," Lochte explained, "to achieve the goal, to go straight ahead without any interruptions, any faltering. This attitude is not possible with men." (Albrecht, however, reportedly was submitted to intense pressure by her comrades to exploit her relationship with the banker, and the plan was only to kidnap him rather than kill him.) After many years of observing German terrorists, Lochte concluded, in his comments to MacDonald, that women would not hesitate to shoot at once if they were cornered. "For anyone who loves his life," he told MacDonald, "it is a good idea to shoot the women terrorists first." In his view, woman terrorists feel they need to show that they can be even more ruthless than men.

Germany's neo-Nazi groups also have included female members, who have played major roles, according to MacDonald. For example, Sibylle Vorderbrügge, 26, joined a notorious neo-Nazi group in 1980 after becoming infatuated with its leader. She then became a bomb-throwing terrorist expressly to please him. According to MacDonald, she was a good example to Christian Lochte of how women become very dedicated to a cause, even more than men. "One day she had never heard of the neo-Nazis, the next she was a terrorist." Lochte commented, "One day she had no interest in the subject; the next she was 100 percent terrorist; she became a fighter overnight."

Female Motivation for Terrorism

What motivates women to become terrorists? Galvin suggests that women, being more idealistic than men, may be more impelled to perpetrate terrorist activities in response to failure to achieve change or the experience of death or injury to a loved one. Galvin also argues that the female terrorist enters into terrorism with different motivations and expectations than the male terrorist. In contrast to men, who Galvin characterizes as being enticed into terrorism by the promise of "power and glory," females embark on terrorism "attracted by promises of a better life for their children and the desire to meet people's needs that are not being met by an intractable establishment." Considering that females are less likely than males to have early experience with guns, terrorist membership is therefore a more active process for women than for men because women have more to learn. In the view of Susana Ronconi, one of Italy's most notorious and violent terrorists in the 1970s, the ability to commit violence did not have anything to do with gender. Rather, one's personality, background, and experience were far more important.

Companionship is another motivating factor in a woman's joining a terrorist group. MacDonald points out that both Susanna Ronconi and Ulrike Meinhof "craved love, comradeship, and emotional support" from their comrades.

Feminism has also been a motivating ideology for many female terrorists. Many of them have come from societies in which women are repressed, such as Middle Eastern countries and North Korea, or Catholic countries, such as in Latin America, Spain, Ireland, and Italy. Even Germany was repressive for women when the Baader-Meinhof Gang emerged.

CONCLUSION

Terrorist Profiling

In profiling the terrorist, some generalizations can be made on the basis on this examination of the literature on the psychology and sociology of terrorism published over the past three decades. One finding is that, unfortunately for profiling purposes, there does not appear to be a single terrorist personality . This seems to be the consensus among terrorism psychologists as well as political scientists and sociologists. The personalities of terrorists may be as diverse as the personalities of people in any lawful profession. There do not appear to be any visibly detectable personality traits that would allow authorities to identify a terrorist.

Another finding is that the terrorist is not diagnosably psychopathic or mentally sick. Contrary to the stereotype that the terrorist is a psychopath or otherwise mentally disturbed, the terrorist is actually quite sane, although deluded by an ideological or religious way of viewing the world. The only notable exceptions encountered in this study were the German anarchist terrorists, such as the Baader-Meinhof Gang and their affiliated groups. The German terrorists seem to be a special case, however, because of their inability to come to terms psychologically and emotionally with the shame of having parents who were either passive or active supporters of Hitler.

The highly selective terrorist recruitment process explains why most terrorist groups have only a few pathological members. Candidates who exhibit signs of psychopathy or other mental illness are deselected in the interest of group survival. Terrorist groups need members whose behavior appears to be normal and who would not arouse suspicion. A member who exhibits traits of psychopathy or any noticeable degree of mental illness would only be a liability for the group, whatever his or her skills. That individual could not be depended on to carry out the assigned mission. On the contrary, such an individual would be more likely to sabotage the group by, for example, botching an operation or revealing group secrets if captured. Nor would a psychotic member be likely to enhance group solidarity. A former PKK spokesman has even stated publicly that the PKK's policy was to exclude psychopaths.

This is not to deny, however, that certain psychological types of people may be attracted to terrorism. In his examination of autobiographies, court records, and rare interviews, Jerrold M. Post (1990:27) found that "people with particular

60

personality traits and tendencies are drawn disproportionately to terrorist careers." Authors such as Walter Laqueur, Post notes, "have characterized terrorists as action-oriented, aggressive people who are stimulus-hungry and seek excitement." Even if Post and some other psychologists are correct that individuals with narcissistic personalities and low self-esteem are attracted to terrorism, the early psychological development of individuals in their pre-terrorist lives does not necessarily mean that terrorists are mentally disturbed and can be identified by any particular traits associated with their early psychological backgrounds. Many people in other high-risk professions, including law enforcement, could also be described as "action-oriented, aggressive people who are stimulus-hungry and seek excitement." Post's views notwithstanding, there is actually substantial evidence that terrorists are quite sane.

Although terrorist groups are highly selective in whom they recruit, it is not inconceivable that a psychopathic individual can be a top leader or *the* top leader of the terrorist group. In fact, the actions and behavior of the ANO's Abu Nidal, the PKK's Abdullah Ocalan, the LTTE's Velupillai Prabhakaran, the FARC's Jorge Briceño Suárez, and Aum Shinrikyo's Shoko Asahara might lead some to believe that they all share psychopathic or sociopathic symptoms. Nevertheless, the question of whether any or all of these guerrilla/terrorist leaders are psychopathic or sociopathic is best left for a qualified psychologist to determine. If the founder of a terrorist group or cult is a psychopath, there is little that the membership could do to remove him, without suffering retaliation. Thus, that leader may never have to be subjected to the group's standards of membership or leadership.

In addition to having normal personalities and not being diagnosably mentally disturbed, a terrorist's other characteristics make him or her practically indistinguishable from normal people, at least in terms of outward appearance. Terrorist groups recruit members who have a normal or average physical appearance. As a result, the terrorist's physical appearance is unlikely to betray his or her identity as a terrorist, except in cases where the terrorist is well known, or security personnel already have a physical description or photo. A terrorist's physical features and dress naturally will vary depending on race, culture, and nationality. Both sexes are involved in a variety of roles, but men predominate in leadership roles. Terrorists tend to be in their twenties and to be healthy and strong; there are relatively few older terrorists, in part because terrorism is a physically demanding occupation. Training alone requires considerable physical fitness. Terrorist leaders are older, ranging from being in their thirties to their sixties.

The younger terrorist who hijacks a jetliner, infiltrates a government building, lobs a grenade into a sidewalk café, attempts to assassinate a head of state, or detonates a body-bomb on a bus will likely be appropriately dressed and acting normal before initiating the attack. The terrorist needs to be inconspicuous in order to approach the target and then to escape after carrying out the attack, if escape is part of the plan. The suicide terrorist also needs to approach a target inconspicuously. This need to appear like a normal citizen would also apply to the FARC, the LTTE, the PKK, and other guerrilla organizations, whenever they use commandos to carry out urban terrorist operations. It should be noted that regular FARC, LTTE, and PKK members wear uniforms and operate in rural areas. These three groups do, however, also engage in occasional acts of urban terrorism, the LTTE more than the FARC and PKK. On those occasions, the LTTE and PKK terrorists wear civilian clothes. FARC guerrillas are more likely to wear uniforms when carrying out their acts of terrorism, such as kidnappings and murders, in small towns.

Terrorist and guerrilla groups do not seem to be identified by any particular social background or educational level. They range from the highly educated and literate intellectuals of the 17 November Revolutionary Organization (17N) to the scientifically savvy "ministers" of the Aum Shinrikyo terrorist cult, to the peasant boys and girls forcibly inducted into the FARC, the LTTE, and the PKK guerrilla organizations.

Most terrorist leaders have tended to be well educated. Examples include Illich Ramírez Sánchez ("The Jackal") and the Shining Path's Abimael Guzmán Reynoso, both of whom are currently in prison. Indeed, terrorists are increasingly well educated and capable of sophisticated, albeit highly biased, political analysis. In contrast to Abu Nidal, for example, who is a relatively uneducated leader of the old generation and one who appears to be motivated more by vengefulness and greed than any ideology, the new generation of Islamic terrorists, be they key operatives such as the imprisoned Ramzi Yousef, or leaders such as Osama bin Laden, are well educated and motivated by their religious ideologies. The religiously motivated terrorists are more dangerous than the politically motivated terrorists because they are the ones most likely to develop and use weapons of weapons of mass destruction (WMD) in pursuit of their messianic or apocalyptic visions. The level of intelligence of a terrorist group's leaders may determine the longevity of the group. The fact that the 17 November group has operated successfully for a quarter century must be indicative of the intelligence of its leaders.

In short, a terrorist will look, dress, and behave like a normal person, such as a university student, until he or she executes the assigned mission. Therefore, considering that this physical and behavioral description of the terrorist could describe almost any normal young person, terrorist profiling based on personality, physical, or sociological traits would not appear to be particularly useful.

If terrorists cannot be detected by personality or physical traits, are there other early warning indicators that could alert security personnel? The most important indicator would be having intelligence information on the individual, such as a "watch list," a description, and a photo, or at least a threat made by a terrorist group. Even a watch-list is not fool-proof, however, as demonstrated by the case of Sheikh Omar Abdel Rahman, who, despite having peculiar features and despite being on a terrorist watch-list, passed through U.S. Customs unhindered.

Unanticipated stress and nervousness may be a hazard of the profession, and a terrorist's nervousness could alert security personnel in instances where, for example, a hijacker is boarding an aircraft, or hostage-takers posing as visitors are infiltrating a government building. The terrorist undoubtedly has higher levels of stress than most people in lawful professions. However, most terrorists are trained to cope with nervousness. Female terrorists are known to be particularly cool under pressure. Leila Khaled and Kim Hyun Hee mention in their autobiographies how they kept their nervousness under control by reminding themselves of, and being totally convinced of, the importance of their missions.

Indeed, because of their coolness under pressure, their obsessive dedication to the cause of their group, and their need to prove themselves to their male comrades, women make formidable terrorists and have proven to be more dangerous than male terrorists. Hizballah, the LTTE, and PKK are among the groups that have used attractive young women as suicide body-bombers to great effect. Suicide body-bombers are trained to be totally at ease and confident when approaching their target, although not all suicide terrorists are able to act normally in approaching their target.

International terrorists generally appear to be predominately either leftist or Islamic. A profiling system could possibly narrow the statistical probability that an unknown individual boarding an airliner might be a terrorist if it could be accurately determined that most terrorists are of a certain race, culture, religion, or nationality. In the absence of statistical data, however, it cannot be determined here whether members of any particular race, religion, or nationality are responsible for most acts of international terrorism. Until those figures become available, smaller-scale terrorist group profiles might be more useful. For example, a case could be made that U.S. Customs personnel should give extra scrutiny to the passports of young foreigners claiming to be "students" and meeting the following general description: physically fit males in their early twenties of Egyptian, Jordanian, Yemeni, Iraqi, Algerian, Syrian, or Sudanese nationality, or Arabs bearing valid British passports, in that order. These characteristics generally describe the core membership of Osama bin Laden's Arab "Afghans" (see Glossary), also known as the Armed Islamic Movement (AIM), who are being trained to attack the United States with WMD.

Terrorist Group Mindset Profiling

This review of the academic literature on terrorism suggests that the psychological approach by itself is insufficient in understanding what motivates terrorists, and that an interdisciplinary approach is needed to more adequately understand terrorist motivation. Terrorists are motivated not only by psychological factors but also very real political, social, religious, and economic factors, among others. These factors vary widely. Accordingly, the motivations, goals, and ideologies of ethnic separatist, anarchist, social revolutionary, religious fundamentalist, and new religious terrorist groups differ significantly. Therefore, each terrorist group must be examined within its own cultural, economic, political, and social context in order to better understand the motivations of its individual members and leaders and their particular ideologies.

Although it may not be possible to isolate a so-called terrorist personality, each terrorist group has its own distinctive mindset. The mindset of a terrorist group reflects the personality and ideology of its top leader and other circumstantial traits, such as typology (religious, social revolutionary, separatist, anarchist, and so forth), a particular ideology or religion, culture, and nationality, as well as group dynamics.

Jerrold Post dismisses the concept of a terrorist mindset on the basis that behavioral scientists have not succeeded in identifying it. Post confuses the issue, however, by treating the term "mindset" as a synonym for personality. The two terms are not synonymous. One's personality is a distinctive pattern of thought, emotion, and behavior that define one's way of interacting with the physical and social environment, whereas a mindset is a fixed mental attitude or a fixed state of mind.

In trying to better define mindset, the term becomes more meaningful when considered within the context of a group. The new terrorist recruit already has a personality when he or she joins the group, but the new member acquires the group's mindset only after being fully indoctrinated and familiarized with its ideology, point of view, leadership attitudes, ways of operating, and so forth. Each group will have its own distinctive mindset, which will be a reflection of the top leader's personality and ideology, as well as group type. For example, the basic mindset of a religious terrorist group, such as Hamas and Hizballah, is Islamic fundamentalism. The basic mindset of an Irish terrorist is anti-British sectarianism and separatism. The basic mindset of an ETA member is anti-Spanish separatism. The basic mindset of a 17 November member is antiestablishment, anti-US, anti-NATO, and anti-German nationalism and Marxism-Leninism. And the basic mindset of an Aum Shinrikyo member is worship of Shoko Asahara, paranoia against the Japanese and U.S. governments, and millenarian, messianic apocalypticism.

Terrorist group mindsets determine how the group and its individual members view the world and how they lash out against it. Knowing the mindset of a group enables a terrorism analyst to better determine the likely targets of the group and its likely behavior under varying circumstances. It is surprising, therefore, that the concept of the terrorist mindset has not received more attention by terrorism specialists. It may not always be possible to profile the individual leaders of a terrorist group, as in the case of the 17 November Revolutionary Organization, but the group's mindset can be profiled if adequate information is available on the group and there is an established record of activities and pronouncements. Even though two groups may both have an Islamic fundamentalist mindset, their individual mindsets will vary because of their different circumstances.

One cannot assume to have a basic understanding of the mindset of a terrorist group without having closely studied the group and its leader(s). Because terrorist groups are clandestine and shadowy, they are more difficult to analyze than guerrilla groups, which operate more openly, like paramilitary organizations. A terrorist group is usually much smaller than a guerrilla organization, but the former may pose a more lethal potential threat to U.S. security interests than the latter by pursuing an active policy of terrorist attacks against U.S. interests. A guerrilla group such as the FARC may kidnap or kill an occasional U.S. citizen or citizens as a result of unauthorized actions by a hard-line front commander, but a terrorist group such as the 17 November Revolutionary Organization does so as a matter of policy.

Although Aum Shinrikyo, a dangerous cult, is on U.S. lists of terrorist groups and is widely feared in Japan, it still operates openly and legally, even though a number of its members have been arrested, some have received prison sentences, and others, including Shoko Asahara, have been undergoing trial. It can probably be safely assumed that Aum Shinrikyo will resume its terrorist activities, if not in Japan then elsewhere. Indeed, it appears to be reorganizing, and whatever new form in which this hydra-headed monster emerges is not likely to be any more pleasant than its former incarnation. The question is: what is Aum Shinrikyo planning to help bring about the apocalypse that it has been predicting for the new millennium?

Knowing the mindset of a terrorist group would better enable the terrorism analyst to understand that organization's behavior patterns and the active or potential threat that it poses. Knowing the mindsets, including methods of operation, of terrorist groups would also aid in identifying what group likely perpetrated an unclaimed terrorist action and in predicting the likely actions of a particular group under various circumstances. Indeed, mindset profiling of a terrorist group is an essential mode of analysis for assessing the threat posed by the group. A terrorist group's mindset can be determined to a significant extent through a database analysis of selective features of the group and patterns in its record of terrorist attacks. A computer program could be designed to replicate the mindset of each terrorist group for this purpose.

Promoting Terrorist Group Schisms

All terrorist and guerrillas groups may be susceptible to psychological warfare aimed at dividing their political and military leaders and factions. Guerrilla organizations, however, should not be dealt with like terrorist groups. Although the FARC, the LTTE, and the PKK engage in terrorism, they are primarily guerrilla organizations, and therefore their insurgencies and accompanying terrorism are likely to continue as long as there are no political solutions. In addition to addressing the root causes of a country's terrorist and insurgency problems, effective counterterrorist and counterinsurgency strategies should seek not only to divide a terrorist or guerrilla group's political and military factions but also to reduce the group's rural bases of support through rural development programs and establishment of civil patrols in each village or town.

Another effective counterterrorist strategy would be the identification and capture of a top hard-line terrorist or guerrilla leader, especially one who exhibits psychopathic characteristics. Removing the top hard-liners of a terrorist group would allow the group to reassess the policies pursued by its captured leader and possibly move in a less violent direction, especially if a more politically astute leader assumes control. This is what appears to be happening in the case of the PKK, which has opted for making peace since the capture of its ruthless, hard-line leader, Abdullah Ocalan. A government could simultaneously help members of urban terrorist groups to defect from their groups, for example through an amnesty program, as was done so effectively in Italy. A psychologically sophisticated policy of promoting divisions between political and military leaders as well as defections within guerrilla and terrorist groups is likely to be more effective than a simple military strategy based on the assumption that all members and leaders of the group are hard-liners. A military response to terrorism unaccompanied by political countermeasures is likely to promote cohesion within the group. The U.S. Government's focus on bin Laden as the nation's number one terrorist enemy has clearly raised his profile in the Islamic world and swelled the membership ranks of al-Qaida. Although not yet martyred, bin Laden has become the Ernesto "Che" Guevara of Islamic fundamentalism. As Post (1990:39) has explained:

> When the autonomous cell comes under external threat, the external danger has the consequence of reducing internal divisiveness and uniting the group against the outside enemy....Violent societal counteractions can transform a tiny band of insignificant persons into a major opponent of society, making their "fantasy war," to use Ferracuti's apt term, a reality."

How Guerrilla and Terrorist Groups End

A counterterrorist policy should be tailor-made for a particular group, taking into account its historical, cultural, political, and social context, as well as the context of what is known about the psychology of the group or its leaders. The motivations of a terrorist group—both of its members and of its leaders—cannot be adequately understood outside its cultural, economic, political, and social context. Because terrorism is politically or religiously motivated, a counterterrorist policy, to be effective, should be designed to take into account political or religious factors. For example, terrorists were active in Chile during the military regime (1973-90), but counterterrorist operations by democratic governments in the 1990s have reduced them to insignificance. The transition from military rule to democratic government in Chile proved to be the most effective counterterrorist strategy.

In contrast to relatively insignificant political terrorist groups in a number of countries, Islamic terrorist groups, aided by significant worldwide support among Muslim fundamentalists, remain the most serious terrorist threat to U.S. security interests. A U.S. counterterrorist policy, therefore, should avoid making leaders like Osama bin Laden heroes or martyrs for Muslims. To that end, the eye-for-an-eye Israeli policy of striking back for each act of terrorism may be highly counterproductive when applied by the world's only superpower against Islamic terrorism, as in the form of cruise-missile attacks against, or bombings of, suspected terrorist sites. Such actions, although politically popular at home, are seen by millions of Muslims as attacks against the Islamic religion and by people in many countries as superpower bullying and a violation of a country's sovereignty. U.S. counterterrorist military attacks against elusive terrorists may serve only to radicalize large sectors of the Muslim population and damage the U.S. image worldwide.

Rather than retaliate against terrorists with bombs or cruise missiles, legal, political, diplomatic, financial, and psychological warfare measures may be more effective. Applying pressure to state sponsors may be especially effective. Cuba and Libya are two examples of terrorist state sponsors that apparently concluded that sponsoring terrorists was not in their national interests. Iran and Syria may still need to be convinced.

Jeanne Knutson was critical of the reactive and ad hoc nature of U.S. counterterrorism policy, which at that time, in the early 1980s, was considered an entirely police and security task, as opposed to "...a *politically* rational, comprehensive strategy to deal with *politically* motivated violence." She found this policy flawed because it dealt with symptoms instead of root causes and instead of eradicating the causes had increased the source of political violence. She charged that this policy routinely radicalized, splintered, and drove underground targeted U.S. groups, thereby only confirming the "we-they" split worldview of these groups. Unfortunately, too many governments still pursue purely military strategies to defeat political and religious extremist groups.

Abroad, Knutson argued, the United States joined military and political alliances to support the eradication of internal dissident groups without any clear political rationale for such a stance. She emphasized that "terrorists are individuals who commit crimes for *political* reasons," and for this reason "the political system has better means to control and eliminate their activities and even to attack their root causes than do the police and security forces working alone." Thus, she considered it politically and socially unwise to give various national security agencies, including the Federal Bureau of Investigation (FBI), the political role of choosing targets of political violence. She advocated "a necessary stance of neutrality toward national dissident causes—whether the causes involve the territory of historical friend or foe." She cited the neutral U.S. stance toward the Irish Republican Army (IRA) as a case study of how to avoid anti-U.S. terrorism. Her views still seem quite relevant.

Goals of a long-range counterterrorism policy should also include deterring alienated youth from joining a terrorist group in the first place. This may seem an impractical goal, for how does one recognize a potential terrorist, let alone deter him or her from joining a terrorist group? Actually, this is not so impractical in the cases of guerrilla organizations like the FARC, the LTTE, and the PKK, which conscript all the young people in their rural areas of operation who can be rounded up. A counter strategy could be approached within the framework of advertising and civic-action campaigns. A U.S. government-sponsored mass media propaganda campaign undertaken in the Colombian countryside, the Kurdish enclaves, and the Vanni region of Sri Lanka and tailor-made to fit the local culture and society probably could help to discredit hard-liners in the guerrilla/terrorist groups sufficiently to have a serious negative impact on their recruitment efforts. Not only should all young people in the region be educated on the realities of guerrilla life, but a counterterrorist policy should be in place to inhibit them from joining in the first place. If they are inducted, they should be helped or encouraged to leave the group.

The effectiveness of such a campaign would depend in part on how sensitive the campaign is culturally, socially, politically, and economically. It could not succeed, however, without being supplemented by civic-action and rural security programs, especially a program to establish armed self-defense civil patrols among the peasantry. The Peruvian government was able to defeat terrorists operating in the countryside only by creating armed self-defense civil patrols that became its eyes and ears. These patrols not only provided crucial intelligence on the movements of the Shining Path and Tupac Amaru terrorists, but also enabled the rural population to take a stand against them.

There is little evidence that direct government intervention is the major factor in the decline of terrorist groups. Clearly, it was an important factor in certain cases, such as the RAF and with various urban Marxist-Leninist group in Latin America where massive governmental repression was applied (but at unacceptably high cost in human rights abuses). Social and psychological factors may be more important. If, for security reasons, a terrorist group becomes too isolated from the population, as in the case of the RAF and the Uruguayan Tupamaros, the group is prone to losing touch with any base of support that it may have had. Without a measure of popular support, a terrorist group cannot survive. Moreover, if it fails to recruit new members to renew itself by supporting or replacing an aging membership or members who have been killed or captured, it is likely to disintegrate. The terrorist groups that have been active for many years have a significant base of popular support. Taylor and Qualye point out that despite its atrocious terrorist violence, the Provisional IRA in 1994 continued to enjoy the electoral support of between 50,000 and 70,000 people in Northern Ireland. The FARC, the LTTE, and the PKK continue to have strong popular support within their own traditional bases of support.

In the cases of West German and Italian terrorism, counterterrorist operations undoubtedly had a significant impact on terrorist groups. Allowing terrorists an exit can weaken the group. For example, amnesty programs, such as those offered by the Italian government, can help influence terrorists to defect. Reducing support for the group on the local and national levels may also contribute to reducing the group's recruitment pool. Maxwell Taylor and Ethel Quayle have pointed out that penal policies in both countries, such as allowing convicted terrorists reduced sentences and other concessions, even including daytime furloughs from prison to hold a normal job, had a significant impact in affecting the long-term reduction in terrorist violence. Referring to Italy's 1982 Penitence Law, Taylor and Quayle explain that "This law effectively depenalized serious terrorist crime through offering incentives to terrorists to accept their defeat, admit their guilt and inform on others so that the dangers of terrorist violence could be diminished." Similarly, Article 57 of the German Penal Code offers the possibility of reduction of sentence or suspension or deferment of sentence when convicted terrorists renounce terrorism. Former terrorists do not have to renounce their ideological convictions, only their violent methods. To be sure, these legal provisions have not appealed to hard-core terrorists, as evidenced by the apparent reactivation of the Italian Red Brigades in 1999. Nevertheless, for countries with long-running insurgencies, such as Colombia, Sri Lanka, and Turkey, amnesty programs for guerrillas are very important tools for resolving their internal wars.

With regard to guerrilla/terrorist organizations, a major question is how to encourage the political wing to constrain the military wing, or how to discredit or neutralize the military branch. The PKK should serve as an ongoing case study in this regard. Turkey, by its policy of demonizing the PKK and repressing the Kurdish population in its efforts to combat it instead of seeking a political solution, only raised the PKK's status in the eyes of the public and lost the hearts and minds of its Kurdish population. Nevertheless, by capturing Ocalan and by refraining thus far from making him a martyr by hanging him, the Turkish government has inadvertently allowed the PKK to move in a more political direction as advocated by its political leaders, who now have a greater voice in decision-making. Thus, the PKK has retreated from Turkey and indicated an interest in pursuing a political as opposed to a military strategy. This is how a guerrilla/terrorist organization should end, by becoming a political party, just as the M-19 did in Colombia and the Armed Forces of National Liberation (FALN) did in El Salvador.

APPENDIX

SOCIOPSYCHOLOGICAL PROFILES: CASE STUDIES

Exemplars of International Terrorism in the Early 1970s

Renato Curcio

Significance: Imprisoned leader of the Italian Red Brigades.

Background: The background of Renato Curcio, the imprisoned former main leader of the first-generation Red Brigades (Brigata Rosse), provides some insight into how a university student became Italy's most wanted terrorist. The product of an extramarital affair between Renato Zampa (brother of film director Luigi Zampa) and Yolanda Curcio, Renato Curcio was born near Rome on September 23, 1941. His early years were a difficult time for him and his mother, a housemaid, whose itinerant positions with families required long separations. In April 1945, Curcio's beloved uncle, Armando, a Fiat auto worker, was murdered in a Fascist ambush. A poor student, Curcio failed several subjects in his first year of high school and had to repeat the year. He then resumed vocational training classes until moving to Milan to live with his mother. He enrolled in the Ferrini Institute in Albenga, where he became a model student. On completing his degree in 1962, he won a scholarship to study at the new and innovative Institute of Sociology at the University of Trento, where he became absorbed in existential philosophy. During the mid-1960s, he gravitated toward radical politics and Marxism as a byproduct of his interest in existentialism and the self. By the late 1960s, he had become a committed revolutionary and Marxist theoretician. According to Alessandro Silj, three political events transformed him from a radical to an activist and ultimately a political terrorist: two bloody demonstrations at Trento and a massacre by police of farm laborers in 1968. During the 1967-69 period, Curcio was also involved in two Marxist university groups: the Movement for a Negative University and the publication *Lavoro Politico* (Political Work). Embittered by his expulsion from the radical Red Line faction of *Lavoro Politico* in August 1969, Curcio decided to drop out of Trento and forego his degree, even though he already had passed his final examinations. Prior to transferring his bases of activities to Milan, Curcio married, in a Catholic ceremony, Margherita (Mara) Cagol, a Trentine sociology major, fellow radical, and daughter of a prosperous Trento merchant. In Milan Curcio became a full-fledged terrorist. The Red Brigades was formed in the second half of 1970 as a result of the merger of Curcio's Proletarian Left and a radical student and worker group. After getting arrested in February 1971 for occupying a vacant house, the Curcios and the most militant members of the Proletarian Left went completely underground and organized the Red Brigades and spent the next three years, from 1972 to 1975, engaging in a series of bombings and kidnappings of prominent figures. Curcio was captured but freed by Margherita in a raid on the prison five months later. Three weeks after the dramatic prison escape, Margherita was killed in a shootout with the Carabinieri. Curcio was again captured in January 1976, tried, and convicted, and he is still serving a 31-year prison sentence for terrorist activities.

An insight into Curcio's (1973:72) motivation for becoming a terrorist can be found in a letter to his mother written during his initial prison confinement:

> Yolanda dearest, mother mine, years have passed since the day on which I set out to encounter life and left you alone to deal with life. I have worked, I have studied, I have fought....Distant memories stirred. Uncle Armando who carried me astride his shoulders. His limpid and ever smiling eyes that peered far into the distance towards a society of free and equal men. And I loved him like a father. And I picked up the rifle that only death, arriving through the murderous hand of the Nazi-fascists, had wrested from him.... My enemies are the enemies of humanity and of intelligence, those who have built and build their accursed fortunes on the material and intellectual misery of the people. Theirs is the hand that has banged shut the door of my cell. And I cannot be but proud. But I am not merely an "idealist" and it is not enough for me to have, as is said, "a good conscience." For this reason I will continue to fight for communism even from the depths of a prison.

Leila Khaled

Position: First Secretary of the PFLP's Palestinian Popular Women's Committees (PPWC).

Background: Khaled was born on April 13, 1948, in Haifa, Palestine. She left Haifa at age four when her family fled the Israeli occupation and lived in impoverished exile in a United Nations Relief and Works Agency (UNRWA) refugee camp in Sour, Lebanon. By age eight, she had become politically aware of the Palestinian plight. Inspired by a Palestinian revolutionary of the 1930s, Izz Edeen Kassam, she decided to become a revolutionary "in order to liberate my people and myself." The years 1956-59 were her period of political apprenticeship as an activist of the Arab Nationalist Movement (ANM). By the summer of 1962, she was struggling to cope with national, social, class, and sexual oppression but, thanks to her brother's financial support, finally succeeded in attending the American University of Beirut (AUB) in 1962-63, where she scored the second highest average on the AUB entrance exam.

While an AUB student, Khaled received what she refers to as her "real education" in the lecture hall of the Arab Cultural Club (ACC) and in the ranks of the ANM and the General Union of Palestinian Students (GUPS). Her "intellectual companion"at AUB was her American roommate, with whom she would have heated political arguments. In the spring of 1963, Khaled was admitted into the ANM's first paramilitary contingent of university students and was active in ANM underground activities. For lack of funding, she was unable to continue her education after passing her freshman year in the spring of 1963.

In September 1963, Khaled departed for Kuwait, where she obtained a teaching position. After a run-in with the school's principal, who called her to task for her political activities on behalf of the Palestine Liberation Organization (PLO), she returned to Lebanon in late June 1964. She returned to the school in Kuwait that fall but was demoted to elementary teaching. The U.S. invasions of the Dominican Republic and Vietnam in 1965 solidified her hatred of the U.S. Government. The death of Ernesto "Che" Guevara on October 9, 1967, convinced her to join the revolution.

When Fatah renewed its military operations on August 18, 1967, Khaled attempted to work through Fatah's fund-raising activities in Kuwait to liberate Palestine. She pleaded with Yasir Arafat's brother, Fathi Arafat, to be allowed to join Al-Assifah, Fatah's military wing. She found an alternative to Fatah, however, when the Popular Front for the Liberation of Palestine (PFLP) hijacked an El-Al airplane in July 1968, an action that inspired her to seek contacts with the PFLP in Kuwait. She succeeded when PFLP representative Abu Nidal, whom she described as "a tall, handsome young man" who was "reserved and courteous," met her in a Kuwaiti bookstore. After performing fund-raising for the PFLP, she was allowed to join its Special Operations Squad and underwent intensive training. In her first mission, she hijacked a TWA plane on a flight from Rome to Athens on August 29, 1969, and diverted it to Damascus, where all 113 passengers were released unharmed. Although her identity was revealed to the world by the Syrians, she continued her terrorist career by training to commandeer an El-Al plane. When Jordan's King Hussein launched a military offensive against the Palestinian resistance in Amman in February 1970, Khaled fought in the streets alongside PFLP comrades. That March, in preparation for another hijacking, she left Amman and underwent at least three secret plastic surgery operations over five months by a well-known but very reluctant plastic surgeon in Beirut.

While Khaled was discussing strategy with Dr. Wadi Haddad in his Beirut apartment on July 11, 1970, the apartment was hit by two rockets in the first Israeli attack inside Lebanon, injuring the man's wife and child. On September 6, 1970, Khaled and an accomplice attempted to hijack an El-Al flight from Amsterdam with 12 armed security guards aboard but were overpowered. He was shot to death, but she survived and was detained in London by British police. After 28 days in detention, she was released in a swap for hostages from hijacked planes and escorted on a flight to Cairo and then, on October 12, to Damascus.

Following her release, Khaled went to Beirut and joined a combat unit. In between fighting, she would tour refugee camps and recruit women. She married an Iraqi PFLP member, Bassim, on November 26, 1970, but the marriage was short-lived. She returned to the same Beirut plastic surgeon and had her former face mostly restored. She barely escaped a bed-bomb apparently planted by the Mossad, but her sister was shot dead on Christmas Day 1976. After fading from public view, she surfaced again in 1980, leading a PLO delegation to the United Nations Decade for Women conference in Copenhagen. She attended university in Russia for two years in the early 1980s, but the PFLP ordered her to return to combat in Lebanon before she had completed her studies.

Khaled married a PFLP physician in 1982. She was elected first secretary of the Palestinian Popular Women's Committees (PPWC) in 1986. At the beginning of the 1990s, when she was interviewed by Eileen MacDonald, she was living in the Yarmuk refugee camp in Damascus, still serving as PPWC first secretary and "immediately recognizable as the young Leila."

Since then, Khaled has been living in Amman, Jordan, where she works as a teacher, although still a PFLP member. She was allowed by Israel briefly to enter Palestinian-ruled areas in the West Bank, or at least the Gaza Strip, in February 1996, to vote on amending the Palestinian charter to remove its call for Israel's destruction. She was on a list of 154 members of the Palestine National Council (PNC), an exile-based parliament, who Israel approved for entrance into the Gaza Strip. Khaled said she had renounced terrorism. However, she declined an invitation to attend a meeting in Gaza with President Clinton in December 1998 at which members of the PNC renounced portions of the PLO charter calling for the destruction of Israel. "We are not going to change our identity or our history," she explained to news media.

Kozo Okamoto

Significance: The sole surviving Rengo Sekigun (Japanese Red Army) terrorist of the PFLP's Lod (Tel Aviv) Airport massacre of May 30, 1972, who remains active.

Background: Kozo Okamoto was born in southwestern Japan in 1948. He was the youngest of six children, the son of a retired elementary school principal married to a social worker. The family was reportedly very close when the children were young. His mother died of cancer in 1966, and his father remarried. He is not known to have had a disturbed or unusual childhood. On the contrary, he apparently had a normal and happy childhood. He achieved moderate success at reputable high schools in Kagoshima. However, he failed to qualify for admission at Kyoto University and had

Kozo Okamoto (presumably on right) with three other captured PFLP comrades, 1997. (AP Photo courtesy of www.washingtonpost.com)

to settle for the Faculty of Agriculture at Japan's Kagoshima University, where his grades were mediocre. While a university student, he was not known to be politically active in extremist groups or demonstrations, although he belonged to a student movement and a peace group and became actively concerned with environmental issues. However, Okamoto's older brother, Takeshi, a former student at Kyoto University, introduced him to representatives of the newly formed JRA in Tokyo in early 1970. Soon thereafter, Takeshi participated in the hijacking of a Japan Air Lines jet to Korea. Takeshi's involvement in that action compelled his father to resign his job. Although Kozo had promised his father that he would not follow in his brother's footsteps, Kozo became increasingly involved in carrying out minor tasks for the JRA. Kozo Okamoto was attracted to the JRA more for its action-oriented program than for ideological reasons.

In late February 1972, Okamoto traveled to Beirut, where the JRA said he could meet his brother, and then underwent seven weeks of terrorist training by PFLP personnel in Baalbek. After he and his comrades traveled through Europe posing as tourists, they boarded a flight to Lod Airport on May 30, 1972. Unable to commit suicide as planned following the Lod Airport massacre, Okamoto was captured and made a full confession only after being promised that he would be allowed to kill himself. During his trial, he freely admitted his act and demonstrated no remorse; he viewed himself as a soldier rather than a terrorist, and to him Lod Airport was a military base in a war zone. Psychiatrists who examined Okamoto certified that he was absolutely sane and rational. To be sure, Okamoto's courtroom speech, including his justification for slaughtering innocent people and his stated hope that he and his two dead comrades would become, in death, "three stars of Orion," was rather bizarre.

By 1975, while in solitary confinement, Okamoto began identifying himself to visitors as a Christian. When his sanity began to deteriorate in 1985, he was moved to a communal cell. That May, he was released as a result of an exchange of Palestinian prisoners for three Israeli soldiers, under a swap conducted by the Popular Front for the Liberation of Palestine—General Command (PFLP-GC) . He arrived to a hero's welcome in Libya on May 20, and was met by JRA leader Fusako Shigenobu. He apparently has continued to operate with the PFLP-GC. On February 15, 1997, he and five JRA comrades were arrested in Lebanon and accused of working with the PFLP-GC and training PFLP-GC cadres in the Bekaa Valley outside Baalbek. According to another report, they were arrested in a Beirut apartment. That August, he and four of his comrades were sentenced to three years in jail (minus time already served and deportation to an undisclosed location) for entering the country with forged passports.

Exemplars of International Terrorism in the Early 1990s

Mahmud Abouhalima

Significance: World Trade Center bomber.

Background: Mahmud Abouhalima was born in a ramshackle industrial suburb 15 miles south of Alexandria in 1959, the first of four sons of a poor but stern millman, a powerful weight lifter. Mahmud was known as an ordinary, well-rounded, cheerful youth who found comfort in religion. He prayed hard and shunned alcohol. He studied education at Alexandria University and played soccer in his spare time. He developed a deep and growing hatred for Egypt because of his belief that the country offered little hope for his generation's future. As a teenager, he began to hang around with members of an outlawed Islamic Group (al-Jama al-Islamiyya), headed by Sheikh Omar Abdel Rahman. In 1981 Abouhalima quit school and left Egypt. He reportedly fought against the Soviets in Afghanistan. In September 1991, now an Afghan veteran, he was granted a tourist visa to visit Germany. In Munich he sought political asylum, claiming that he faced persecution in Egypt because of his membership in the Muslim Brotherhood (Al Ikhwan al Muslimun). He subsequently made his way to the United States and worked as a taxi driver in Brooklyn, New York. He also allegedly ran a phony coupon-redemption scam. This operation and a similar one run by Zein Isa, a member of the ANO in St. Louis, supposedly funneled about $200 million of the annual $400 million in fraudulent coupon losses allegedly suffered by the industry back to the Middle East to fund terrorist activities, although the figure seems a bit high. On February 26, 1993, the day of the WTC bombing, he was seen by several witnesses with Mohammed A. Salameh at the Jersey City storage facility. Tall and red-haired, Abouhalima ("Mahmud the Red"), 33, was captured in his native Egypt not long after the bombing. He was "hands-on ringleader" and the motorist who drove a getaway car. He is alleged to have planned the WTC bombing and trained his co-conspirators in bomb-testing. He was sentenced to 240 years in federal prison.

Sheikh Omar Abdel Rahman

Significance: World Trade Center bombing co-conspirator.

Background: Omar Abdel Rahman was born in 1938, blinded by diabetes as an infant. He became a religious scholar in Islamic law at Cairo's al-Azhar University. By the 1960s, he had become increasingly critical of Egypt's government and its institutions, including al-Azhar University, which he blamed for failing to uphold true Islamic law. One of the defendants accused of assassinating Egyptian President Anwar Sadat on October 6, 1981, Dr. Abdel Rahman was considered an accessory because of his authorization of the assassination through the issuance of a fatwa or Islamic judicial decree, to the assassins. However, he was acquitted because of the ambiguity of his role. In the 1980s, made unwelcome by the Egyptian government, he traveled to Afghanistan, Britain, Pakistan, Saudi Arabia, Sudan, Switzerland, and the United States, exhorting young Muslims to join the mujahideen to fight the Soviets in Afghanistan. Sheikh Abdel Rahman's activities also included leading a puritanical Islamic fundamentalist movement (Al Jamaa al Islamiyya) aimed at overthrowing the regime of President Hosni Mubarak. The movement's methods included terrorist attacks against foreign tourists visiting archaeological sites in Egypt. The sheik has described American and other Western tourists in Egypt as part of a "plague" on his country.

Sheikh Omar Abdel Rahman
(Photo courtesy of Middle East Intelligence Bulletin, Vol. 3, No. 6, June 2001)

In 1990, after a brief visit back to Egypt, Abdel Rahman fled to Sudan. Later that year, the blind cleric, despite being on the U.S. official list of terrorists, succeeded in entering the United States with a tourist visa obtained at the U.S. Embassy in Sudan. He became the prayer leader of the small El Salem Mosque in Jersey City, New Jersey, where many of the WTC bombing conspirators attended services. He preached violence against the United States and pro-Western governments in the Middle East. Abdel Rahman maintained direct ties with mujahideen fighters and directly aided terrorist groups in Egypt, to whom he would send messages on audiotape. He served as spiritual mentor of El Sayyid A. Nosair, who assassinated Jewish Defense League founder Rabbi Meir Kahane on November 5, 1990. (Nosair, whose conviction was upheld by a Federal appeals court panel on August 16, 1999, knew many members of the WTC bombing group and was visited by some of them in jail.)

Following the WTC bombing on February 26, 1993, Abdel Rahman was implicated in that conspiracy as well as in a plot to bomb other public places in New York, including the Holland and Lincoln tunnels and the United Nations building. He was also implicated in a plot to assassinate U.S. Senator Alfonse d'Amato (R., N.Y.) and United Nations Secretary General Boutros-Ghali. Abdel Rahman and seven others were arrested in connection with this plot in June 1993. In a 1994 retrial of 1981 riot cases in Egypt, Abdel Rahman was convicted in absentia and sentenced to seven years in prison.

On October 1, 1995, Sheikh Abdel Rahman and nine other Islamic fundamentalists were convicted in a federal court in New York of conspiracy to destroy U.S. public buildings and structures. Abdel Rahman was convicted of directing the conspiracy and, under a joint arrangement with Egypt, of attempting to assassinate Mubarak. His conviction and those of his co-conspirators were upheld on August 16, 1999. Despite his imprisonment, at least two Egyptian terrorist groups—Islamic Group (Gamaa Islamiya) and al-Jihad (see al-Jihad)—continue to regard him as their spiritual leader. The Gamaa terrorists who massacred 58 tourists near Luxor, Egypt, in November 1997 claimed the attack was a failed hostage takeover intended to force the United States into releasing Abdel Rahman. He is currently serving a life sentence at a federal prison in New York.

Mohammed A. Salameh

Significance: A World Trade Center bomber.

Background: Mohammed A. Salameh was born near Nablus, an Arab town on the West Bank, on September 1, 1967. In his final years in high school, Salameh, according to his brother, "became religious, started to pray and read the Koran with other friends in high school. He stopped most of his past activities and hobbies....He was not a fundamentalist. He was interested in Islamic teachings." According to another source, Salameh comes from a long line of guerrilla fighters on his mother's side. His maternal grandfather fought in the 1936 Arab revolt against British rule in Palestine, and even as an old man joined the PLO and was jailed by the Israelis. A maternal uncle was arrested in 1968 for "terrorism" and served 18 years in an Israeli prison before he was released and deported, making his way to Baghdad, where he became number two in the "Western Sector," a PLO terrorist unit under Iraqi influence. Mohammed Salameh earned a degree from the Islamic studies faculty of the University of Jordan. His family went into debt to buy him an airline ticket to the United States, where he wanted to obtain an MBA. Salameh entered the United States on February 17, 1988, on a six-month tourist visa, and apparently lived in Jersey City illegally for the next five years. He apparently belonged to the Masjid al-Salam Mosque in Jersey City, whose preachers included fundamentalist Sheikh Omar Abdel Rahman. Slight and bearded, naive and manipulable, Salameh was arrested in the process of returning to collect the deposit on the van that he had rented to carry the Trade Center bombing materials. On March 4, 1993, Salameh, 26, was charged by the FBI with "aiding and abetting" the WTC bombing on February 26, 1993. He is also believed to be part of the group that stored the explosive material in a Jersey City storage locker.

Ahmed Ramzi Yousef

Significance: Mastermind of the World Trade Center bombing.

Background: Yousef, whose real name is Abd-al-Basit Balushi, was born either on May 20, 1967, or April 27, 1968, in Kuwait, where he grew up and completed high school. His Pakistani father is believed to have been an engineer with Kuwaiti Airlines for many years. Yousef is Palestinian on his mother's side; his grandmother is Palestinian. He considers himself Palestinian.

In 1989 Yousef graduated from Britain's Swansea University with a degree in engineering. Yousef is believed to have trained and fought in the Afghan War. He and bin Laden reportedly were linked at least as long ago as 1989. In that year, Yousef went to the Philippines and introduced himself as an emissary of Osama bin Laden, sent to support that country's radical Islamic movement, specifically the fundamentalist Abu Sayyaf group. When Iraqi President Saddam Hussein's army invaded Kuwait in August 1990, Yousef was known as a collaborator. After disappearing in Kuwait in 1991, he is next known to have reappeared in the Philippines in December 1991, accompanied by a Libyan missionary named Mohammed abu Bakr, the leader of the Mullah Forces in Libya. Yousef stayed for three months providing training to Abu Sayyaf guerrillas in the southern Philippines.

When he arrived from Pakistan at John F. Kennedy Airport on September 1, 1992, without a visa, Yousef, who was carrying an Iraqi passport, applied for political asylum. Often described as slender, Yousef is six feet tall, weighs 180 pounds, and is considered white, with an olive complexion. He was sometimes clean shaven, but wears a beard in his FBI wanted poster. Despite his itinerant life as an international terrorist, Yousef is married and has two daughters. A Palestinian friend and fellow terrorist, Ahmad Ajaj, who was traveling with Yousef on September 1, 1992, although apparently at a safe distance, was detained by passport control officers at John F. Kennedy Airport for carrying a false Swedish passport. Ajaj was carrying papers containing formulas for bomb-making material, which prosecutors said were to be used to destroy bridges and tunnels in New York.

Ahmed Ramzi Yousef
(Photo courtesy of
www.terrorismfiles.org/individuals/ramzi_
yousef.html/)

Yousef was allowed to stay in the United States while his political asylum case was considered. U.S. immigration officials apparently accepted his false claim that he was a victim of the Gulf War who had been beaten by Iraqi soldiers because the Iraqis suspected that he had worked for Kuwaiti resistance. Yousef moved into an apartment in Jersey City with roommate Mohammad Salameh (*q.v.*). After participating in the Trade Center bombing on February 26, 1993, Yousef, then 25 or 26 years old, returned to Manila, the Philippines, that same day. In Manila, he plotted "Project Bojinka," a plan to plant bombs aboard U.S. passenger airliners in 1995, using a virtually undetectable bomb that he had created. He was skilled in the art of converting Casio digital watches into timing switches that use light bulb filaments to ignite cotton soaked in nitroglycerine explosive. He carried out a practice run on a Philippine Airlines Flight 434 bound for Tokyo on December 9, 1994. A wearer of contact lenses, Yousef concealed the nitroglycerin compound in a bottle normally used to hold saline solution. His bomb killed a Japanese tourist seated near the explosive, which he left taped under a seat, and wounded 10 others. In March 1993, prosecutors in Manhattan indicted Yousef for his role in the WTC bombing. On January 6, 1995, Manila police raided Yousef's room overlooking Pope John Paul II's motorcade route into the city. Yousef had fled the room after accidentally starting a fire while mixing chemicals. Police found explosives, a map of the Pope's route, clerical robes, and a computer disk describing the plot against the Pope, as well as planned attacks against U.S. airlines. Yousef's fingerprints were on the material, but he had vanished, along with his girlfriend, Carol Santiago. Also found in his room was a letter threatening Filipino interests if a comrade held in custody were not released. It claimed the "ability to make and use chemicals and poisonous gas... for use against vital institutions and residential populations and the sources of drinking water." Yousef's foiled plot involved blowing up eleven U.S. commercial aircraft in midair. The bombs were to be made of a stable, liquid form of nitroglycerin designed to pass through airport metal detectors.

For most of the three years before his capture in early 1995, Yousef reportedly resided at the bin Laden-financed Bayt Ashuhada (House of Martyrs) guest house in Peshawar, Pakistan. On February 8, 1995, local authorities arrested Yousef in Islamabad in the Su Casa guest house, also owned by a member of the bin Laden family. Yousef had in his possession the outline of an even greater international terrorist campaign that he was planning, as well as bomb-making products, including two toy cars packed with explosives and flight schedules for United and Delta Airlines. His plans included using a suicide pilot (Said Akhman) to crash a light aircraft filled with powerful explosives into the CIA headquarters in Langley, Virginia, as well as blowing up 11 U.S. airliners simultaneously as they approached U.S. airports. He was then turned over to the FBI and deported to the United States. On June 21, 1995, Yousef told federal agents that he had planned and executed the WTC bombing.

On September 6, 1996, Yousef was convicted in a New York Federal District Court for trying to bomb U.S. airliners in Asia in 1995. On January 8, 1998, he was sentenced to 240 years in prison. He has remained incarcerated in the new "supermax" prison in Florence, Colorado. His cellmates in adjoining cells in the "Bomber Wing" include Timothy McVeigh, the right-wing terrorist who blew up a federal building in Oklahoma City on April 19, 1995, and Ted Kaczynski, the sociopathic loner known as the Unabomber. The polyglot Yousef has discussed languages with Kaczynski, who speaks Spanish, French, and German, and taught him some Turkish.

Ethnic Separatist Groups

Irish Terrorists

According to a middle-level IRA officer interviewed by *Newsweek* in 1988, the IRA has plenty of recruits. Each potential enlistee is kept under scrutiny for as long as a year before being allowed to sign up. The Provos are paranoid about informers, so hard drinkers and loudmouths are automatically disqualified from consideration. H.A. Lyons, a Belfast psychiatrist who frequently works with prisoners, told *Newsweek* that the IRA's political murderers are "fairly normal individuals," compared with nonpolitical killers. "They regard themselves as freedom fighters,"adding that they feel no remorse for their actions, at least against security forces. As the IRA officer explained to *Newsweek*:

> The killing of innocent civilians is a thing that sickens all volunteers, and it must and will stop. But I can live with the killing [of security forces]. There is an occupying army which has taken over our country. I see no difference between the IRA and World War II resistance movements.

Rona M. Fields noted in 1976 that Belfast "terrorists" are most often adolescent youths from working-class families. By the 1990s, however, that appeared to have changed. According to the profile of Irish terrorists, loyalist and republican, developed by Maxwell Taylor and Ethel Quayle (1994), "The person involved in violent action is likely to be up to 30 years old, or perhaps a little older and usually male." Republican and loyalist leaders tend to be somewhat older. The terrorist is invariably from a working class background, not because of some Marxist doctrine but because the loyalist and republican areas of Northern Ireland are primarily working class. Quite likely, he is unemployed. "He is either living in the area in which he was born, or has recently left it for operational reasons." His education is probably limited, because he probably left school at age 15 or 16 without formal qualifications. However, according to Taylor and Quayle, recruits in the early 1990s were becoming better educated. Before becoming involved in a violent action, the recruit probably belonged to a junior wing of the group for at least a year. Although not a technically proficient specialist, he is likely to have received weapons or explosives training. The profile notes that the recruits are often well dressed, or at least appropriately dressed, and easily blend into the community. "Northern Ireland terrorists are frequently articulate and give the impression of being worldly," it states. At the psychological level, Taylor found "a lack of signs of psychopathology, at least in any overt clinical sense" among the members. Irish terrorists can easily justify their violent actions "in terms of their own perception of the world," and do not even object to being called terrorists, although they refer to each other as volunteers or members.

The Provisional Irish Republican Army (PIRA) is generally a homegrown, grassroots organization. In the late 1980s, some members of the PIRA were as young as 12 years of age, but most of those taking part in PIRA operations were in the twenties. Front-line bombers and shooters were younger, better educated, and better trained than the early members were. The PIRA recruits members from the streets.

Kurdistan Workers' Party (PKK) and Abdullah Ocalan

Group/Leader Profile:

The Kurdistan Workers' Party (Parte Krikaranc Kordesian/Partia Karkaris Kurdistan-PKK) originated in 1972 with a small group of Marxist-oriented university activists in Ankara known as "Apocus." The principal founder of the student-based Apocular group, Abdullah Ocalan ("Apo"—Uncle) was a former student (expelled) in political science at Ankara University, who was prominent in the underground Turkish Communist Party. Ocalan (pronounced Oh-ja-lan or

URGE'ah-lohn) was born in 1948 in the village of Omerli in the southeastern Turkish province of Urfa, the son of an impoverished Kurdish farmer and a Turkish mother. In 1974 Apocus formed a university association whose initial focus was on gaining official recognition for Kurdish language and cultural rights. Over the next four years, Ocalan organized the association into the PKK while studying revolutionary theories. In 1978 he formally established the PKK, a clandestine Marxist-Leninist Kurdish political party. During his trial in June 1999, Ocalan blamed harsh Turkish laws for spawning the PKK in 1978, and then

Abdullah Ocalan
(Photo courtesy of CNN.com, Time.com)

for its taking up arms in 1984. "These kinds of laws give birth to rebellion and anarchy," he said. The language ban—now eased—"provokes this revolt."

Several of the founders of the PKK were ethnic Turks. One of the eleven founders of the PKK was Kesire Yildirim, the only female member. She later married Ocalan, but they became estranged when she began questioning his policies and tactics. (She left him in 1988 to join a PKK breakaway faction in Europe.) Unlike other Kurdish groups in the Middle East, the PKK advocated the establishment of a totally independent Kurdish Marxist republic, Kurdistan, to be located in southeastern Turkey.

In about 1978, influenced by Mao Zedong's revolutionary theory, Ocalan decided to leave the cities and establish the PKK in rural areas. He fled Turkey before the 1980 military coup and lived in exile, mostly in Damascus and in the Lebanese plains under Syrian control, where he set up his PKK headquarters and training camps. In 1983 he recruited and trained at least 100 field commandos in the Bekaa Valley in Lebanon, where the PKK maintains its Masoum Korkmaz guerrilla training base and headquarters. The PKK's army, the People's Liberation Army of Kurdistan (ARGK), began operating in August 1984. The PKK created the National Liberation Front of Kurdistan (ERNK) in 1985 to bolster its recruitment, intelligence, and propaganda activities.

The PKK's early radical agenda, including its antireligious rhetoric and violence, alienated the PKK from much of the Kurdish peasantry. Citing various sources, Kurdish specialist Martin van Bruinessen reports that although the PKK had won little popular sympathy by the early 1990s with its brutally violent actions, "It gradually came to enjoy the grudging admiration of many Kurds, both for the prowess and recklessness of its guerrilla fighters and for the courage with which its arrested partisans stood up in court and in prison.... By the end of 1990, it enjoyed unprecedented popularity in eastern Turkey, although few seemed to actively support it." Ocalan is reportedly regarded by many Kurds as a heroic freedom fighter. However, the "silent majority" of Kurds living in Turkey reportedly oppose the PKK and revile Ocalan.

The charismatic Ocalan was unquestioningly accepted by devoted PKK members, and the PKK reportedly lacked dissenting factions, at least until the early 1990s. The PKK's Leninist structure constrained any internal debate. However, in March 1991 Ocalan admitted at a press conference that he was facing a challenge from a faction within the PKK that wanted him to work for autonomy within Turkey instead of a separate Kurdish state and recognition of the PKK as a political force. When Ocalan, who is said to speak very little Kurdish, agreed to this position and announced a cease-fire in March 1993, the decision was not unanimous, and there was dissension within the PKK leadership over it.

The PKK's recruitment efforts mainly have targeted the poorer classes of peasants and workers, the latter group living in the standard apartment ghettos on the fringes of Turkey's industrial cities. According to a Turkish survey in the southeast cited by Barkey and Fuller, of the 35 percent of those surveyed who responded to a question on how well they knew members of the PKK, 42 percent claimed to have a family member in the PKK. The Turkish government has maintained that the PKK recruits its guerrillas forcibly and then subjects them to "brainwashing" sessions at training camps in Lebanon. According to the official Ankara Journalist Association, "members of the organization are sent into armed clashes under the influence of drugs. [PKK leaders] keep them under the influence of drugs so as to prevent them from seeing the reality." Scholars also report that the PKK has forced young men to join. In November 1994, the PKK's former American spokesperson, Kani Xulum, told James Ciment that the PKK recruits only those who understand "our strategies and aims" and "we're careful to keep psychopaths" out of the organization. The PKK has laws regarding military conscription. At its 1995 congress, the PKK decided not to recruit youth younger than 16 to fight and to make military service for women voluntary. By the mid-1990s, PKK volunteers increasingly came from emigre families in Germany and the rest of Europe and even Armenia and Australia.

Since it began operating, the PKK's ranks have included a sprinkling of female members.
However, according to O'Ballance, "Its claim that they lived and fought equally side by side with their male colleagues can be discounted, although there were some exceptions. Women were employed mainly on propaganda, intelligence, liaison and educational tasks. The PKK claimed that women accounted for up to 30 percent of its strength." In April 1992, the ARGK claimed that it had a commando force of some 400 armed women guerrillas in the mountains of northern Iraq. James Ciment reported in 1996 that approximately 10 percent of PKK guerrillas are women. Thomas Goltz, a journalist specializing in Turkey, reports that beginning in the mid-1990s, "Many female recruits were specially trained as suicide bombers for use in crowded urban environments like Istanbul's bazaar and even on the beaches favored by European tourists along the Turkish Riviera." For example, a 19-year-old suicide female commando wounded eight policemen in a suicide attack in Istanbul in early July 1999.

The well-funded PKK's recruitment efforts have probably been aided significantly by its mass media outlets, particularly Med-TV, a PKK-dominated Kurdish-language TV station that operates by satellite transmission out of Britain. Ocalan himself often participated, by telephone, in the Med-TV talk shows, using the broadcasts to Turkey and elsewhere to convey messages and make announcements. Med-TV commands a wide viewership among the Kurds in southeast Turkey.

Barkey and Fuller describe the PKK as "primarily a nationalist organization," but one still with ties to the Left, although it claimed to have abandoned Marxism-Leninism by the mid-1990s. They report that, according to some Kurdish observers, "Ocalan has begun to show considerably more maturity, realism, and balance since 1993," moving away from ideology toward greater pragmatism. Barley and Graham confirm that the PKK "has been undergoing a significant shift in its political orientation" since the mid-1990s, including moving away from its anti-Islamism and "toward greater reality in its assessment of the current political environment" and the need to reach a political settlement with Turkey.

The PKK leadership's seemingly psychotic vengeful streak became an issue in the assassination of Olaf Palme, the prime minister of Sweden, who was shot and killed while walking in a Stockholm street on February 28, 1986. PKK members immediately became the prime suspects because of the group's extremist reputation. According to John Bulloch and Harvey Morris, "The motive was thought to be no more than a Swedish police determination that the PKK was a terrorist organization, and that as a result a visa had been refused for Ocalan to visit the country, which has a large and growing Kurdish minority." On September 2, 1987, PKK militant Hasan Hayri Guler became the prime suspect. According to *Hurriyet*, a Turkish newspaper, Hasan Hayri Guler reportedly was sent to Stockholm with orders to assassinate Palme in retaliation for the death of a PKK militant in Uppsala, Sweden. (The PKK denied the accusation and hinted that Turkish security forces may have been behind Palme's murder.)

In late 1998, Syria, under intense pressure from Turkey, closed the PKK camps and expelled Ocalan, who began an odyssey through various nations in search of political asylum. In February 1999, he was captured in Kenya and flown to Turkey.

Ocalan had the reputation of being a dogmatic, strict, and hard disciplinarian, even tyrannical. Scholars Henri J. Barkey and Graham E. Fuller, citing a Turkish book, describe him as:

> secretive, withdrawn, suspicious, and lacking in self-confidence. He does not like group discussion; his close associates reportedly seem uncomfortable around him. He does not treat others as equals and he often demeans his subordinates in front of others, demands self-confessions from his lieutenants, and keeps his distance from nearly everyone.

The ruthlessness with which Kurdish collaborators and PKK defectors were treated by the PKK reflected Ocalan's brutish attitude. Some PKK defectors have also alleged intimidation of guerrillas within PKK camps and units in the field. "If anyone crosses [Ocalan], either with eyes or attitude, he is accused of creating conflict," one defector was quoted by a Danish weekly. "The sinner is then declared a contra-guerrilla, and his punishment is death." According to the *Turkish Daily News*, Ocalan underlined his personal hunger for absolute power at the helm of the PKK in a party publication in 1991 as follows:

> I establish a thousand relationships every day and destroy a thousand political, organizational, emotional and ideological relationships. No one is indispensable for me. Especially if there is anyone who eyes the chairmanship of the PKK. I will not hesitate to eradicate them. I will not hesitate in doing away with people.

Ocalan has also been described as "a smiling, fast-talking and quick-thinking man," but one who "still follows an old Stalinist style of thinking, applying Marxist principles to all problems...." He is reportedly given to exaggeration of his importance and convinced that he and his party alone have the truth. Turkish journalists who have interviewed Ocalan have come away with the impression of a "megalomaniac" and "sick" man who has no respect for or understanding of the "superior values of European civilization." A December 1998 issue of the *Turkish Daily News* quoted Ocalan as saying in one of his many speeches:

> Everyone should take note of the way I live, what I do and what I don't do. The way I eat, the way I think, my orders and even my inactivity should be carefully studied. There will be lessons to be learned from several generations because Apo is a great teacher.

Ocalan's capture and summary trial initially appeared to have radicalized the PKK. The return of two senior PKK members to the main theater of operations following Ocalan's capture seemed to indicate that a new more hard-line approach was emerging within the PKK leadership. Ali Haidar and Kani Yilmaz, former PKK European representatives, were summoned back to the PKK's main headquarters, now located in the Qandil Mountain Range straddling Iraq and Iran. *Jane's Defence Weekly* reports that their return suggested that the PKK's military wing exercises new authority over the PKK's political or diplomatic representatives, whose approach was seen as failing in the wake of Ocalan's capture. (In addition to Haidar and Yilmaz, the PKK's ruling six-member Presidential Council includes four other senior and long-serving PKK commanders: Cemil Bayik ("Cuma"), Duran Kalkan ("Abbas"), Murat Karayillan ("Cemal"), and Osman Ocalan ("Ferhat")). However, on August 5, 1999, the

PKK's Presidential Council declared that the PKK would obey Ocalan's call to abandon its armed struggle and pull out of Turkey. Whether all the PKK groups would do the same or whether the PKK's gesture merely amounted to a tactical retreat remained to be seen. In any case, the rebels began withdrawing from Turkey in late August 1999.

The PKK remains divided between political and military wings. The political wing favors a peaceful political struggle by campaigning for international pressure on Ankara. It is supported by hundreds of thousands of Kurds living in Europe. The military wing consists of about 4,500 guerrillas operating from the mountains of Turkey, northern Iraq, and Iran. It favors continuing the war and stepping up attacks if Ocalan is executed. Karayillan, a leading military hard-liner, is reportedly the most powerful member of the Council and slated to take over if Ocalan is executed.

Liberation Tigers of Tamil Eelam (LTTE)

Group Profile

Background

The LTTE is widely regarded as the world's deadliest and fiercest guerrilla/terrorist group and the most ferocious guerrilla organization in South Asia. It is the only terrorist group to have assassinated three heads of government—Indian Prime Minister Rajiv Gandhi in 1991, Sri Lankan President Ranasinghe Premadasa in 1993, and former Prime Minister Dissanayake in 1994. It has also assassinated several prominent political and military figures. The LTTE's ill-conceived Gandhi assassination, however, resulted in the LTTE's loss of a substantial logistical infrastructure, and also the loss of popular support for the LTTE among mainstream Indian Tamils. In 1999 the LTTE made two threats on the life of Sonia Gandhi, who has nevertheless continued to campaign for a seat in parliament.

Also known as the Tamil Tigers, the LTTE is a by-product of Sri Lanka's ethnic conflict between the majority Sinhalese people and the minority ethnic Tamils, whose percentage of the island's population has been reported with figures ranging from 7 per cent to 17 percent. As a result of government actions that violated the rights of the Tamils in Sri Lanka in the 1948-77 period, a large pool of educated and unemployed young people on the island rose up against the government in 1972, under the leadership of the reputed military genius, Velupillai Prabhakaran. The Tigers and other Tamil militant groups realized the importance of creating an exclusively Tamil northern province for reasons of security, and began their campaign for the independence of Tamil Eelam, in the northern part of the island.

Founders of the military youth movement, Tamil New Tigers, formed the Liberation Tigers of Tamil Eelam on May 5, 1976. In one of its first major terrorist acts, it destroyed an Air Ceylon passenger jet with a time bomb in September 1978. The LTTE is only one of five groups, albeit the supreme one, that have achieved dominance over more than 35 Tamil guerrilla groups. Nationalism has remained the driving force behind the Tiger Movement.

The Tamil guerrilla movement is mainly composed of groups known as the Tigers, a term applied to the movement's numerous factions. According to Robert C. Oberst,

The groups, commonly called 'Tigers,' are shadowy collections of youths which emerged in the early 1980s as full-fledged politico-military organizations. Prior to that time they were loosely organized, and centered around dominant personalities.

The bloody ethnic riots of July 1983 polarized the Sinhalese and Tamil communities and became a watershed in the history of Sri Lanka. The riots started by the Sinhalese were a reaction to the death of 13 soldiers in a Tiger ambush. The end result was that around 500,000 Tamils left for India and the West, seeking asylum. They became the economic backbone of the terrorist campaign, and in the years that followed, the Tigers established offices and cells throughout the world, building a network unsurpassed by any other terrorist group. By 1987 the LTTE had emerged as the strongest militant group in Sri Lanka. More than two generations of Tamil youth have now been indoctrinated with separatism.

Membership Profile

The LTTE is an exclusively ethnic organization consisting almost entirely of Tamil Hindu youth. Although a majority of members of the Tamil guerrilla groups are Hindu, a significant number of Tamil Christians reportedly are in the movement. The early supporters of the Tamil independence movement were in their thirties. Since then, the age level has declined sharply. In the 1970s, quotas on university admissions for Tamils prompted younger Tamils to join the insurgency. By 1980 a majority of LTTE combatants were reportedly between 18 and 25 years of age, with only a few in their thirties. In 1990 approximately 75 percent of the second-generation LTTE membership were below 30 years of age, with about 50 percent between the ages of 15 and 21 and about 25 percent between the ages of 25 and 29. Highly motivated and disciplined, most LTTE fighters are subteenagers, according to an Indian authority.

The majority of the rank and file membership belong to the lower middle class. Almost all LTTE cadres have been recruited from the lower-caste strata of Jaffna society. The Tamil Tigers draw their recruits from the Tamils who live in the northern province and some from the eastern province. The cadres drawn from other

LTTE child soldiers
(Photo courtesy of Asiaweek, July 26, 1996)

areas of the northern and eastern provinces are only lower-rung "troops" who do not hold any place of importance or rank. In 1993 the LTTE reportedly had about 10,000 men in its fighting cadres, all Tamils and Hindus.

Deputy Defense Minister General Anuruddha Ratwatte reported in March 1999 that LTTE recruitment had been limited since early 1998 and reduced in strength

to a fighting cadre of fewer than 3,000, down from 4,000 to 5,000 members. As a result of its depleted manpower strength, the LTTE has become largely dependent on its Baby Brigade, which is comprised of boys and girls of ages ranging from 10 to 16 years. In May 1999, in an apparently desperate plan to establish a Universal People's Militia, the LTTE began to implement compulsory military training of all people over the age of 15 in areas under LTTE control in the Vanni.

Among the world's child combatants, children feature most prominently in the LTTE, whose fiercest fighting force, the Leopard Brigade (Sirasu puli), is made up of children. In 1983 the LTTE established a training base in the state of Pondicherry in India for recruits under 16, but only one group of children was trained. By early 1984, the nucleus of the LTTE Baby Brigade (Bakuts) was formed. The LTTE trained its first group of women in 1985. In October 1987, the LTTE stepped up its recruitment of women and children and began integrating its child warriors

LTTE child combatants
(Photo courtesy of Asiaweek, July 26, 1996)

into other units. LTTE leader Prabhakaran reportedly had ordered the mass conscription of children in the remaining areas under LTTE control, especially in the northeastern Mullaittivu District. From late 1995 to mid-1996, the LTTE recruited and trained at least 2,000 Tamils largely drawn from the 600,000 Tamils displaced in the wake of the operations to capture the peninsula. About 1,000 of these were between 12 and 16 years old. In 1998 Sri Lanka's Directorate of Military Intelligence estimated that 60 percent of LTTE fighters were below 18 and that a third of all LTTE recruits were women. According to an estimate based on LTTE fighters who have been killed in combat, 40 percent of LTTE's force are both males and females between nine and 18 years of age. Since

April 1995, about 60 percent of LTTE personnel killed in combat have been children, mostly girls and boys aged 10 to 16. Children serve everywhere except in leadership positions.

The entire LTTE hardcore and leaders are from Velvettihura or from the "fisher" caste, which has achieved some social standing because of the AK-47s carried by many of its militant members. According to Oberst, many tend to be university-educated, English-speaking professionals with close cultural and personal ties to the West. However, several of the important Tiger groups are led by Tamils who are relatively uneducated and nonprofessional, from a middle-status caste.

LTTE Suicide Commandos

The LTTE has a female military force and uses some females for combat. Indeed, female LTTE terrorists play a key role in the force. An unknown number of LTTE's female commandos are members of the LTTE's elite commando unit known as the Black Tigers. Members of this unit are designated as "suicide commandos" and carry around their necks a glass vial containing potassium cyanide. Suicide is common in Hindu society, and the Tigers are fanatical Hindus. The cyanide capsule, which LTTE members view as the ultimate symbol of bravery and commitment to a cause, is issued at the final initiation ceremony. A LTTE commando who wears the capsule must use it without fail in the event of an unsuccessful mission, or face some more painful form of death at the hands of the LTTE. One of the first reported instances when LTTE members had to carry out their suicide vow was in October 1987, when the LTTE ordered a group of captured leaders being taken to Colombo to commit suicide.

A LTTE child soldier with a cyanide capsule in his hand.
(Photo courtesy of Asiaweek, July 26, 1996)

The Black Tigers include both male and female members. The LTTE "belt-bomb girl" who assassinated Indian Prime Minister Rajiv Gandhi on May 21, 1991, after garlanding him with flowers, was an 18-year-old Sri Lankan Tamil Hindu, who had semtex sachets taped to her body. The blast also killed 17 others, including a LTTE photographer recording the action. Over the subsequent two months of investigations, as many as 25 LTTE members committed suicide to avoid capture.

Although the Gandhi assassination had huge negative repercussions for the LTTE, suicide attacks have remained the LTTE's trademark. On January 31, 1996, a LTTE suicide bomber ran his truck carrying 440 pounds of explosives into the front of the Central Bank of Sri Lanka, killing at least 91 people and wounding 1,400, as well as damaging a dozen office buildings in Sri Lanka's busy financial district. On March 16, 1999, a LTTE "belt-bomb girl" blew herself to bits when she jumped in front of the car of the senior counter-terrorism police officer in an attack just outside Colombo. The car, swerved, however, and escaped the full force of the blast. An accomplice of the woman then killed himself by swallowing cyanide. More recently, on July 29, 1999, a LTTE "belt-bomb girl" assassinated Neelan Tiruchelvam, a Harvard-educated, leading Sri Lankan moderate politician and peacemaker, in Colombo by blowing herself or himself up by detonating a body bomb next to the victim's car window.

Leader Profile
Velupillai Prabhakaran

Position: Top leader of the LTTE.

Velupillai Prabhakaran
(Photo courtesy of Rediff
on the Net, April 3,1999)

Background: Velupillai Prabhakaran was born on November 27, 1954. He is a native of Velvettihurai, a coastal village near Jaffna, where he hails from the "warrior-fisherman" caste. He is the son of a pious and gentle Hindu government official, an agricultural officer, who was famed for being so incorruptible that he would refuse cups of tea from his subordinates. During his childhood, Prabhakaran spent his days killing birds and squirrels with a slingshot. An average student, he preferred historical novels on the glories of ancient Tamil conquerors to his textbooks. As a youth, he became swept up in the growing militancy in the northern peninsula of Jaffna, which is predominately Tamil. After dropping out of school at age 16, he began to associate with Tamil "activist gangs." On one occasion as a gang member, he participated in a political kidnapping. In 1972 he helped form a militant group called the New Tamil Tigers, becoming its co-leader at 21. He imposed a strict code of conduct over his 15 gang members: no smoking, no drinking, and no sex. Only through supreme sacrifice, insisted Prabhakaran, could the Tamils achieve their goal of Eelam, or a separate homeland. In his first terrorist action, which earned him nationwide notoriety, Prabhakaran assassinated Jaffna's newly elected mayor, a Tamil politician who was a member of a large Sinhalese political party, on July 27, 1973 [some sources say 1975]. Prabhakaran won considerable power and prestige as a result of the deed, which he announced by putting up posters throughout Jaffna to claim responsibility. He became a wanted man and a disgrace to his pacifist father. In the Sri Lankan underworld, in order to lead a gang one must establish a reputation for sudden and decisive violence and have a prior criminal record. Qualifying on both counts, Prabhakaran then was able to consolidate control over his gang, which he renamed Liberation Tigers of Tamil Eelam on May 5, 1976.

In Tamil Nadu, Prabhakaran's exploits in the early 1980s turned him into a folk hero. His fierce eyes glared from calendars. Gradually and ruthlessly, he gained control of the Tamil uprising. Prabhakaran married a fiery beauty named Mathivathani Erambu in 1983. Since then, Tigers have been allowed to wed after five years of combat. Prabhakaran's wife, son, and daughter (a third child may also have been born) are reportedly hiding in Australia.

The LTTE's charismatic "supremo," Prabhakaran has earned a reputation as a military genius. A portly man with a moustache and glittering eyes, he has also been described as "Asia's new Pol Pot," a "ruthless killer," a "megalomaniac," and an "introvert," who is rarely seen in public except before battles or to host farewell banquets for Tigers setting off on suicide missions. He spends time planning murders of civilians, including politicians, and perceived Tamil rivals. Prabhakaran is an enigma even to his most loyal commanders. Asked who his heroes are, Prabhakaran once named actor Clint Eastwood. He has murdered many of his trusted commanders for suspected treason. Nevertheless, he inspires fanatical devotion among his fighters.

Prabhakaran and his chief intelligence officer and military leader, Pottu Amman, are the main LTTE leaders accused in Rajiv Gandhi's assassination. On January 27, 1998, the Colombo High Court issued warrants for the arrest of Prabhakaran, Amman, and eight others accused of killing 78 persons and destroying the Central Bank Building by the bomb explosion in 1996 and perpetrating other criminal acts between July 1, 1995, and January 31, 1996. Prabhakaran has repeatedly warned the Western nations providing military support to Sri Lanka that they are exposing their citizens to possible attacks.

Social Revolutionary Groups

Abu Nidal Organization (ANO)

(aka Fatah—The Revolutionary Council, Black June Organization, Arab Revolutionary Brigades, Revolutionary Organization of Socialist Muslims)

Group Profile

Since 1974 the Abu Nidal Organization (ANO) is said to have killed more than 300 people and wounded more than 650 in 20 countries. In recent years, however, as Abu Nidal has become little more than a symbolic head of the ANO, the ANO appears to have passed into near irrelevance as a terrorist organization.

By mid-1984 the ANO had about 500 members. A highly secretive, mercenary, and vengeful group, ANO has carried out actions under various aliases on several continents on behalf of Middle East intelligence organizations, such as those of Iraq, Syria, Iran, and Libya, as well as other terrorist groups, such as the Shi'ites in southern Lebanon. For many of its attacks, the ANO has used its trademark Polish W.Z.63 submachine gun. Relying primarily on highly motivated young

Palestinian students, Abu Nidal has run a highly disciplined and professional organization, but one held together by terror; many members have been accused of treason, deviation, or desertion and eliminated.

For Abu Nidal, the enemy camp comprises everyone who opposes the forceful liberation of Palestine. Together with Zionism and imperialism, a special place in this pantheon is occupied by those in the Arab world supporting the political process, whether Arab regimes or Arafat's PLO. Abu Nidal's Fath (Revolutionary Council) sees itself as the true heir of the authentic Fath, which must be saved from the "founding fathers" (Arafat and his cohorts) who betrayed its heritage. Abu Nidal's Fath represents a model of secular Palestinian fundamentalism, whose sacred goal is the liberation of Palestine.

In 1976-78 Abu Nidal began to establish a corps of dormant agents by forcing young Palestinian students on scholarships in Europe to become his agents. After a short training period in Libya, Iraq, or Syria, they were sent abroad to remain as dormant agents for activation when needed. Despite the ruthlessness of ANO terrorism, ANO members may have a very conservative appearance. Robert Hitchens, a British journalist and reportedly one of the few foreigners to have met Abu Nidal, was highly impressed by the cleanliness of Abu Nidal's headquarters in Baghdad, and by the "immaculate dress of his men," who were "all clean-shaven and properly dressed," as well as very polite.

Recruiting is highly selective. In the early 1980s, members typically came from families or hometowns of earlier members in Lebanon, but by the mid-1980s the ANO began to increase recruitment by drawing from refugee camps. Graduates of the first training program would be driven to southern Lebanon, where they would undergo several weeks of military training. A few weeks later, they would be driven to Damascus airport, issued new code names, and flown to Tripoli, where they would be transferred to ANO training camps.

In the mid-1980s, Abu Nidal continued to recruit from Arab students studying in Europe. Madrid has served as an important source for recruiting these students.

In the 1987-92 period, most of Abu Nidal's trainees at his camp located 170 kilometers south of Tripoli continued to be alienated Palestinian youths recruited from Palestinian refugee camps and towns in Lebanon. They were flown to Libya on Libyan military transports from the Damascus airport in groups of about 100. Abu Nidal's recruitment efforts were directed at very young students, whom he would promise to help with education, career prospects, and families. In addition to paying them a good salary, he lauded the students for fulfilling their duty not just to Palestine but to the whole Arab nation by joining his organization, which he claimed was inspired by the noblest Arab virtues.

The selection process became very serious once the new recruits arrived at ANO training camps in Libya. New recruits were made to sign warrants agreeing to be executed if any intelligence connection in their backgrounds were later to be discovered. They were also required to write a highly detailed autobiography for their personal file, to be used for future verification of the information provided. While still on probation, each new recruit would be assigned to a two-man cell with his recruiter and required to stand guard at the Abu Nidal offices, distribute the Abu Nidal magazine, or participate in marches and demonstrations. Some were ordered to do some intelligence tasks, such as surveillance or reporting on neighborhood activities of rival organizations. New recruits were also required to give up alcohol, cigarettes, drugs, and women. They were ordered never to ask the real name of any Abu Nidal member or to reveal their own, and to use only codenames. Throughout their training, recruits were drilled in and lectured on the ANO's ten fundamental principles: commitment, discipline, democratic centralism, obedience to the chain of command, initiative and action, criticism and self-criticism, security and confidentiality, planning and implementation, assessment of experience gained, and thrift. Infractions of the rules brought harsh discipline. Recruits suspected of being infiltrators were tortured and executed.

According to the *Guardian*, by the late 1990s the ANO was no longer considered an active threat, having broken apart in recent years in a series of feuds as Abu Nidal became a recluse in his Libyan haven. According to the *New York Times*, Abu Nidal still had 200 to 300 followers in his organization in 1998, and they have been active in recent years, especially against Arab targets. As of early 1999, however, there were reports that the ANO was being torn apart further by internal feuds, defections, and lack of financing. Half of Abu Nidal's followers in Lebanon and Libya reportedly had defected to Yasser Arafat's Fatah movement and moved to the Gaza Strip.

Sabri al-Banna ("Abu Nidal")
(Photo courtesy of The Washington Post, 1999)

Leader Profile
Abu Nidal

Position: Leader of the ANO.

Background: Abu Nidal was born Sabri al-Banna in May 1937 in Jaffa, Palestine, the son of a wealthy orange grower, Khalil al-Banna, and of his eighth wife. His father was reputed to be one of the wealthiest men in Palestine, primarily from dealing in property. Abu Nidal's family also had homes in Egypt, France, and Turkey. His father died in 1945, when Sabri was attending a French mission school in Jaffa. His more devout older brothers then enrolled him in a private Muslim school in Jerusalem for the next two years, until the once wealthy family was forced into abject poverty. The Israeli government confiscated all of the al-Banna land in 1948, including more than 6,000 acres of orchards. After living in a refugee camp in Gaza for nine months, the family moved to Nablus on the West Bank, when Sabri al-Banna was 12 years old. An average student, he graduated from high school in Nablus in 1955.

That year Sabri joined the authoritarian Arab nationalist and violence-prone Ba'ath Party. He also enrolled in the engineering department of Cairo University, but two years later returned to Nablus without having graduated. In 1958 he got a demeaning job as a common laborer with the Arabian-American Oil Company (Aramco) in Saudi Arabia. In 1960 he also set up an electronic contracting shop in Riyadh. His character traits at that time included being an introvert and stubborn. In 1962, while back in Nablus, he married and then returned with his wife to Saudi Arabia. Political discussions with other Palestinian exiles in Saudi Arabia inspired him to become more active in the illegal Ba'ath Party and then to join Fatah. In 1967 he was fired from his Aramco job because of his political activities, imprisoned, and tortured by the Saudis, who then deported him to Nablus. As a result of the Six-Day War and the entrance of Israeli forces into Nablus, he formed his own group called the Palestine Secret Organization, which became more militant in 1968 and began to stir up trouble. He moved his family to Amman, where he joined Fatah, Yasser Arafat's group and the largest of the Palestinian commando organizations.

In 1969 Abu Nidal became the Palestinian Liberation Organization's (PLO) representative in Khartoum, and while there he apparently first came in contact with Iraqi intelligence officers. In August 1970, he moved to Baghdad, where he occupied the same post, and became an agent of the Iraqi intelligence service. After the 1973 Arab-Israeli War, he left Fatah to start his own organization. With Iraqi weapons, training, and intelligence support, his first major act of terrorism was to seize the Saudi Arabian Embassy in Paris on September 5, 1973. Later Iraqi officials reportedly admitted that they had commissioned Abu Nidal to carry out the operation.

During 1973-74, the relationship between Abu Nidal and Arafat worsened. Abu Nidal himself has suggested that he left Fatah because of the PLO's willingness to accept a compromise West Bank state instead of the total liberation of Palestine. By mid-1974 Abu Nidal was replaced because of his increasing friendliness with his Iraqi host. In October 1974, Iraq sponsored the Rejection Front. Abu Nidal did not join, however, because of his recent expulsion from the PLO, and he was organizing his own group, the Fatah Revolutionary Council, with the help of the Iraqi leadership. In 1978 Abu Nidal began to retaliate for his ouster from the PLO by assassinating the leading PLO representatives in London, Kuwait, and Paris. He subsequently assassinated the leading PLO representative in Brussels in 1981 and the representatives in Bucharest, Romania, in 1984. Other attempts failed. In 1983 Abu Nidal's hitmen in Lisbon also assassinated one of Arafat's most dovish advisers.

In addition to his terrorist campaign against the PLO, Abu Nidal carried out attacks against Syria. He organized a terrorist group called Black June (named after the month the Syrian troops invaded Lebanon) that bombed Syrian embassies and airline offices in Europe, took hostages at a hotel in Damascus, and attempted to assassinate the Syrian foreign minister. In November 1983, Saddam expelled Abu Nidal from Iraq because of pressure applied by the United States, Jordan, and the United Arab Emirates—all allies of Iraq in the ongoing war against Iran.

Abu Nidal moved his headquarters to Syria. From late 1983 to 1986, Hafiz al-Assad's government employed ANO to carry out two main objectives: to intimidate Arafat and King Hussein, who were considering taking part in peace plans that excluded Syria, and to attempt to assassinate Jordanian representatives (mainly diplomats). Between 1983 and 1985, the ANO attacked Jordanians in Ankara, Athens, Bucharest, Madrid, New Delhi, and Rome, as well as bombed offices in these capitals. The Gulf states, mainly Saudi Arabia, Kuwait, and the United Arab Emirates were also attacked because they were late in paying him protection money. Other ANO attacks included the machine-gun massacres of El Al passengers at the Vienna and Rome airports on December 27, 1985.

Abu Nidal's relationship with Syria weakened, however, because Assad treated him as a contract hitman rather than a Palestinian leader and because Britain, the Soviet Union, and the United States applied intense pressures on Assad's regime to end terrorism. After Syrian intelligence caught one of Abu Nidal's lieutenants at the Damascus airport carrying sensitive documents and found weapons that he had stored in Syria without their knowledge, Syria expelled Abu Nidal in 1987. After the expulsion, he moved to Libya.

Abu Nidal appeared to be more secure in Libya. He followed the same pattern that he had established in Iraq and Syria. He organized attacks on the enemies of his friends (Libya's enemies included the United States, Egypt, and the PLO), bombed the U.S. Embassy in Cairo, hijacked planes, and gunned down 21 Jews at an Istanbul synagogue. In Libya, however, internal feuds ripped ANO apart. In 1989-90 hundreds died in battles between Abu Nidal and dissidents supported by the PLO, who sought to take control of his operations in Libya and Lebanon.

A curious feature of Abu Nidal's terrorism is that more than 50 percent of it has been directed against Arab and Palestinian rivals. The ANO's vicious war against the PLO has led to Arab claims that it was secretly manipulated by Israel's Mossad secret service. According to this seemingly far-fetched hypothesis, the Mossad penetrated Abu Nidal's organization and has manipulated Abu Nidal to carry out atrocities that would discredit the Palestinian cause. The hypothesis is based on four main points: Abu Nidal killings have damaged the Palestinian cause to Israel's advantage, the suspicious behavior of some of Abu Nidal's officials, the lack of attacks on Israel, lack of involvement in the Intifada, and Israel's failure to retaliate against Abu Nidal's groups. Another distinctive feature of Abu Nidal's terrorism is that the ANO has generally not concerned itself with captured ANO members, preferring to abandon them to their fate rather than to attempt to bargain for their release. These traits would seem to suggest that the ANO has been more a product of its leader's paranoid psychopathology than his ideology. Abu Nidal's paranoia has also been evident in interviews that he has supposedly given, in which he has indicated his belief that the Vatican was responsible for his fallout with Iraq and is actively hunting down his organization. Wary of being traced or blown up by a remote-controlled device, he allegedly never speaks on a telephone or two-way radio, or drinks anything served to him by others.

In recent years, the aging and ailing Abu Nidal has slipped into relative obscurity. On July 5, 1998, two days after 10 ANO members demanded his resignation as ANO chief, the Egyptians arrested Abu Nidal, who was carrying a Tunisian passport under a false name. Egyptian security officers eventually ordered the 10 dissident members of his group out of Egypt. Abu Nidal was rumored to be undergoing treatment in the Palestinian Red Crescent Society Hospital in the Cairo suburb of Heliopolis. In mid-December 1998, he went from Egypt to Iraq after fleeing a hospital bed in Cairo, where he had quietly been undergoing treatment for leukemia.

Abu Nidal's physical description seems to vary depending on the source. In 1992 Patrick Seale described Abu Nidal as "a pale-skinned, balding, pot-bellied man, with a long thin nose above a gray mustache." One trainee added that Abu Nidal was not very tall and had blue-green eyes and a plump face.

Popular Front for the Liberation of Palestine-General Command (PFLP-GC)

Group Profile

Ahmad Jibril, a Palestinian who had served as a captain in the Syrian army before joining
first the Fatah and later the PFLP, became disillusioned with the PFLP's emphasis on ideology over action and for being too willing to compromise with Israel. Consequently, in August 1968 Jibril formed the PFLP-GC as a breakaway faction of the PFLP. The PFLP-GC is a secular, nationalist organization that seeks to replace Israel with a "secular democratic" state. Like the PFLP, the PFLP-GC has refused to accept Israel's continued existence, but the PFLP-GC has been more strident and uncompromising in its opposition to a negotiated solution to the Palestinian conflict than the PFLP and, unlike the PFLP, has made threats to assassinate Yasir Arafat. Terrorist actions linked to the PFLP-GC have included the hang-glider infiltration of an operative over the Lebanese border in November 1987, the hijacking of four jet airliners on September 6, 1970, and the bombing of a Pan Am Boeing 747 over Lockerbie, Scotland, in 1988, causing 270 deaths. Libyan agents were later charged for the Pan Am bombing, but Jibril and his PFLP-GC have continued to be suspected of some involvement, such as planning the operation and then giving it to the Libyans. In recent years, the PFLP-GC, weakened by reduced support from Syria and Jibril's health problems, has not been associated with any major international terrorist action. Its activities have focused on guerrilla attacks against Israeli forces in southern Lebanon.

In 1991 the PFLP-GC had about 500 members and was attempting to recruit new members. It is known that the PFLP looks for support from the working classes and middle classes, but little has been reported about the PFLP-GC's membership composition. The PFLP-GC's presence in the West Bank and Gaza is negligible, however.

The PFLP has a strict membership process that is the only acceptable form of recruitment. Although it is unclear whether the PFLP-GC uses this or a similar process, the PFLP's recruiting program is nonetheless described here briefly. A PFLP cell, numbering from three to ten members, recruits new members and appoints one member of a comparably sized PFLP circle to guide PFLP trainees through their pre-membership period. Cells indoctrinate new recruits through the study of PFLP literature and Marxist-Leninist theory. Prior to any training and during the training period, each recruit is closely monitored and evaluated for personality, ability, and depth of commitment to the Palestinian cause. To qualify for membership, the applicant must be Palestinian or Arab, at least 16 years old, from a "revolutionary class," accept the PFLP's political program and internal rules, already be a participant in one of the PFLP's noncombatant organizations, and be prepared to participate in combat. To reach "trainee" status, the new recruit must submit an application and be recommended by at least two PFLP members, who are held personally responsible for having recommended the candidate. Trainees undergo training for a period of six months to a year. On completing training, the trainee must be formally approved for full membership.

The PFLP-GC political leadership is organized into a General Secretariat, a Political Bureau, and a Central Committee. The PFLP-GC is currently led by its secretary general, Ahmad Jibril. Other top leaders include the assistant secretary general, Talal Naji; and the Political Bureau secretary, Fadl Shururu.

In August 1996, Syrian President Hafiz al-Asad reportedly asked PFLP-GC chief Ahmad Jibril to leave Syria and go to Iran. However, Jibril apparently was not out of Syria for long. On May 14, 1999, a delegation representing the leadership of the PFLP-GC, led by PFLP-GC Secretary General Ahmad Jibril and comprising PFLP-GC Assistant Secretary General Talal Naji, PFLP-GC Political Bureau Secretary Fadl Shururu, and Central Committee Member Abu Nidal 'Ajjuri, met in Damascus with Iranian President Muhammad Khatami and his delegation, who paid a state visit to the Syrian Arab Republic. Several senior PFLP-GC members quit the group in August 1999 because of Jibril's hard-line against peace negotiations.

The PFLP-GC is not known to have been particularly active in recent years, at least in terms of carrying out major acts of terrorism. However, if one of its state sponsors, such as Iran, Libya, and Syria, decides to retaliate against another nation for a perceived offense, the PFLP-GC could be employed for that purpose. The group retains dormant cells in Europe and has close ties to the JRA and Irish terrorists.

Leader Profile
Ahmad Jibril

Position: Secretary General of the PFLP-GC.

Background: Ahmad Jibril was born in the town of Yazur, on land occupied in 1938. Following the Arab-Israeli War in 1948, his family moved to Syria. Late in the second half of the 1950s, he, like other Palestinians, joined the Syrian Army. He attended military college and eventually became a demolitions expert and a captain. While remaining an active officer in the Syrian Army, Jibril tried to form his own militant organization, the Palestine Liberation Front (PLF), with a few young Palestinians on the eve of the June 1967 war. Since that time, Jibril has been characterized by two basic constants: not offending or distancing himself from Syria and maintaining a deep-seated hostility toward Fatah and Yasir Arafat. After a brief membership in George Habbash's PFLP, in October 1968 Jibril formed the PFLP-GC, which became known for its military explosives technology.

Ahmad Jibril
(Photo courtesy of The
Washington Post, 1999)

After a long period of suffering and poverty, Jibril had the good fortune in the mid-1970s of becoming acquainted with Libya's Colonel Muammar al-Qadhafi in the wake of the downing of a Libyan civilian plane by Israeli fighters over the Sinai. Jibril offered to retaliate, and Qadhafi reportedly gave him millions of dollars to buy gliders and launch kamikaze attacks on an Israeli city. After sending the pilots to certain communist countries for training in suicide missions, Jibril met with Qadhafi and returned the money, saying that twice that amount was needed. Impressed by Jibril's honesty, Qadhafi immediately gave him twice the amount.

Despite his huge quantities of weapons and money, Jibril still suffered from low popularity among Palestinians and a lack of presence in the occupied West Bank and Gaza Strip. Reasons cited for his low popularity included his having grown up in Syrian Army barracks, the nature of his alliance with Syria, and the Fatah movement's isolation of him from the Palestinian scene. Jibril suffered a major setback in 1977, when the PFLP-GC split. In 1982 Jibril fled Beirut in 1982 and began a closer association with Libyan agencies, taking charge of liquidating a large number of Libyan opposition figures and leaders overseas. In early 1983, Jibril suddenly began identifying with Iran, which welcomed him. Eventually, he moved his headquarters and operations center to Tehran. The PFLP-GC began engaging in intelligence operations for Iran among Palestinians in various countries.

Revolutionary Armed Forces of Colombia (FARC)

Group Profile

The membership of the Revolutionary Armed Forces of Colombia (Fuerzas Armadas Revolucionarias de Colombia—FARC) has always come primarily from the countryside. Sociologist James Peter says that 80 percent of the FARC's members are peasants, which explains its vitality and development over time. Most FARC members reportedly are poorly educated, young people from rural areas and who are more attracted to the FARC for its relatively good salary and revolutionary adventurism than for ideology. Many are teenagers, both male and female. Many poor farmers and teenagers join the FARC out of boredom or simply because it pays them about $350 a month, which is $100 more than a Colombian Army conscript. Others may be more idealistic. For example, Ramón, a 17-year-old guerrilla, told a *Washington Post* reporter in February 1999 that "I do not know the word 'Marxism,' but I joined the FARC for the cause of the country...for the cause of the poor." The FARC has relied on forced conscription in areas where it has had difficulties recruiting or in instances in which landowners are unable to meet FARC demands for "war taxes." In early June 1999, the FARC's Eduardo Devía ("Raul Reyes") pledged to a United Nations representative not to recruit or kidnap more minors.

Although the FARC has traditionally been a primarily peasant-based movement, its membership may have broadened during the 1990s as a result of the steadily expanding area under FARC control. Timothy P. Wickham-Crowley points out that "The most striking single feature of the Colombian guerrilla experience, especially but not only for the FARC, is how thoroughly the entire guerrilla experience has been rooted in local experiences in the countryside." Wickham-Crowley qualifies that traditional characteristic, however, by noting that, according to FARC leader Manuel Marulanda, "there had been an appreciable broadening of the guerrillas' ranks, now including a larger number of urbanites: workers, intellectuals, students, professionals, doctors, lawyers, professors, and priests." If true, this would be surprising considering that the FARC's increasingly terrorist actions, such as mass kidnappings, have had the effect of shifting public opinion in Colombia from apathy toward the isolated rural guerrilla groups to increasing concern and a hardening of attitudes toward the guerrillas.

According to some analysts, the insurgent organization has approximately 20,000 fighters organized in at least 80 fronts throughout the country, which are especially concentrated in specific areas where the FARC has managed to establish a support base within the peasant population. However, that figure is at the higher end of estimates. In 1999 the FARC reportedly had approximately 15,000 heavily armed combatants. The National Army's intelligence directorate puts the figure even lower, saying that the insurgent group has close to 11,000 men—seven blocs that comprise a total of 61 fronts, four columns, and an unknown number of mobile companies.

The FARC was not known to have any women combatants in its ranks in the 1960s, but by the 1980s women were reportedly fighting side by side with FARC men without any special privileges. By 1999 a growing number of FARC troops were women.

In contrast to most other Latin American guerrilla/terrorist groups, FARC leaders generally are poorly educated peasants. The formal education of current FARC leader Manuel Marulanda consists of only four years of grammar school. His predecessor, Jocobo Arenas, had only two years of school. Wickham-Crowley has documented the peasant origins of FARC leaders and the organization in general, both of which were a product of the La Violencia period in 1948, when the government attempted to retake the "independent republics" formed by peasants.

Marulanda's power is limited by the Central General Staff, the FARC's main decision-making body, formed by seven members, including Marulanda. The other six are Jorge Briceño Suárez ("Mono Jojoy"), Guillermo León Saenz Vargas ("Alfonso Cano"), Luis Eduardo Devía ("Raúl Reyes"), Rodrigo Londoño Echeverry ("Timochenko" or "Timoleón"), Luciano Marín Arango ("Iván Márquez"), and Efraín Guzmán Jiménez. Raúl Reyes, Joaquín Gómez and Fabian Ramírez, who have led lengthy military and political careers within the insurgent ranks, have been present during the peace talks with the government in 1999. Raúl Reyes is in charge of finances and international policy; Fabian Ramírez is a commander with the Southern Bloc, one of the organization's largest operations units; and Joaquín Gómez is a member of the Southern Bloc's General Staff.

At the beginning of the 1980s, the FARC leadership decided to send about 20 of its best youth to receive training in the military academies of the now former Soviet Union. The FARC's new second-generation of guerrilla leaders—those young FARC members who completed political-military training abroad and are beginning to assume important military responsibilities—have been educated more for waging war than making peace. Since the mid-1990s, these second-generation FARC military leaders have been gradually assuming greater military responsibilities and taking over from the FARC's first-generation leaders.

The division between so-called moderates and hard-liners within the FARC leadership constitutes a significant vulnerability, if it can be exploited. Whereas Marulanda represents the supposedly moderate faction of the FARC and favors a political solution, Jorge Briceño ("Mono Jojoy") represents the FARC hard-liners who favor a military solution. Marulanda must know that he will not live long enough to see the FARC take power. Thus, he may prefer to be remembered in history as the FARC leader who made peace possible. However, should Marulanda disappear then Mono Jojoy and his fellow hard-liners will likely dominate the FARC. Mono Jojoy, who does not favor the peace process, reportedly has been the primary cause of a rupture between the FARC's political and military branches.

Leader Profiles
Pedro Antonio Marín/Manuel Marulanda Vélez

Position: FARC founder and commander in chief.

Pedro Antonio Marín
(Photo courtesy of www.geocities.com/Capit olHill/Lobby/6433/04.html)

Background:　　Since its inception in May 1966, the FARC has operated under the leadership of Pedro Antonio Marín (aka "Manuel Marulanda Vélez" or "Tirofijo"—Sure Shot). Marín was born into a peasant family in Génova, Quindío Department, a coffee-growing region of west-central Colombia. He says he was born in May 1930, but his father claimed the date was May 12, 1928. He was the oldest of five children, all brothers. His formal education consisted of only four years of elementary school, after which he went to work as a woodcutter, butcher, baker, and candy salesman. His family supported the Liberal Party. When a civil war erupted in 1948 following the assassination of a Liberal president, Marín and a few cousins took to the mountains. On becoming a guerrilla, Marín adopted the pseudonym of Manuel Marulanda Vélez in tribute to a trade unionist who died while opposing the dispatch of Colombian troops to the Korean War.

A professional survivor, an experienced tactician, and a determined commander, Marulanda Vélez has been officially pronounced dead several times in army communiqués, but he has always reappeared in guerrilla actions. Although only five feet tall, he is a charismatic guerrilla chieftain who has long been personally involved in combat and has inspired unlimited confidence among his followers. He ascended to the top leadership position after the death of Jocobo Arenas from a heart attack in 1990. He is reported to be a member of the Central Committee of the Communist Party of Colombia (Partido Comunista de Colombia—PCC), which has historically been associated with the FARC. According to author Alfredo Rangel Suárez, Marulanda "is not a theoretician by any means, but he is very astute and has a great capacity for command and organization." Rangel Suárez believes that Marulanda is a hardcore Marxist-Leninist. However, Marulanda's peasant origins and his innate sense of military strategy have earned him nationwide recognition as a leader among politicians, leftists, and other guerrilla groups.

Marulanda is not known to have ever married, although he reportedly has numerous children by liaisons with various women. According to journalist María Jimena Duzán, Marulanda lives simply, like a peasant, and without any luxuries, such as cognac. However, he smokes cigarettes.

Jorge Briceño Suárez ("Mono Jojoy")

Position: Second in command of the FARC; commander, Eastern Bloc of the FARC; member, FARC General Secretariat since April 1993.

Background: Jorge Briceño Suárez was born in the Duda region of Colombia, in the jurisdiction of Uribe, Meta Department, in 1949. His father was the legendary guerrilla Juan de la Cruz Varela, and his mother was a peasant woman, Romelia Suárez. He grew up and learned to read and write within the FARC. For years, he was at the side of Manuel Marulanda Vélez ("Tirofijo"—Sureshot), who is considered his tutor and teacher. Mono Jojoy is a jovial-looking, heavy-set man who wears a handlebar moustache and who normally wears a simple green camouflage uniform and a black beret. He is another of the new second-generation FARC military chiefs who was born in the FARC. Both he and "Eliécer" created the FARC's highly effective school for "special attack tactics," which trains units to strike the enemy without suffering major casualties. Mono Jojoy is credited with introducing the Vietnam War-style specialized commandos that consist of grouping the best men of each front in order to assign them specific high-risk missions. He is one of the most respected guerrilla leaders within FARC ranks. He became second in command when Marulanda succeeded Jocobo Arenas in 1990.

Unlike the other commanders who came to the FARC after university-level studies, Mono Jojoy learned everything about guerrilla warfare in the field. He easily moves among the Departments of Boyacá, Cundinamarca, and Meta. He is said to know the Sumapaz region "like the palm of his hand." He is known as a courageous guerrilla, who is obsessed with attacking the Public Force, has little emotion, and is laconic. His great military experience helps to compensate for his low intellectual level. He is said to be unscrupulous and to advocate any form of warfare in pursuit of power, including dialoging with the government as a ruse. Under his command, the Eastern Bloc has earned record amounts of cocaine-trafficking profits. He is opposed to extradition of Colombians, including his brother, Germán Briceño Suárez ("Grannobles"), a FARC hard-liner who was charged on July 21, 1999, in the slayings of three U.S. Indian rights activists, who were executed in early 1999. He is contemptuous of the prospect of U.S. military intervention, noting that U.S. soldiers would not last three days in the jungle. However, he would welcome U.S. economic assistance to rural development projects, such as bridge-building.

Germán Briceño Suárez ("Grannobles")

Position: Commander, 10th, 28th, 38th, 45th, and 56th fronts.

Background: Germán Briceño, younger brother of Jorge Briceño Suárez, was born in the Duda region of Colombia, in the jurisdiction of Uribe, Meta Department, in 1953. His father was the legendary guerrilla Juan de la Cruz Varela, and his mother was a peasant woman, Romelia Suárez. At the recommendation of his brother, Germán Briceño became an official member of the FARC in 1980. Even from that early date, Germán Briceño showed himself to be more of a fighter and bolder than his older brother, despite the latter's own reputation for boldness. Germán Briceño was promoted rapidly to commander of the FARC's 30th Front in Cauca Department. After founding a combat training school in that department's Buenos Aires municipality, he began to be known for his meanness. He was reportedly suspended temporarily from the FARC for his excesses against the peasants and his subordinates, but later readmitted as a commander, thanks to his brother. However, he was transferred to Vichada Department, where he engaged in weapons trafficking and extortion of taxes from coca growers and drug traffickers.

In 1994, after being promoted to his brother's Western Bloc staff, Germán Briceño took over command of the 10th Front, which operates in Arauca Department and along the Venezuelan border. Since then he has also assumed command of the 28th, 38th, 45th, and 56th fronts, operating in the economically and militarily important departments of Arauca, Boyaca, and Casanare. In 1994 he reportedly participated, along with his brother, in the kidnappings and murders of American missionaries Stephen Welsh and Timothy van Dick; the kidnapping of Raymond Rising, an official from the Summer Linguistics Institute; and the kidnappings of industrialist Enrique Mazuera Durán and his son, Mauricio, both of whom have U.S. citizenship. Germán Briceño is also accused of kidnapping British citizen Nigel Breeze, and he is under investigation for the murder of two Colombian Marine Infantry deputy officers and for the kidnappings of Carlos Bastardo, a lieutenant from the Venezuelan navy, as well as about a dozen cattlemen from Venezuela's Apure State. His kidnap victims in Arauca have included the son of Congressman Adalberto Jaimes; and Rubén Dario López, owner of the Arauca convention center, along with his wife. He has also ordered the murders of young women who were the girlfriends of police or military officers.

On February 23, 1999, Germán Briceño also kidnapped, without FARC authorization, three U.S. indigenous activists in Arauca and murdered them a week later in Venezuelan territory. The incident resulted in the breaking off of contact between the FARC and the U.S. Department of State. After a so-called FARC internal investigation, he was exonerated, again thanks to his brother, and a guerrilla named Gildardo served as the fall guy. Germán Briceño recovered part of his warrior's reputation by leading an offensive against the army in March and April 1999 that resulted in the deaths of 60 of the army's soldiers. On July 30, 1999, however, Germán Briceño once again carried out an unauthorized action by hijacking a Venezuela Avior commercial flight with 18 people on board (they were released on August 8).

"Eliécer"

Position: A leading FARC military tactician.

Background: "Eliécer" was born in the FARC in 1957, the son of one of the FARC's founders. He walked through the Colombian jungles at the side of his father. Tall, white, and muscular, he is a member of the so-called second-generation of the FARC. One the FARC's most highly trained guerrillas, he received military training in the Soviet Union. The late FARC ideologist Jocobo Arenas singled out Eliécer for this honor. An outstanding student, Eliécer was awarded various Soviet decorations. He then went to East Germany, where he not only received military training but also learned German and completed various political science courses. Following his stay in East Germany, he received guerrilla combat experience in Central America. Commander "Eliécer" became the FARC's military chief of Antioquia Department at the end of 1995. A modern version of Manuel Marulanda, Eliécer is regarded as cold, calculating, a very good conversationalist, cultured, and intuitive. By 1997 he was regarded as one of the FARC's most important tacticians. He and "Mono Jojoy"created the FARC's highly effective school for "special attack tactics," which trains units to strike the enemy without suffering major casualties. In Antioquia Eliécer was assigned to work alongside Efraín Guzmán ("El Cucho"), a member of the FARC Staff and a FARC founder who was 60 years old in 1996.

Revolutionary Organization 17 November (17N)

Group Profile

Since the group's initial appearance with the assassination of U.S. official Richard Welch in an Athens suburb with a Colt .45-caliber magnum automatic pistol on December 23, 1975, no known member of the shadowy Revolutionary Organization 17 November (Epanastatiki Organosi 17 Noemvri—17N) has been apprehended. Thus, the membership and internal dynamics of this small, mysterious, and well-disciplined group remain largely unknown.

It has been claimed in some news media that the identity of no member of 17N is known to Greek, American, or European police and intelligence agencies. However, the group's ability to strike with impunity at its chosen targets for almost a quarter century without the apprehension of a single member has reportedly made Western intelligence agencies suspect it of being the instrument of a radicalized Greek intelligence service, the GYP, according to the *Observer* [London]. According to one of the *Observer's* sources, Kurdish bomber Seydo Hazar, 17N leaders work hand-in-glove with elements of the Greek intelligence service. According to the *Observer*, 17N has sheltered the PKK by providing housing and training facilities for its guerrillas. Police were kept away from PKK training camps by 17N leaders who checked the identity of car license plates with Greek officials. Funds were obtained and distributed to the PKK by a retired naval commander who lives on a Greek military base and is a well-known sympathizer of 17N.

What little is known about 17N derives basically from its target selection and its rambling written communiqués that quote Balzac or historical texts, which a member may research in a public library. Named for the 1973 student uprising in

Greece protesting the military regime, the group is generally believed to be an ultranationalist, Marxist-Leninist organization that is anti-U.S., anti-Turkey, anti-rich Greeks, anti-German, anti-European Union (EU), and anti-NATO, in that order. It has also been very critical of Greek government policies, such as those regarding Cyprus, relations with Turkey, the presence of U.S. bases in Greece, and Greek membership in NATO and the European Union (EU). In its self-proclaimed role as "vanguard of the working class," 17N has also been critical of Greek government policies regarding a variety of domestic issues. One of the group's goals is to raise the "consciousness of the masses" by focusing on issues of immediate concern to the population. To these ends, the group has alternated its attacks between so-called "watchdogs of the capitalist system" (i.e., U.S. diplomatic and military personnel and "secret services") and "servants of the state" (such as government officials, security forces, or industrialists). It has been responsible for numerous attacks against U.S. interests, including the assassination of four U.S. officials, the wounding of 28 other Americans, and a rocket attack on the U.S. Embassy compound in Athens in February 1996. The group justified its assassination of Welch by blaming the CIA for "contributing to events in Cyprus" and for being "responsible for and supporting the military junta."

Unlike most European Marxist-Leninist terrorist groups that are in their third or fourth generation of membership, the 17N group has been able to retain its original hard-core members. In 1992, according to 17N expert Andrew Corsun, the group's hard-core members were most likely professionals such as lawyers, journalists, and teachers in their late thirties and early forties. If that is the case, most of the group's core membership, which he estimated to be no more than twenty, would today be mostly in their forties. Moreover, the 17N communiques, with a five-pointed star and the name "17N," typically come from the same typewriter that issued the movement's first proclamation in 1975, shortly before Welch's execution. According to the prosecutor who examined the files on 17N accumulated by late Attorney General Dhimitrios Tsevas, the group comprises a small circle of members who are highly educated, have access and informers in the government, and are divided into three echelons: General Staff, operators, and auxiliaries. The core members are said to speak in the cultivated Greek of the educated.

There appears to be general agreement among security authorities that the group has between 10 and 25 members, and that its very small size allows it to maintain its secrecy and security. The origin of the group is still somewhat vague, but it is believed that its founders were part of a resistance group that was formed during the 1967-75 military dictatorship in Greece. It is also believed that Greek Socialist Premier Andreas Papendreou may have played some hand in its beginnings. After democracy returned to Greece in 1975, it is believed that many of the original members went their own way. N17 is considered unique in that it appears not to lead any political movement.

One of the group's operating traits is the fact that more than 10 of its attacks in Athens, ranging from its assassination of U.S. Navy Captain George Tsantes on November 15, 1983, to its attack on the German ambassador's residence in early 1999, took place in the so-called Khalandhri Triangle, a triangle comprising apartment blocks under construction in the suburb of Khalandhri and situated between Kifisias, Ethinikis Antistaseos, and Rizariou. The terrorists are believed by authorities to know practically every square foot of this area. Knowing the urban terrain intimately is a basic tenet of urban terrorism, as specified by Carlos Marighella, author of *The Minimanual of the Urban Guerrilla*.

The continuing hard-core membership is suggested by the fact that the group murdered Cosfi Peraticos, scion of a Greek shipping family, in June 1997 with the same Colt .45 that it used to assassinate Richard Welch in 1975. The group has actually used the Colt .45 in more attacks than those in 1975 and 1997 (see Table 6, Appendix). Since the Welch assassination, its signature Colt .45 has been used to kill or wound at least six more of its 20 victims, who include three other American officials and one employee, two Turkish diplomats, and 13 Greeks. The rest have been killed by another Colt .45, bombs, and anti-tank missiles. The group's repeated use of its Colt .45 and typewriter suggests a trait more typical of a psychopathic serial killer. In the political context of this group, however, it appears to be symbolically important to the group to repeatedly use the same Colt .45 and the same typewriter.

Authorities can tell that the people who make bombs for the 17N organization were apparently trained in the Middle East during the early 1970s. For example, in the bombing of a bank branch in Athens on June 24, 1998, by the May 98 Group, the bomb, comprised of a timing mechanism made with two clocks and a large amount of dynamite, was typical of devices used by 17N, according to senior police officials.

Religious Fundamentalist Groups

Al-Qaida

Group Profile

In February 1998, bin Laden announced the formation of an umbrella organization called the Islamic World Front for the Struggle against the Jews and the Crusaders (Al-Jabhah al-Islamiyyah al-`Alamiyyah li-Qital al-Yahud wal-Salibiyyin). Among the announced members of this terrorist organization are the Egyptian Al-Jama'a al-Islamiyyah, the Egyptian Al-Jihad, the Egyptian Armed Group, the Pakistan Scholars Society, the Partisan Movement for Kashmir, the Jihad Movement in Bangladesh, and bin Laden's Afghan military wing of the Advice and Reform Commission (Bodansky: 316). Unlike most terrorist groups, Al-Qaida is more of a home base and financier for a global network of participating Islamic groups.

According to Bodansky (308-9), bin Laden and his close advisers live in a three-chamber cave in eastern Afghanistan, in the mountains near Jalalabad. One room is used as bin Laden's control and communications center and is equipped with a state-of-the-art satellite communications system, which includes, in addition to a satellite telephone, a desktop computer, at least a couple laptops, and fax machines. Another room is used for storage of weapons such as AK-47s, mortars, and machine guns. A third room houses a large library of Islamic literature and three cots. His immediate staff occupy cave bunkers in nearby mountains.

Bin Laden is ingratiating himself with his hosts, the Taliban, by undertaking a massive reconstruction of Qandahar. In the section reserved for the Taliban elite, bin Laden has built a home of his own, what Bodansky (312) describes as "a massive stone building with a tower surrounded by a tall wall on a side street just across from the Taliban's "foreign ministry" building." Bin Laden's project includes the construction of defensive military camps around the city. In addition, in the mountains east of Qandahar, bin Laden is building bunkers well concealed and fortified in mountain ravines.

After the U.S. cruise missile attack against his encampment on August 20, 1998, bin Laden began building a new headquarters and communications center in a natural cave system in the Pamir Mountains in Kunduz Province, very close to the border with Tajikistan. According to Bodansky (312-13), the new site will be completed by the first half of 2000.

Bodanksy (326) reports that, since the fall of 1997, bin Laden has been developing chemical weapons at facilities adjacent to the Islamic Center in Soba, one of his farms located southwest of Khartoum, Sudan. Meanwhile, since the summer of 1998 bin Laden has also been preparing terrorist operations using biological, chemical, and possibly radiological weapons at a secret compound near Qandahar.

By 1998 a new generation of muhajideen was being trained at bin Laden's camps in eastern Afghanistan and Pakistan. Bin Laden's Afghan forces consist of more than 10,000 trained fighters, including almost 3,000 Arab Afghans, or Armed Islamic Movement (AIM), which is also known as the International Legion of Islam. According to Bodansky (318-19), Egyptian intelligence reported that these Arab Afghans total 2,830, including 177 Algerians, 594 Egyptians, 410 Jordanians, 53 Moroccans, 32 Palestinians, 162 Syrians, 111 Sudanese, 63 Tunisians, 291 Yemenis, 255 Iraqis, and others from the Gulf states. The remaining 7,000 or so fighters are Bangladeshis, Chechens, Pakistanis, Tajiks, Uzbeks, and other nationalities. Bodansky (318) reports that the 5,000 trainees at one training center in Afghanistan are between 16 and 25 years of age and from all over the world. The Martyrdom Battalions are composed of human bombs being trained to carry out spectacular terrorist operations.

Leader Profiles:

Osama bin Laden ("Usama bin Muhammad bin Laden, Shaykh Usama bin Laden, the Prince, the Emir, Abu Abdallah, Mujahid Shaykh, Hajj, the Director")

Position: Head of Al-Qaida.

Background: Usamah bin Mohammad bin Laden, now known in the Western world as Osama bin Laden, was born on July 30, 1957, in Riyadh, Saudi Arabia, the seventeenth son of Mohammad bin Laden. The late Mohammad bin Laden rose from peasant origins in Yemen to become a small-time builder and contractor in Saudi Arabia and eventually the wealthiest construction contractor in Saudi Arabia.. He had more than 50 children from several wives. Osama bin Laden's mother was reportedly a Palestinian. Depending on the source of information, she was the least or most favored of his father's ten wives,

Osama bin Laden
(AP Photo; www.cnn.com)

and Osama was his father's favorite son. He was raised in the Hijaz in western Saudi Arabia, and ultimately al Medina Al Munawwara. The family patriarch died in the late 1960s, according to one account, but was still active in 1973, according to another account. In any case, he left his 65 children a financial empire that today is worth an estimated $10 billion. The Saudi bin Laden Group is now run by Osama's family, which has publicly said it does not condone his violent activities.

After being educated in schools in Jiddah, the main port city on the Red Sea coast, bin Laden studied management and economics in King Abdul Aziz University, also in Jiddah, from 1974 to 1978. As a student, he often went to Beirut to frequent nightclubs, casinos, and bars. However, when his family's construction firm was rebuilding holy mosques in the sacred cities of Mecca and Medina in 1973, bin Laden developed a religious passion for Islam and a strong belief in Islamic law. In the early 1970s, he began to preach the necessity of armed struggle and worldwide monotheism, and he also began to associate with Islamic fundamentalist groups.

Bin Laden's religious passion ignited in December 1979, when the Soviet Union invaded Muslim Afghanistan. Bin Laden's worldview of seeing the world in simplistic terms as a struggle between righteous Islam and a doomed West prompted him to join the mujahideen in Pakistan, just a few days after the invasion. In the early 1980s, he returned home to fund, recruit, transport, and train a volunteer force of Arab nationals, called the Islamic Salvation Front (ISF), to fight alongside the existing Afghan mujahideen. He co-founded the Mujahideen Services Bureau (Maktab al-Khidamar) and transformed it into an international network that recruited Islamic fundamentalists with special knowledge, including engineers, medical doctors, terrorists, and drug smugglers. In addition, bin Laden volunteered the services of the family construction firm to blast new roads through the mountains. As commander of a contingent of Arab troops, he experienced combat against the Soviets first-hand, including the siege of Jalalabad in 1986—one of the fiercest battles of the war, and he earned a reputation as a fearless fighter. Following that battle, bin Laden and other Islamic leaders concluded that they were victims of a U.S. conspiracy to defeat the jihad in Afghanistan and elsewhere.

By the time the Soviet Union had pulled out of Afghanistan in February 1989, bin Laden was leading a fighting force known as "Afghan Arabs," which numbered between 10,000 and 20,000. That year, after the Soviets were forced out of Afghanistan, bin Laden disbanded the ISF and returned to the family construction business in Saudi Arabia. However, now he was a celebrity, whose fiery speeches sold a quarter million cassettes. The Saudi government rewarded his hero status with numerous government construction contracts. Following Iraq's invasion of Kuwait on August 2, 1990, bin Laden urged the Saudi government not to compromise its Islamic legitimacy by inviting infidel Americans into Saudi Arabia to defend the country, but he was ignored..

Although bin Laden, unlike most other Islamic leaders, remained loyal to the regime while condemning the U.S. military and economic presence as well as the Iraqi invasion, Saudi officials increasingly began to threaten him to halt his criticism. Consequently, bin Laden and his family and a large band of followers moved to Sudan in 1991. While living modestly in Sudan, bin Laden established a construction company employing many of his former Afghan fighters. In addition to building roads and infrastructure for the Sudanese government, he ran a farm producing sunflower seeds and a tannery exporting goat hides to Italy. Sudan served as a base for his terrorist operations. In 1992 his attention appears to have been directed against Egypt, but he also claimed responsibility that year for attempting to bomb U.S. soldiers in Yemen, and again for attacks in Somalia in 1993. He also financed and help set up at least three terrorist training camps in cooperation with the Sudanese regime, and his construction company worked directly with Sudanese military officials to transport and supply terrorists training in such camps. During the 1992-96 period, he built and equipped 23 training camps for mujahideen. While in Sudan, he also established a supposedly detection-proof financial system to support Islamic terrorist activities worldwide.

In the winter of 1993, bin Laden traveled to the Philippines to support the terrorist network that would launch major operations in that country and the United States. In 1993–94, having become convinced that the House of al-Saud was no longer legitimate, bin Laden began actively supporting Islamic extremists in Saudi Arabia. His calls for insurrection prompted Saudi authorities to revoke his Saudi citizenship on April 7, 1994, for "irresponsible behavior," and he was officially expelled from the country. He subsequently established a new residence and base of operations in the London suburb of Wembley, but was forced to return to Sudan after a few months to avoid being extradited to Saudi Arabia. In early 1995, he began stepping up activities against Egypt and Saudi Arabia.

In mid-May 1996, pressure was applied by the Saudi government on Sudan to exert some form of control over bin Laden. That summer, he uprooted his family again, returning to Afghanistan on board his unmarked, private C-130 military transport plane. Bin Laden established a mountain fortress near the city of

Kandahar southwest of Jalalabad, under the protection of the Afghan government. From this location, he continues to fund his training camps and military activities. In particular, bin Laden continues to fund the Kunar camp, which trains terrorists for Al-Jihad and Al-Jama' ah al-Islamiyyah. After attending a terrorism summit in Khartoum, bin Laden stopped in Tehran in early October 1996 and met with terrorist leaders, including Abu Nidal, to discuss stepping up terrorist activities in the Middle East.

A mysterious figure whose exact involvement with terrorists and terrorist incidents remains elusive, bin Laden has been linked to a number of Islamic extremist groups and individuals with vehement anti-American and anti-Israel ideologies. His name has been connected to many of the world's most deadly terrorist operations, and he is named by the U.S. Department of State as having financial and operational connections with terrorism. Some aspects of bin Laden's known activities have been established during interviews, mainly with Middle Eastern reporters and on three occasions of the release of fatwas (religious rulings) in April 1996, February 1997, and February 1998. Each threatened a jihad against U.S. forces in Saudi Arabia and the Holy Lands, and each called for Muslims to concentrate on "destroying, fighting and killing the enemy."Abdul-Bari Atwan, editor of *al-Quds al-Arabi* [London], who interviewed bin Laden at his Afghan headquarters in the Khorassan mountains, reports that:

> The mujahideen around the man belong to most Arab states, and are of different ages, but most of them are young. They hold high scientific degrees: doctors, engineers, teachers. They left their families and jobs and joined the Afghan Jihad. There is an open front, and there are always volunteers seeking martyrdom. The Arab mujahideen respect their leader, although he does not show any firmness or leading gestures. They all told me that they are ready to die in his defense and that they would take revenge against any quarter that harms him.

A tall (6'4" to 6'6"), thin man weighing about 160 pounds and wearing a full beard, bin Laden walks with a cane. He wears long, flowing Arab robes fringed with gold, and wraps his head in a traditional red-and-white checkered headdress. He is said to be soft-spoken, extremely courteous, and even humble. He is described in some sources as ordinary and shy. He speaks only Arabic. Because he has dared to stand up to two superpowers, bin Laden has become an almost mythic figure in the Islamic world. Thanks to the ineffectual U.S. cruise missile attack against his camps in Afghanistan following the bombings in Kenya and Tanzania in August 1998, thousands of Arabs and Muslims, seeing him as a hero under attack by the Great Satan, have volunteered their service.

In 1998 bin Laden married his oldest daughter to Mullah Muhammad Omar, the Taliban's leader. He himself married a fourth wife, reportedly a young Pushtun related to key Afghan leaders. Thus, Bodansky points out, now that he is related to the Pushtun elite by blood,
the ferocious Pushtuns will defend and fight for him and never allow him to be surrendered to outsiders. Bin Laden's son Muhammad, who was born in 1985, rarely leaves his father's side. Muhammad has already received extensive military and terrorist training and carries his own AK-47. He serves as his father's vigilant personal bodyguard.

Ayman al-Zawahiri

Position: Bin Laden's second in command and the undisputed senior military commander.

Background: Al-Zawahiri, who claims to be the supreme leader of the Egyptian Jihad, is responsible for converting bin Laden to Islamic fundamentalism.

Subhi Muhammad Abu-Sunnah ("Abu-Hafs al-Masri")

Position: Military Commander of al-Qaida.

Background: A prominent Egyptian fundamentalist leader. He has close ties to bin Laden and has accompanied him on his travels to Arab and foreign countries. He also helped to establish the al-Qaida organization in Afghanistan in early 1991. He moved his activities with bin Laden to Sudan and then backed to Afghanistan.

Hizballah (Party of God)
Alias: Islamic Jihad

Group Profile

Hizballah, an extremist political-religious movement based in Lebanon, was created and sponsored by a contingent of 2,000 Iranian Revolutionary Guards (IRGs) dispatched to Lebanon by Iran in July 1982, initially as a form of resistance to the Israeli presence in southern Lebanon. Hizballah's followers are Shia Muslims, who are strongly anti-Western and anti-Israeli and totally dedicated to the creation of an Iranian-style Islamic Republic in Lebanon and the removal of non-Islamic influences in the area. Hizballah's following mushroomed in 1982 as both the Iranians and their local allies in Lebanon indoctrinated young and poor Shia peasants and young people in West Beirut's poor Shia suburbs through films, ideological seminars, and radio broadcasts. The Islamic fundamentalist groups in Lebanon have been most successful in recruiting their followers among the slum dwellers of south Beirut. By late 1984, Hizballah is thought to have absorbed all the known major extremist groups in Lebanon.

Hizballah's worldview, published in a 1985 manifesto, states that all Western influence is
detrimental to following the true path of Islam. In its eyes, the West and

particularly the United States, is the foremost corrupting influence on the Islamic world today: thus, the United States is known as "the Great Satan." In the same way, the state of Israel is regarded as the product of Western imperialism and Western arrogance. Hizballah believes that the West installed Israel in the region in order to continue dominating it and exploiting its resources. Thus, Israel represents
the source of all evil and violence in the region and is seen as an outpost of the United States in the heart of the Islamic Middle East. In Hizballah's eyes, Israel must, therefore, be eradicated.
Hizballah sees itself as the savior of oppressed and dispossessed Muslims.

Hizballah's central goals help to explain the nature and scope of its use of terrorism.
These include the establishment of an exclusively Shia, Iran-style Islamic state in Lebanon; the complete destruction of the state of Israel and the establishment of Islamic rule over Jerusalem and Palestine; and an implacable opposition to the Middle East peace process, which it has tried to sabotage through terrorism.

The typical Hizballah member in 1990 was a young man in his late teens or early twenties, from a lower middle-class family. In Hizballah's first years, many members were part-time soldiers. By 1990, however, most of the militia and terrorist group members were believed to be full-time "regulars." In the early 1980s, Hizballah used suicide commandos as young as 17, including a beautiful Sunni girl, who killed herself and two Israeli soldiers. In the last decade or so, however, Hizballah has been using only more mature men for special missions and attacks, while continuing to induct youths as young as 17 into its guerrilla ranks. Hizballah's military branch includes not only members recruited from the unemployed, but also doctors, engineers, and other professionals. In 1993 Iranian sources estimated the number of Hizballah's fighters at 5,000 strong, plus 600 citizens from Arab and Islamic countries; the number of the party's political cadres and workers was estimated at 3,000 strong. Within this larger guerrilla organization, Hizballah has small terrorist cells organized on an informal basis. They may consist of the personal following of a particular leader or the relatives of a single extended family.

Hizballah is divided between moderates and radicals. Shaykh Muhammud Husayn Fadlallah, Hizballah's spiritual leader, is considered a moderate leader. The radical camp in 1997 was led by Ibrahim Amin and Hasan Nasrallah. The latter is now Hizballah's secretary general.

Leader Profile

Imad Fa'iz Mughniyah

Position: Head of Hizballah's Special Operations Command.

Background: Imad Mughniyah was born in about 1961 in southern Lebanon. He has been wanted by the FBI since the mid-1980s. He is a charismatic and extremely violent individual. His physical description, according to Hala Jaber (1997:120), is "short and chubby with a babyish face." Mughniyah served in the PLO's Force 17 as a highly trained security man specializing in explosives. In 1982, after his village in southern Lebanon was occupied by Israeli troops, he and his family took refuge in the southern suburbs of Beirut, where he was soon injured by artillery fire. Disillusioned by the PLO, he joined the IRGs. His first important task apparently was to mastermind the bombing of the Israeli Embassy in Buenos Aires in 1982, in which 22 people were killed. On September 2, 1999, Argentina's Supreme Court issued an arrest warrant for Mughniyah for ordering that bombing. His next important tasks, on behalf of Syria and Iran, were the truck bombings that killed 63 people at the U.S. Embassy in Beirut, Lebanon, in April 1983, and another 241 U.S. Marines and sailors at their barracks near Beirut airport the following October; the hijacking of an American airliner in 1985, in which one American was killed; and the 1995 hijacking of TWA flight 847 from Athens to Rome. He also kidnapped most of the Americans who were held hostage in Lebanon, including William Buckley, who was murdered, as well as the British envoy, Terry Waite. In December 1994, his brother was killed by a car bomb placed outside his shop in Beirut.

In mid-February 1997, the pro-Israeli South Lebanese Army radio station reported that Iran's intelligence service dispatched Mughniyah to Lebanon to directly supervise the reorganization of Hizballah's security apparatus concerned with Palestinian affairs in Lebanon and to work as a security liaison between Hizballah and Iranian intelligence. Mughniyah also reportedly controls Hizballah's security apparatus, the Special Operations Command, which handles intelligence and conducts overseas terrorist acts. Operating out of Iran, Lebanon, and Syria, Mughniyah is known to frequently travel on Middle East Airlines (MEA), whose ground crews include Hizballah members. Although he uses Hizballah as a cover, he reports to the Iranians.

Islamic Resistance Movement (Hamas)

Group Profile

In December 1987, when the Palestinian uprising (Intifada) erupted, Sheikh Ahmed Yassin and other followers of the Muslim Brotherhood Society (Jama'at al-Ikhwan al-Muslimin—MB), who had been running welfare, social, and educational services through their mosques, immediately established the Islamic Resistance Movement (Harakat al Muqawana al Islamiyyah—Hamas). Hamas's militant wing Al Qassam ('Izz al-Din al-Qassam) played a major role in the Intifada. Responsible for attacks on Israeli soldiers, Hamas gained a reputation for ruthlessness and unpredictability.

During the Intifada, two main organizational trends toward decentralization of Hamas developed: Hamas's political leadership moved to the neighboring Arab states, mainly Jordan; and grass-roots leaders, representing young, militant activists, attained increased authority and increased freedom of action within their areas of operation. Hamas's leadership remains divided between those operating inside the Occupied Territories and those operating outside, mainly from Damascus. Mahmoud el-Zahar, Hamas's political leader in Gaza, operated openly until his arrest in early 1996 by Palestinian security forces.

Impatient with the PLO's prolonged efforts to free the Occupied Territories by diplomatic means, in November 1992 Hamas formed an alliance with Iran for support in the continuation of the Intifada. That December, 415 Palestinians suspected of having links with Hamas were expelled from Israel into Lebanon, where they were refused refugee status by Lebanon and neighboring Arab states. They remained for six months in a desert camp until international condemnation of the deportations forced Israel to agree to their return. In September 1993, Hamas opposed the peace accord between Israel and the Palestine Liberation Organization (PLO) and maintained a campaign of violence within Israel aimed at disrupting the Middle East peace process. Its militant wing, Al-Qassam, claimed responsibility for two bomb attacks within Israel in April 1994 and for a further bus bombing in Tel Aviv in October 1994. All were carried out by suicide bombers.

The most persistent image of Hamas in the Western media is that of a terrorist group comprised of suicide bombers in the occupied territories and a radical terrorist faction in Damascus. However, Hamas is also a large socioreligious movement involved in communal work within the Palestinian refugee camps and responsible for many civic-action projects. It runs a whole range of cultural, educational, political, and social activities based on mosques and local community groups. In 1996 most of Hamas's estimated $70 million annual budget was going to support a network of hundreds of mosques, schools, orphanages, clinics, and hospitals in almost every village, town, and refugee camp on the West Bank and Gaza Strip. Consequently, Hamas has massive grass-roots support.

In 1993 Hamas's support reportedly varied from more than 40 percent among the Gaza population as a whole to well over 60 percent in certain Gaza refugee camps, and its support in the West Bank varied from 25 percent to as much as 40 percent. Hamas was reported in early 1996 to enjoy solid support among 15 percent to 20 percent of the 2 million Palestinians in Gaza and the West Bank. According to Professor Ehud Sprinzak of Hebrew University, Hamas is so popular among 20 to 30 percent of Palestinians not because it has killed and wounded hundreds of Israelis but because it has provided such important community services for the Palestinian population. Moreover, Hamas activists live among the poor and have a reputation for honesty, in contrast with many Palestine Liberation Organization (PLO) activists. Hamas supporters reportedly cross both tribal patterns and family patterns among Palestinians. The same family often has brothers in both the PLO and Hamas.

Hamas's social services also provide both a cover and a recruiting ground for young Hamas terrorists. Hamas members have been recruited from among believers at Hamas-run mosques, which are also used for holding meetings, organizing demonstrations, distributing leaflets, and launching terrorist attacks. Hamas's ability to recruit leading West Bank religious activists into its leadership ranks has broadened its influence.

The Suicide Bombing Strategy

Sprinzak points out that Hamas's opposition to the peace process has never led it to pursue a strategy of suicide bombing. Rather, the group has resorted to this tactic as a way of exacting tactical revenge for humiliating Israeli actions. For example, in a CBS "60 Minutes" interview in 1997, Hassan Salameh, arch terrorist of Hamas, confirmed that the assassination of Yehiya Ayash ("The Engineer") by Israelis had prompted his followers to organize three suicide bombings that stunned Israel in 1996. Salameh thus contradicted what former Labor Party prime minister Shimon Peres and other Israeli leaders had contended, that the bombings resulted from a strategic decision by Hamas to bring down the Israeli government. According to Sprinzak, the wave of Hamas suicide bombings in late 1997, the third in the series, started in response to a series of Israeli insults of Palestinians that have taken place since the beginning of 1997, such as unilateral continuation of settlements. Similarly, Sprinzak notes, Hamas did not initially pursue a policy of bombing city buses. Hamas resorted to this tactic only after February 1994, when Baruch Goldstein, an Israeli physician and army reserve captain, massacred 29 Palestinians praying in a Hebron shrine. The professor's policy prescriptions for reducing Hamas's incentives to commit terrorist atrocities against Israel are to recognize that Hamas is a Palestinian fact of life and to desist from aggressive policies such as unilateral continuation of settlements and assassination of Hamas leaders.

Hamas thrives on the misery and frustration of Palestinians. Its charter, Jerrold Post notes, is pervaded with paranoid rhetoric. The harsh Israeli blockade of Palestinian areas has only strengthened Hamas.

Selection of Suicide Bombers

Hamas's suicide bombers belong to its military wing, Al-Qassam. The Al-Qassam brigades are composed of small, tightly knit cells of fanatics generally in their mid- to late twenties. In Hamas, selection of a suicide bomber begins with members of Hamas's military cells or with members of the Palestinian Islamic Jihad, who circulate among organizations, schools, and mosques of the refugee camps in the West Bank and the Gaza Strip. The recruiter will broach the subject of dying for Allah with a group of students and watch the students' reactions. Students who seem particularly interested in the discussion are immediately singled out for possible "special merit."

In almost every case, these potential bombers--who range in age from 12 to 17 years--have a relative or close friend who was killed, wounded, or jailed during the Israeli occupation. Bombers are also likely to have some longstanding personal frustration, such as the shame they suffered at the hands of friends who chastised them for not throwing stones at the Israeli troops during the Intifada. Theirs is a strong hatred of the enemy that can only be satisfied through a religious act that gives them the courage to take revenge. The suicide bombers are of an age to be regarded by the community as old enough to be responsible for their actions but too young to have wives and children. Hamas claims that its suicide bombers repeatedly volunteer to be allowed to be martyrs. These young persons, conditioned by years of prayer in Hamas mosques, believe that as martyrs they will go to heaven.

These aspiring suicide bombers attend classes in which trained Islamic instructors focus on the verses of the Koran and the Hadith, the sayings of the Prophet that form the basis of Islamic law and that idealize and stress the glory of dying for Allah. Students are promised an afterlife replete with gold palaces, sumptuous feasts, and obliging women. Aside from religion, the indoctrination includes marathon sessions of anti-Israeli propaganda. Students entering the program quickly learn that "the Jews have no right to exist on land that belongs to the Muslims." Students are assigned various tasks to test their commitment. Delivering weapons for use in clandestine activities is a popular way to judge the student's ability to follow orders and keep a secret. Some students are even buried together in mock graves inside a Palestinian cemetery to see if the idea of death spooks them. Students who survive this test are placed in graves by themselves and asked to recite passages from the Koran. It is at this stage that the recruits, organized in small groups of three to five, start resembling members of a cult, mentally isolated from their families and friends.

The support granted by Hamas to the families of suicide bombers and others killed in clashes with Israel are considered vital to Hamas's military operations because they play an important role in recruiting. Graduates of Hamas's suicide schools know that their supreme sacrifice will see their families protected for life. For someone used to a life of poverty, this is a prized reward. Hamas awards monthly stipends in the range of $1,000 to the families of the bombers. Scholarships for siblings and foodstuffs are also made available. Hamas pays for the resettlement of all suicide bomber families who lose their homes as a result of Israeli retribution.

Before embarking on his or her final mission directly from a mosque, the young suicide bomber spends many days chanting the relevant scriptures aloud at the mosque. The mantras inculcate a strong belief in the bomber that Allah and Heaven await. For example, a favorite verse reads: "Think not of those who are slain in Allah's way as dead. No, they live on and find their sustenance in the presence of their Lord." This belief is strong enough to allow the bomber to mingle casually among his intended victims without showing any nervousness.

To ensure the utmost secrecy, a bomber learns how to handle explosives only right before the mission. This practice also minimizes the time in which the bomber could have second thoughts about his martyrdom that could arise from using explosives over time. In the past, it was common for the bomber to leave a written will or make a videotape. This custom is no longer practiced because the General Security Service, the secret service, known by its initials in Hebrew as Shin Bet, has arrested other suicide bombers on the basis of information left on these records. In November 1994, the names of 66 Al-Qassam Brigade Martyrs, along with their area of residence, date of martyrdom, and means of martyrdom, were published for the first time. In the late 1990s, the name or the picture of the bomber is sometimes not even released after the suicide attack. Hamas has even stopped publicly celebrating successful suicide attacks. Nevertheless, pictures of past suicide bombers hang on the walls of barber shops inside the refugee camps, and small children collect and trade pictures of suicide bombers. There is even a teenage rock group known as the "Martyrs" that sings the praises of the latest bombers entering heaven.

In late 1997, Iran reportedly escalated its campaign to sabotage the Middle East peace process by training Palestinian suicide bombers. The two suicide bombers who carried out an attack that killed 22 Israelis on January 22, 1998, reportedly had recently returned from training in Iran. After their deaths, the Iranian government reportedly made payments to the families of both men. On September 5, 1999, four Hamas terrorists, all Israeli Arabs who had been recruited and trained in the West Bank, attempted to carry out a mission to bomb two Jerusalem-bound buses. However, both bombs apparently had been set to explode much earlier than planned, and both exploded almost simultaneously in the terrorists' cars, one in Tiberias and another in Haifa, as they were en route to their targets.

Leader Profiles

Sheikh Ahmed Yassin

Significance: Hamas founder and spiritual leader.

Background: Ahmed Yassin was born near Ashqelan in the south of Palestine in 1937. After the

1948 Israeli occupation, he lived as a refugee in the Shati camp in Gaza. He became handicapped and confined to a wheelchair in 1952 as a result of an accident. He is also blind and nearly deaf. He received a secondary school education in Gaza and worked as a teacher and preacher there from 1958 until 1978. His association with the Islamic fundamentalist Muslim Brotherhood organization began in the 1950s. He founded the Islamic Center in Gaza in 1973. In 1979, influenced by the 1979 Islamic revolution in Iran, he established Gaza's Islamic Society (Mujamma') and was its director until 1984. Although he was allowed to use the Israeli media to criticize Yasir Arafat and the PLO, Yassin was jailed for 10 months in 1984 for security reasons. He was a well-respected Muslim Brotherhood leader in Gaza running welfare and educational services in 1987 when the Palestinian uprising, Intifada, against Israeli occupation began. He shortly thereafter formed Hamas. He was arrested in May 1989 and sentenced in Israel to life imprisonment for ordering the killing of Palestinians who had allegedly collaborated with the Israeli Army. He was freed in early October 1997 in exchange for the release of two Israeli agents arrested in Jordan after a failed assassination attempt there against a Hamas

Sheikh Ahmed Yassin
(Photo courtesy of The News-Times,
January 28, 1998)

leader. Yassin then returned to his home in Gaza. He spent much of the first half of 1998 on a fund-raising tour of Sudan, Yemen, Saudi Arabia, Qatar, Kuwait, United Arab Republics, Iran, and Syria, during which he also received medical treatment in Egypt. Two countries, Saudi Arabia and Iran, reportedly pledged between $50 million and $300 million for Hamas's military operations against Israel. After his tour, and in frail health, Yassin returned to Gaza.

Mohammed Mousa ("Abu Marzook")

Significance: Member, Hamas Political Bureau.

Background: Mohammed Mousa was born in 1951 in Rafah, the Gaza Strip. He completed his basic education in the Gaza Strip, studied engineering at Ein

Shams University in Cairo, and graduated in 1977. He worked as manager of a factory in the United Arab Emirates (UAE) until 1981. He then moved to the United States to pursue his doctorate and lived with his family in Falls Church, Virginia, and Brooklyn, New York, for almost 14 years prior to his arrest in 1995. In the early 1980s, he became increasingly involved with militant Muslims in the United States and elsewhere. He co-founded an umbrella organization called the Islamic Association for Palestine (IAP) and became head of its governing council. The IAP, now headquartered in Richardson, Texas, established offices in Arizona, California, and Indiana. Beginning in 1987, Mousa allegedly was responsible for launching Hamas terrorist attacks against Israel. In 1989 he became the founding president of the United Association of Studies and Research (UASR), allegedly a covert branch of Hamas responsible for disseminating propaganda and engaging in strategic and political planning, located in Springfield, Virginia. In 1991 he earned a Ph.D. degree in Industrial Engineering. That year he was elected as Chairman of the Hamas Political Bureau, as a result of the arrest of Sheikh Ahmed Yassin in 1989. Known as an ambitious and charismatic figure, Mousa reorganized Hamas by centralizing political, military, and financial control under his leadership and developing foreign funding. Traveling freely between the United States and Europe, Iran, Jordan, Sudan, and Syria, he allegedly helped to establish a large, clandestine financial network as well as death squads that allegedly were responsible for the murder or wounding of many Israelis and suspected Palestinian collaborators. He led the resumption of suicide bombings in protest of the 1993 Oslo accords. In early 1995, under U.S. pressure, Jordanian authorities expelled him from Amman, where he had set up a major Hamas support office. After leaving Amman, he traveled between Damascus and Dubai in the United Arab Emirates, among other places.

On July 28, 1995, Mousa arrived at John F. Kennedy Airport in New York on a flight from London and was detained by Immigration and Naturalization Service (INS) agents for being on a "watch list" of suspected terrorists. Three days later, Israel formally requested Mousa's extradition to face criminal charges of terrorism and conspiracy to commit murder. FBI agents arrested Mousa on August 8, 1995, pending an extradition hearing, and he was jailed at the Federal Metropolitan Correction Center in Manhattan. Mousa dropped his objection to extradition 18 months later, saying he would rather "suffer martyrdom in Israel than fight extradition through an unjust U.S. court system." Mahmoud Zahar, a top Hamas official in Gaza, then threatened the United States if Mousa were extradited. Wishing to avoid terrorist retaliation, Israel withdrew its extradition request on April 3, 1997. Mousa was thereupon deported to Jordan on May 6, 1997. In August 1999, Jordanian authorities closed the Hamas office in Amman and, on September 22, arrested Mousa and two of his fellow Hamas members. Mousa, who was reportedly holding Yemeni citizenship and both Egyptian and Palestinian travel documents, was again deported.

Emad al-Alami

Significance: A Hamas leader.

Background: Al-Alami was born in the Gaza Strip in 1956. An engineer, he became overall leader of Hamas after the arrest of Mohammed Mousa in 1995. However, in early 1996 he reportedly had less control over all elements of Hamas than Mousa had had. He was based mainly in Damascus, from where he made trips to Teheran.

Mohammed Dief

Position: Al-Qassam leader.

Background: Mohammed Dief is believed to have assumed command of the military brigades of Hamas (Al-Qassam) following the death of Yahya Ayyash ("The Engineer"), who was killed on January 5, 1996. Dief reportedly leads from a small house on the Gaza Strip, although he is known to travel frequently to both Lebanon and Syria. He is currently among the most wanted by Israeli authorities.

Al-Jihad Group
(a.k.a.: al-Jihad, Islamic Jihad, New Jihad Group, Vanguards of the Conquest, Tala'i' al-Fath)

Group Profile

The al-Jihad Organization of Egypt, also known as the Islamic Group, is a militant offshoot of the Muslim Brotherhood movement, an anti-Western Islamic organization that has targeted Egyptian government officials for assassination since its founding in 1928. In 1981 Sheikh 'Umar Abd al-Rahman (also known as Omar Abdel Rahman), al-Jihad's blind theologian at the University of Asyut, issued a fatwa, or religious edict, sanctioning the assassination of President Anwar al-Sadat.

In 1981 more than half of al-Jihad's membership were students or teachers from vocational centers and at least eight universities. However, some of the 302 al-Jihad members arrested in December 1982 for coup-plotting in the wake of Sadat's assassination included members of the Air Force military intelligence, Army central headquarters, the Central Security Services, and even the Presidential Guard. Others included employees at strategic jobs in broadcasting, the telephone exchange, and municipal services.

Since 1998 there has been a change in the declared policy of the Al-Jihad group. In addition to its bitter ideological conflict with the "heretical" Egyptian government, the organization began calling for attacks against American and Israeli targets. Nassar Asad al-Tamini of the Islamic Jihad, noting the apparent ease with which biological weapons can be acquired, has suggested using them against Israel. In the eyes of the al-Jihad group, the United States and Israel are the vanguard of a worldwide campaign to destroy Islam and its believers, with the help of the current Egyptian government. This changed attitude was the result of, among other things, the Egyptian al-Jihad's joining the coalition of Islamic fundamentalist terrorist organizations led by the Afghans. The collaboration between the Egyptian organizations and Al-Qaida played a key role in the formation of Osama bin Laden's "Islamic Front for Jihad against the Jews and the Crusaders." Ayman al-Zawahiri, al-Jihad's leader, who was sentenced in absentia to death or to life imprisonment on April 18, 1999, is a close associate of Osama bin Laden and one of the founders of the "Islamic Front for Jihad against the Crusaders and the Jews."

The movement basically seeks to challenge the West on an Islamic basis and establish an Islamic caliphate. However, the goals of the various al-Jihad groups differ in regard to the Palestinian issue. Islamic Jihad wants to liberate Palestine. Others give priority to establishing an Islamic state as a prerequisite for the liberation of Palestine. Islamic Jihad is very hostile toward Arab and Islamic regimes, particularly Jordan, which it considers puppets of the imperialist West. In the spring of 1999, the Islamic Group's leadership and governing council announced that it was giving up armed struggle. Whether that statement was a ruse remains to be seen.

The social background of the al-Jihad remains unclear because the group has never operated fully in public. By the mid-1990s, intellectuals occupied important positions in the leadership of the al-Jihad movements in both Jordan and the Occupied Territories, where it is a powerful force in the unions of engineers, doctors, and students. Their power among workers continues to be weak.

New Religious Groups

Aum Shinrikyo

Group/Leader Profile

The investigation into the sarin gas attack on the Tokyo subway on March 20, 1995, opened a window on Shoko Asahara's cult, Aum Shinrikyo. In 1995 Aum Shinrikyo claimed to have 10,000 supporters in Japan and 30,000 in Russia. Whereas doomsday cults previously had carried out mass suicides, Aum Shinrikyo set itself apart from them by inflicting mass murder on the general public.

What seems most remarkable about this apocalyptic cult is that its leading members include Japan's best and brightest: scientists, computer experts, lawyers and other highly trained professionals. But according to cult expert Margaret Singer of the University of California at Berkeley, these demographics are not unusual. "Cults actively weed out the stupid and the psychiatric cases and look for people who are lonely, sad, between jobs or jilted," she says. Many observers also suggest that inventive minds turn to Aum Shinrikyo as an extreme reaction against the corporate-centered Japanese society, in which devotion to one's job is valued over individual expression and spiritual growth.

Japan's school system of rote memorization, in which individualism and critical thinking and analysis are systematically suppressed, combined with crowded cities and transportation networks, have greatly contributed to the proliferation of cults in Japan, and to the growth of Aum Shinrikyo in particular. Aum Shinrikyo is one of at least 180,000 minor religions active in Japan. There is general agreement that the discipline and competitiveness required of Japan's education system made Aum Shinrikyo seem very attractive to bright university graduates. It provided an alternative life-style in which recruits could rebel against their families, friends, and "the system."

Numerous Aum Shinrikyo members were arrested on various charges after the sarin attack on the Tokyo subway system in 1995. According to Manabu Watanabe, none of them claimed innocence; rather, many of them confessed their crimes and showed deep remorse. "These people were proven to be sincere and honest victims of Asahara, the mastermind," Watanabe comments. Aum Shinrikyo became active again in 1997, when the Japanese government decided not to ban it. In 1998 Aum Shinrikyo had about 2,000 members, including 200 of the 380 members who had been arrested.

The story of Aum Shinrikyo is the story of Shoko Asahara, its charismatic and increasingly psychopathic leader. Asahara, whose real name is Chizuo Matsumoto, was born in 1955, the fourth son of a poor weaver of *tatami* mats, in the small rural village of Yatsushiro on Japan's main southern island of Kyushu. Afflicted with infantile glaucoma, he was blind in one eye and had diminished vision in the other. At age six, he was sent to join his blind older brother at a government-funded boarding school for the blind. Because he had limited vision in one eye, however, he soon developed influence over the blind students, who would pay him for services such as being a guide. Already at that early age, he exhibited a strong tendency to dominate people. His activities as a violence-prone, judo-proficient con artist and avaricious bully had earned him the fear of his classmates, as well as $3,000, by the time he graduated from high school in 1975.

After graduation, Asahara established a lucrative acupuncture clinic in Kumamoto. However, his involvement in a fight in which several people were injured forced him to leave the island for Tokyo in 1977. His stated ambitions at the time included serving as supreme leader of a robot kingdom and even becoming prime minister of Japan. In Tokyo he again found work as an acupuncturist and also attended a prep school to prepare for the highly competitive Japanese college entrance examinations, which he nevertheless failed. He also began taking an interest in religion, taught himself Chinese, and studied the revolutionary philosophy of Mao Zedong. In the summer of 1977, Asahara met Tomoko Ishii, a young college student; they married in January 1978, and the first of their six children was born in 1979. In 1978 Asahara opened a Chinese herbal medicine and acupuncture clinic southeast of Tokyo and reportedly earned several hundred thousand dollars from the business. In 1981 he joined a new religion called Agon Shu, known for its annual Fire Ceremony and fusing of elements of Early Buddhism, Tantric Buddhism, and Hindu and Taoist yoga. In 1982 he was arrested and convicted for peddling fake Chinese cures and his business collapsed as a result. Bankrupted, Asahara reportedly earned nearly $200,000 from a hotel scam that year.

In 1984 Asahara quit Agon Shu and, with the help of a few followers who also left Agon Shu, created a yoga training center called Aum, Inc. By the mid-1980s, the center had more than 3,000 followers, and in 1985 Asahara began promoting himself as a holy man. After a spiritual voyage through the Himalayas, he promoted himself as having mystical powers and spiritual bliss.

Beginning in 1986, Aum Shinrikyo began a dual system of membership: ordained and lay. Ordained members had to donate all their belongings, including inheritances, to Aum. Many resisted, and a total of 56 ordained members have been reported as missing or dead, including 21 who died in the Aum Shinrikyo clinic.

In early 1987, Asahara managed to meet the Dalai Lama. Asahara's megalomania then blossomed. In July 1987, he renamed his yoga schools, which were nonreligious, Aum Supreme Truth (Aum Shinri Kyo) and began developing a personality cult. The next year, Asahara expanded his vision to include the salvation not only of Japan but the world. By the end of 1987, Aum Shinrikyo had 1,500 members concentrated in several of Japan's major cities.

In 1988 Aum Shinrikyo began recruiting new members, assigning only attractive and appealing members as recruiters. It found a fertile recruitment ground in Japan's young, college-educated professionals in their twenties and early thirties from college campuses, dead-end jobs, and fast-track careers. Systematically targeting top universities, Aum Shinrikyo leaders recruited brilliant but alienated young scientists from biology, chemistry, engineering, medical, and physics departments. Many, for example, the computer programmers, were "techno-freaks" who spent much of their time absorbed in comics and their computers. Aum Shinrikyo also enlisted medical doctors to dope patients and perform human experiments. The first young Japanese to be free of financial pressures, the Aum Shinrikyo recruits were wondering if there was more to life than job security and social conformity. However, as Aum Shinrikyo members they had no need to think for themselves. According to David Kaplan and Andrew Marshall, "The high-tech children of postindustrial Japan were fascinated by Aum's dramatic claims to supernatural power, its warnings of an apocalyptic future, its esoteric spiritualism."

Aum's hierarchy had been influenced by Japanese animated movies, cyberpunk fiction and science fiction, virtual reality machines, and computer games. For example, Aum Shinrikyo used Isaac Asimov's classic sci-fi epic in the Foundation Series as a high-tech blueprint for the millennium and beyond. Indeed, Asahara modeled himself on Hari Seldon, the key character in the Foundation Series. The fictional Seldon is a brilliant mathematician who discovers "psychohistory," the science of true prediction, and attempts to save humanity from apocalypse by forming a secret religious society, the Foundation, that can rebuild civilization in a millennium. To do this, Seldon recruits the best minds of his time, and, once a hierarchy of scientist-priests is established, they set about preserving the knowledge of the universe. Like Asimov's scientists in the Foundation Series, Asahara preached that the only way to survive was to create a secret order of beings armed with superior intellect, state-of-the-art technology, and knowledge of the future.

To retain its membership, Aum Shinrikyo used mind-control techniques that are typical of cults worldwide, including brutal forms of physical and psychological punishment for various minor transgressions. New members had to terminate all contacts with the outside world and donate all of their property to Aum. This policy outraged the parents of Aum Shinrikyo members. In addition, in 1989 Aum Shinrikyo began to use murder as a sanction on members wishing to leave the sect.

Shoko Asahara
(Photo courtesy of
Reuters/Ho/Archive)

In July 1989, Aum Shinrikyo became more public when Asahara announced that Aum Shinrikyo would field a slate of 25 candidates, including Asahara, in the next election of the lower house of the Japanese parliament. To that end, Aum Shinrikyo formed a political party, Shinrito (Turth Party). All of the Aum Shinrikyo candidates were young professionals between the ages of 25 and 38. In addition, Aum Shinrikyo finally succeeded in getting official recognition as an official religion on August 15, 1989, on a one-year probationary basis.

In the political arena, however, Aum Shinrikyo was a total failure. Its bizarre campaign antics, such as having its followers dance about in front of subway stations wearing huge papier-mâché heads of Asahara, dismayed the public, which gave Aum Shinrikyo a resounding defeat in the 1990 parliamentary elections (a mere 1,783 votes). This humiliation, it is believed, fueled Asahara's paranoia, and he accused the Japanese government of rigging the voting.

Following this public humiliation, Asahara's darker side began to emerge. He began asking his advisers how they might set off vehicle bombs in front of their opponents' offices, and in March 1990, he ordered his chief chemist, Seiichi Endo, to develop a botulin agent.
Beginning that April, when Aum Shinrikyo sent three trucks into the streets of Tokyo to spray poisonous mists, Asahara began to preach a doomsday scenario

to his followers and the necessity for Aum Shinrikyo members to militarize and dedicate themselves to protecting Aum Shinrikyo against the coming Armageddon. That April, an Aum Shinrikyo team sprayed botulin poison on the U.S. naval base at Yokosuka outside Tokyo, where the U.S. 7th Fleet docked, but the botulin turned out to be a defective batch.

To prevent its dwindling membership from falling off further, Aum Shinrikyo began to forcefully prevent members from leaving, and to recruit abroad. The group's efforts in the United States were not successful; in the early 1990s, Aum Shinrikyo had only a few dozen followers in the New York City area..

By late 1992, Asahara was preaching that Armageddon would occur by the year 2000, and that more than 90 percent of Japan's urban populations would be wiped out by nuclear, biological, and chemical weapons of mass destruction. Apparently, Asahara's plan was to develop the weapons of mass destruction needed for making this Armageddon a reality. In 1992 Aum Shinrikyo began purchasing businesses on a worldwide scale. It set up dummy companies, primarily in Russia and the United States, where its investments served as covers to purchase technology, weapons, and chemicals for its weapons program. During 1992-94, Aum Shinrikyo recruited a number of Russian experts in weapons of mass destruction. Aum's Russian followers included employees in Russia's premier nuclear research facility, the I.V. Kurchatov Institute of Atomic Energy, and the Mendeleyev Chemical Institute. Aum's chemical weapons efforts were more successful than its nuclear efforts. After the Gulf War, Aum's scientists began work on sarin and other related nerve agents.

Aum Shinrikyo found that it could recruit at least one member from almost any Japanese or Russian agency or corporation and turn that recruit into its own agent. For example, in late 1994 Aum Shinrikyo needed access to sensitive military secrets held by the Mitsubishi Heavy Industries (MHI) compound in Hiroshima, so Aum Shinrikyo member Hideo Nakamoto, an MHI senior researcher, obtained MHI uniforms, and Yoshihiro Inoue recruited and converted three paratroopers from the 1st Airborne Brigade, an elite Japanese paratrooper unit. Nakamoto then escorted Inoue and the three paratroopers, wearing MHI uniforms, into the high-security facility, where they downloaded megabytes of restricted files on advanced weapons technology from MHI's mainframe. Other sites raided by the squad included the laser-research lab of NEC, Japan's top computer manufacturer, and the U.S. naval base at Yokosuka . Aum's membership lists included more than 20 serving and former members of the Self-Defense Forces.

Aum's sarin attacks were carried out by highly educated terrorists. Aum's minister of science and technology, Hideo Murai, an astrophysicist, led the cult's first sarin attack in the mountain town Matsumoto on June 27, 1994, by releasing sarin gas near the apartment building in which the judge who had ruled against the cult lived. The attack killed seven people and poisoned more than 150 others. Robert S. Robbins and Jerrold M. Post note that: "In 1994 Asahara made the delusional claim that U.S. jets were delivering gas attacks on his followers, a projection of his own paranoid psychology. Asahara became increasingly preoccupied not with surviving the coming war but with starting it." That year, Asahara reorganized Aum, using Japan's government as a model (see Table 7).

Table 7. Aum Shinrikyo's Political Leadership, 1995	
Leadership Entity	Leader
Founder	Shoko Asahara
Household Agency	Tomomasa Nakagawa
Secretariat	Reika Matsumoto
Ministry of Commerce	Yofune Shirakawa
Ministry of Construction	Kiyohide Hayakawa
Ministry of Defense	Tetsuya Kibe
Ministry of Education	Shigeru Sugiura
Ministry of Finance	Hisako Ishii
Ministry of Foreign Affairs	Fumihiro Joyu
Ministry of Healing	Ikuo Hayashi
Ministry of Health and Welfare	Seiichi Endo
Ministry of Home Affairs	Tomomitsu Niimi
Ministry of Intelligence	Yoshihiro Inoue
Ministry of Justice	Yoshinobu Aoyama
Ministry of Labor	Mayumi Yamamoto
Ministry of Post and Telecommunications	Tomoko Matsumoto
Ministry of Science and Technology	Hideo Murai
Ministry of Vehicles	Naruhito Noda
Eastern Followers Agency	Eriko Iida
New Followers Agency	Sanae Ouchi
Western Followers Agency	Kazuko Miyakozawa

Source: Based on information from D.W. Brackett, *Holy Terror: Armageddon in Tokyo*. New York: Weatherhill, 1996, 104.

The five Aum Shinrikyo terrorists who carried out the sarin gas attack on the Tokyo subway on March 20, 1995, included Ikuo Hayashi, 48, head of Aum's Ministry of Healing (aka Medical Treatment Ministry). The other four were all vice ministers of Aum's Ministry of Science and Technology and included: Masato Yokoyama, 31, an applied-physics graduate; Kenichi Hirose, 30, who graduated at the top of his class in applied physics at the prestigious Waseda University; Yasuo Hayashi, 37, an electronics engineer; and Toru Toyoda, a physicist.

Although no motive has been established for Asahara's alleged role in the nerve-gas attacks, some observers suggest that the Tokyo subway attack might have been revenge: all the subway cars struck by the sarin converged at a station beneath a cluster of government offices. Adding credence to this view, Ikuo Hayashi, a doctor who admitted planting gas on one of the Tokyo trains, was quoted in newspapers as saying the goal was to wipe out the Kasumigaseki section of Tokyo, where many government offices are located. "The attack was launched so that the guru's prophecy could come true," Hayashi reportedly told interrogators.

Shoko Egawa, an Aum Shinrikyo critic who has authored at least two books on the cult, observed that Aum Shinrikyo members made no attempt at reviewing the propriety of their own actions during the trial. When their own violations were being questioned, they shifted to generalities, and spoke as if they were objective third parties. Their routine tactics, she notes, included shifting stories into religious doctrine and training, making an issue out of a minor error on the part of the other party, evading the main issue, and feigning ignorance when confronted with critical facts.

Authorities arrested a total of 428 Aum Shinrikyo members, and thousands of others quit. The government also stripped Aum Shinrikyo of its tax-exempt status and declared it bankrupt in 1996. Nevertheless, Aum Shinrikyo retained its legal status as a sect and eventually began to regroup. In 1998 its computer equipment front company had sales of $57 million, and its membership had risen to about 2,000. In December 1998, Japan's Public Security Investigation Agency warned in its annual security review that the cult was working to boost its membership and coffers. "Aum is attempting to re-enlist former members and step up recruiting of new members nationwide. It is also initiating advertising campaigns and acquiring necessary capital," the report said.

Key Leader Profiles

Yoshinobu Aoyama

Position: Aum's minister of justice.

Background: Yoshinobu Aoyama was born in 1960. The son of a wealthy Osaka family, he graduated from Kyoto University Law School, where he was the youngest person in his class to pass the national bar exam. He joined Aum Shinrikyo in 1988 and within two years was its chief counsel. He was arrested in 1990 for violation of the National Land Law, and after being released on bail, he involved himself in an effort to prove his innocence. As Aum's attorney, he led its successful defense strategy of expensive countersuits and legal intimidation of Aum Shinrikyo critics. According to Kaplan and Marshall, "He had longish hair, a robotlike delivery, and darting, nervous eyes that made it easy to underestimate him." He was arrested on May 3, 1995.

According to Shoko Egawa, Aoyama's foremost traits during his trial included shifting responsibility and changing the story; speaking emotionally and becoming overly verbose when advocating Aum Shinrikyo positions, but speaking in a completely unemotional voice and making a purely perfunctory apology when addressing a case of obvious violation of the law; engaging in a lengthy dissertation on religious terms; deploying extended empty explanations and religious theory until the listener succumbed to a loss of patience and forgot the main theme of the discussion; deliberately shifting away from the main discussion and responding in a meandering manner to upset the questioner; resorting to counter-questioning and deceiving the other party by refusing to answer and pretending to explain a premise; and showing a complete absence of any remorse for having served the Aum Shinrikyo cult.

Seiichi Endo

Position: Minister of Health and Welfare.

Background: Seiichi Endo, born in 1960, was Aum's health and welfare minister. As a graduate student in biology at Kyoto University, he did experiments in genetic engineering at the medical school's Viral Research Center. Provided with a small but well-equipped biolab by Aum, he conducted research in biological warfare agents, such as botulism and the Ebola virus. In March 1990, three weeks after voters rejected 25 Aum Shinrikyo members running for legislative office, Endo and three others went on a trip to collect starter botulinum germs on the northern island of Hokkaido, where Endo had studied as a young man. In late 1993, Asahara also assigned Endo the task of making sarin nerve gas. In a 1994 speech made in Moscow, he discussed the use of Ebola as a potential biological warfare agent. Endo produced the impure sarin that was used for the Tokyo subway attack on March 20, 1995. He was arrested on April 26,

1995, and publicly admitted his role in the sarin attacks in the town of Matsumoto on June 27, 1994, and Tokyo on March 20, 1995.

Kiyohide Hayakawa

Position: Asahara's second in command and minister of construction.

Background: A key senior Aum Shinrikyo member, Kiyohide Hayakawa was born in 1949 in Osaka. He was active in leftist causes in the 1960s and during college. He received a master's degree in environmental planning from Osaka University in 1975. He worked in various architecture firms until 1986, when he joined the Aum's precursor group and soon distinguished himself as director of the Aum's Osaka division. Beginning in 1990, he masterminded Aum's attempt to arm itself and promoted its expansion into Russia. After becoming second in command, he spent a lot of time in Russia developing contacts there for the sect's militarization program. During 1992-95, he visited Russia 21 times, spending more than six months there. His visits to Russia became monthly between November 1993 and April 1994. His captured notebooks contain numerous references to nuclear and seismological weapons. Hayakawa participated in the murder of an Aum Shinrikyo member and the family of Attorney Tsutsumi Sakamoto, 33, a tenacious Aum Shinrikyo critic, in 1995. He was arrested on April 19, 1995.

Dr. Ikuo Hayashi

Position: Aum's minister of healing.

Background: Ikuo Hayashi, born in 1947, was the son of a Ministry of Health official. He graduated from Keio University's elite medical school, and studied at Mount Sinai Hospital in the United States before joining the Japanese medical system. Handsome and youthful looking, he was a respected doctor and head of cardiopulmonary medicine at a government hospital just outside Tokyo. His behavior changed after an automobile accident in April 1988, when he fell asleep while driving a station wagon and injured a mother and her young daughter. Despondent, he, along with his wife, an anesthesiologist, joined Aum, whereupon he began treating his patients bizarrely, using Aum Shinrikyo techniques. Forced to resign from his hospital position, Dr. Hayashi was put in charge of Aum's new clinic in Tokyo, where patients tended to live only long enough to be brainwashed and to sign over their property to Aum, according to Kaplan and Marshall.

Hayashi was also appointed Aum's minister of healing. Kaplan and Marshall report that "he coldly presided over the wholesale doping, torture, and death of many followers." His activities included using electric shocks to erase memories of 130 suspicious followers. He participated in the sarin attack on the Tokyo subway March 20, 1995.

Arrested on April 8, 1995, Hayashi was sentenced to life in prison on May 26, 1998, for spraying sarin in the Tokyo subway. In trial witness testimony on November 27, 1998, he said that he felt a dilemma over the crimes that he committed because they clashed with his social values, but he used Aum Shinrikyo doctrines to convince himself. Hayashi claimed he followed Asahara's order to commit murders not only out of fear that if he had disobeyed he would have been killed, but also out of a belief that Asahara had some religious power, that he had the God-like ability to see through a person's past, present, and future. Ikuo allegedly abandoned his faith in Asahara.

Yoshihiro Inoue

Position: Aum's minister of intelligence.

Background: Yoshihiro Inoue was born in 1970, the son of a salaried minor official. Kaplan and Marshall describe him as "a quiet boy of middling intelligence who devoured books on Nostradamus and the supernatural." While a high school student in Kyoto, he attended his first Aum Shinrikyo seminar. He became Aum's minister of intelligence and one of its "most ruthless killers," according to Kaplan and Marshall. Unlike other Aum Shinrikyo leaders, Inoue lacked a university degree, having dropped out of college after several months to dedicate his life to Aum, which he had joined as a high school junior. He was so dedicated to Asahara that he declared that he would kill his parents if Asahara ordered it. Inoue was also so articulate, persuasive, and dedicated that, despite his unfriendly face—lifeless black eyes, frowning mouth, and pouting, effeminate lips—he was able to recruit 300 monks and 1,000 new believers, including his own mother and many Tokyo University students. His captured diaries contain his random thoughts and plans concerning future Aum Shinrikyo operations, including a plan to conduct indiscriminate nerve gas attacks in major U.S. cities, including New York City.

In the spring of 1994, Inoue attended a three-day training program run by the former KGB's Alpha Group outside Moscow, where he learned some useful tips on skills such as kidnapping, murder, and so forth. That summer he became Aum's minister of intelligence, a position that he used as a license to abduct runaway followers, kidnap potential cash donors to the cult, torture Aum Shinrikyo members who had violated some regulation, and steal high-technology secrets. That year, Inoue and Tomomitsu Niimi were ordered to plan a sarin and VX gas attack on the White House and the Pentagon. Beginning on December 28, 1994, Inoue led the first of numerous penetrations of the high-security compound of Mitsubishi Heavy Industries (MHI) in Hiroshima to pilfer weapons secrets. He was arrested on May 15, 1995, when police stopped his car at a roadblock outside of Tokyo. During his trial, he allegedly abandoned his faith in Asahara.

Hisako Ishii

Position: Aum's minister of finance.

Background: Hisako Ishii was born in 1960. She joined Aum's yoga classes in 1984, when she was an "office lady" at a major Japanese insurance company.

One of Asahara's most devoted disciples, she became Aum's minister of finance and was behind the group's business success. She was also his inseparable mistress, until she gave birth to twins.

At her trial, Ishii spoke of her childhood fear of death, the fact that adults failed to initially reply to her questions concerning death, the fact that she trusted Asahara with pure feelings, and her determination to mature as a person within the Aum Shinrikyo framework. She then proceeded to speak of changes which took place after her arrest:

> When I experienced a total collapse of the past more than 10 years during which I had matured within the cult as a religious person, I felt I had died. When all that I had believed I had accomplished within myself was destroyed, and I came to the awareness that all was just a fantasy of Asahara imbued in me, that he is not a true religious being, that he is not a guru, and that the Aum Shinrikyo doctrine was wrong, I experienced a form of death separate from the death of a physical being.

Ishii proceeded to read books banned by the Aum, such as religious books, books on mind-control, and psychology. She testified that as a result she had been resurrected through the process of learning the nature of genuine religion. Despite being impressed by the eloquence of her written statement, Shoko Egawa was dismayed by Ishii's total omission of anything about her feelings for the victims who literally met death as the result of the many crimes committed by the Aum. Although charged with relatively minor offenses, such as concealment of criminals and destruction of evidence, Ishii asserted that she was innocent of each of the charges. She depicted herself merely as an innocent victim taken advantage of by Asahara and stressed her determination to resurrect herself despite all the suffering. She not only refused to testify about her inside knowledge of cult affairs, she cut off any questions of that nature. In May 1998, Ishii announced her resignation from the Aum.

Fumihiro Joyu

Position: Aum's minister of foreign affairs.

Background: Fumihiro Joyu joined Aum Shinrikyo in 1989 at age 26. He had an advanced degree in telecommunications from Waseda University, where he studied artificial intelligence. He quit his promising new career at Japan's Space Development Agency after only two weeks because it was incompatible with his interests in yoga. He became the sect's spokesman and minister of foreign affairs. As Aum's Moscow chief, Joyu ran the cult's large Moscow center at Alexseyevskaya Square. "Joyu didn't try to hide his contempt for his poor Russian flock," Kaplan and Marshall write. They describe him as "a mini–guru, a cruel and arrogant man who later proved to be Aum's most accomplished liar." They add: "...fluent in English, Joyu was looked upon by most Japanese as a dangerously glib and slippery operator with the ability to lie in two languages." However, with his charismatic, boyish good looks he developed admirers among teenage girls from his appearances on television talk shows. He was arrested on October 7, 1995, on perjury charges. He was scheduled to be released from prison at the end of 1999. He has remained devout to Asahara, and was planning to rejoin the Aum Shinrikyo cult.

Takeshi Matsumoto

Position: An Aum Shinrikyo driver.

Background: Born in 1966, Takeshi Matsumoto joined Aum Shinrikyo after telling his parents that he had seen hell. Personable but pathetic, he had dreams of becoming a Grand Prix auto racer. He drove the rental car used to kidnap Kiyoshi Kariya, 68, a notary public whose sister was a runaway Aum Shinrikyo member. Aum Shinrikyo members tortured and murdered Kariya after he refused to reveal his sister's whereabouts. National Police identified Matsumoto from fingerprints on the car rental receipt and put him on their "most-wanted" list. His fingerprints were the legal pretext long sought by the National Police to raid Aum Shinrikyo compounds and offices. While on the run, Matsumoto had Dr. Hayashi surgically remove all of his fingerprints and do some abortive facial plastic surgery as well. However, he was arrested in October 1995 and identified by his palm prints. He pleaded guilty to the abduction and confinement of Kariya.

Hideo Murai

Position: Aum's minister of science and technology, minister of distribution supervision, and "engineer of the apocalypse."

Background: Hideo Murai was born in 1954. After graduating from the Physics Department at Osaka University, he entered graduate school, where he studied X-ray emissions of celestial bodies, excelled at computer programming, and earned an advance degree in astrophysics. In 1987 he joined Kobe Steel and worked in research and development. After reading one of Asahara's books, he lost interest in his career. After a trip to Nepal, he quit Kobe Steel in 1989 and, along with his wife, enlisted in a six-month training course at an Aum Shinrikyo commune, where his life style turned ascetic and focused on Asahara's teachings. He quickly rose through the ranks because of his brilliant scientific background, self-confidence, boldness, and devotion to Asahara. He created such devices as the Perfect Salvation Initiation headgear (an electrode-laden shock cap), which netted Aum Shinrikyo about $20 million, and the Astral Teleporter and attempted unsuccessfully to develop a botulinus toxin as well as nuclear, laser, and microwave weapons technology. In early 1993, Asahara ordered him to oversee Aum's militarization program. "Widely recognized and feared within Aum, Murai," according to Brackett, "had a reputation as a determined and aggressive leader who liked to stir up trouble for other people." He was directly involved in the murder of the Sakamotos and at least one Aum Shinrikyo member. He led the team that attacked judges' apartments in Matsumoto with sarin gas in June 27, 1994, in which seven people were killed and 144 injured. Murai also masterminded the sarin attack on the Tokyo subway on March 20, 1995. David Kaplan and Andrew Marshall describe "the cult's deceptively unassuming science chief" as follows: "At first glance, Murai looked more like a provincial schoolteacher than a mad scientist. He had elfin features etched on a perfectly round face, with a fragile build that suggested he could do harm to no one. But a closer look revealed eyes that turned from benign to beady in a blink. His hair was short but disheveled, and he often looked lost in some unreachable thought." Just before he was to be brought in by police for questioning, Murai was stabbed with a butcher's knife by a Korean gangster on April 23, 1995, on prime-time TV in front of Aum's Tokyo headquarters, and he died six hours later.

Kiyohide Nakada

Position: Vice Minister, Ministry of Home Affairs.

Background: Nakada was born in 1948. He is described as having a shiny, shaven head, clipped mustache, and piercing eyes. His distinguishing feature, which is characteristic of a Japanese *yakuza*, or mobster, is a brilliant tattoo stretching from his neck to his calf. For years, he headed a gang affiliated with the Yamaguchi crime syndicate in the city of Nagoya. When he was serving three years in prison on a firearms charge, his wife joined Aum. Although Nakada disapproved of her joining Aum, he himself turned to Aum Shinrikyo when a doctor gave him three months to live because of a failing liver. After a miraculous recovery, he joined Aum, dissolved his gang, and donated his assets to Aum. Nakada became one of Asahara's two former *yakuza* conduits to the underworld. When Aum Shinrikyo began its militarization program in 1994, he became particularly important in obtaining weapons. He eventually became Tomomitsu Niimi's deputy in Aum's Ministry of Home Affairs, charged with enforcing security within the organization. As head of the Action Squad, he was responsible for abducting and killing defecting sect members and opponents of Aum. He was arrested in April 1995.

Tomomasa Nakagawa

Position: Head of Aum's Household Agency.

Background: Dr. Tomomasa Nakagawa, 29, an Aum Shinrikyo physician, is alleged to have murdered Satoko Sakamoto, 29, and her infant son with injections of potassium chloride, in 1995. Nakagawa joined Aum Shinrikyo while a medical student at Kyoto Prefectural College of Medicine in February 1988. After passing the national medical exam in April 1988 and practicing medicine for a year, he moved into an Aum Shinrikyo commune in August 1989. As head of the Aum's Household Agency, one of his primary duties was to act as personal doctor to Asahara and his family. He was also actively involved in Aum's sarin production.

Tomomitsu Niimi

Position: Aum's minister of home affairs.

Background: Tomomitsu Niimi was born in 1964. As a university student, he read law, as well as the works of Nostradamus and esoteric Buddhist texts. After graduation, he worked at a food company but quit six months later to join Aum. Kaplan and Marshall describe him as "a slender figure with a long neck, shaven head, and a reptilian smirk that seemed permanently etched upon his face."

As Aum's ferocious minister of home affairs, Niimi presided over Aum's mini-police state. His 10-member hit squad, the New Followers Agency, engaged in spying on, abducting, confining, torturing, and murdering runaway members. He is described by Kaplan and Marshall as Aum's "chief hit man" and a sadistic and ruthless head of security. He allegedly participated in various murders and abductions, including the murder of Shuji Taguchi in 1989, the slaying of the Sakamoto family, and the strangling of a pharmacist in January 1994. In February 1994, he was accidentally exposed to some sarin and lapsed into convulsions, but Dr. Nakagawa was able to save him. In the spring of 1994, he attended a three-day training course conducted by veterans of the former KGB's Alpha Group near Moscow. That year, Niimi and Yoshihiro Inoue were ordered to plan a sarin and VX gas attack on the White House and the Pentagon. On September 20, 1994, Niimi and his hit squad attacked Shoko Egawa, author of two books on Aum, with phosgene gas, but she survived. In January 1995, Niimi sprayed Hiroyuki Nakaoka, head of a cult victims' support group, with VX, but he survived after several weeks in a coma. Niimi also participated in the Tokyo subway attack on March 20, 1995. He was arrested on April 12, 1995. He has remained devout to Asahara.

Toshihiro Ouchi

Position: An Aum Shinrikyo operative.

Background: Ouchi joined the Aum Shinrikyo cult in 1985. Physically large and a long-time Aum Shinrikyo member, Ouchi functioned primarily as a leader of cult followers. Many of the followers and ordained priests of the cult with whom he had been personally associated became involved in crimes, and many remain active cult followers. Ouchi was indicted for involvement in two incidents. One case took place in February 1989, and involved the murder of cult follower Shuji Taguchi, who was making an attempt to leave the cult; the second case involved the destruction of a corpse of a cult follower who had passed away during religious training in June 1993. Ouchi's reluctant behavior gave Asahara doubts about his commitment; hence, he condemned Ouchi as a "cancerous growth on the Aum," assigning him to the Russian chapter in September 1993. Nevertheless, Ouchi continued to serve as an executive cult follower. He recruited new followers in Russia and provided guidance to them. During the investigation of the Sakamoto case that began in March 1995, Ouchi was alarmed when he learned that the Aum Shinrikyo was involved. The knowledge undermined his religious beliefs. He reportedly was shocked when he later received a letter from a former cult follower, who was an intimate friend, that discussed the misguided doctrine of Aum. His faith in Aum Shinrikyo shaken, he gradually began to alter his views about people outside the cult. In early April 1995, Russian police arrested Ouchi, who had been serving as Fumihiro Joyu's deputy in Moscow. Kaplan and Marshall report that Ouchi, "a grinning naïf," was described by one academic as "knowing as much about Russia as the farthest star." During his initial trial in Japan, Ouchi expressed repentance and apologized "as a former official of the Aum."

Masami Tsuchiya

Position: Head of Aum's chemical-warfare team.

Background: Masami Tsuchiya was born in 1965. Prior to joining Aum, Tsuchiya was enrolled in a five-year doctoral degree program in organic physics and chemistry at Tsukuba University, one of the top universities in Japan, where his graduate work focused on the application of light to change the structure of molecules. Although described by a professor as "brilliant," Tsuchiya lived in a barren room, was introverted, had no social life, and expressed a desire to become a priest.

Tsuchiya abandoned a career in organic chemistry to join Aum. After suggesting that Aum Shinrikyo produce a Nazi nerve gas called sarin, he was given his own lab (named Satian 7) with 100 workers and a vast chemical plant to develop chemical weapons. As Aum's chief chemist and head of its chemical-warfare team, he played a central role in Aum's manufacture of sarin. Kaplan and Marshall describe Tsuchiya as looking the part of the mad scientist: "His goatee and crew-cut hair framed a broad face with eyebrows that arched high above piercing eyes." Fascinated by Russia's chemical weapons stockpiles, Tsuchiya spent at least three weeks in Russia in 1993, where he is suspected of meeting with experts in biochemical weapons. When he returned to his Mount Fuji lab in the fall of 1993, he began experimenting with sarin, using a Russian formula. He was prepared to build a vast stockpile of nerve agents, such as sarin, blister gas, and others. Although poorly trained workers, leaks of toxic fumes, and repeated setbacks plagued the program, Tsuchiya succeeded in stockpiling 44 pounds of sarin at Satian 7 by mid-June 1994. However, Kaplan and Marshall point out that he was not the only Aum Shinrikyo chemist to make the nerve gas. Tsuchiya also produced other chemical-warfare agents such as VX. He had Tomomitsu Niimi, using a VX syringe, test the VX on several unsuspecting individuals. Police arrested Tsuchiya on April 26, 1995. He has remained devout to Asahara.

TABLES

Table 1. Educational Level and Occupational Background of Right-Wing Terrorists in West Germany, 1980 (In percentages of right-wing terrorists)	
Education:	
Volkschule (elementary)	49
Technical	22
Grammar (high school)	17
University	10
Other	2
TOTAL	100
Occupation:	
Self-employed	8
White collar	9
Skilled worker or artisan	41
Unskilled worker	34
Other (unemployed)	8
TOTAL	100

Source: Based on information from Eva Kolinsky, "Terrorism in West Germany. Pages 75-76 in Juliet Lodge, ed., *The Threat of Terrorism*. Boulder, Colorado: Westview Press, 1988.

Table 2. Ideological Profile of Italian Female Terrorists, January 1970–June 1984

Membership in Extraparliamentary Political Organizations Prior to Becoming a Terrorist	Number of Terrorists	Percentage of Total Terrorists
Left	73	91.0
Right	7	9.0
TOTAL	80	100.0
Terrorist Group Affiliation	Number of Terrorists	Percentage of Total Terrorists
Early Left[1]	40	9.0
Early Right[2]	10	2.2
Late Left[3]	366	82.2
Late Right[4]	29	6.5
TOTAL	445	100.0

1. Partisan Action Groups, Nuclei of Armed Proletarians. Red Brigades, 22 October.
2. Compass, Mussolini Action Squads, National Front, National Vanguard, New Order, People's Struggle, Revolutionary Action Movement.
3. Front Line, Red Brigades, Revolutionary Action, Union of Communist Combatants, Worker Autonomy, et alia.
4. Let Us Build Action, Nuclei of Armed Revolutionaries, Third Position.

Source: Based on information from Leonard Weinberg and William Lee Eubank, "Italian Women Terrorists," *Terrorism: An International Journal*, 9, No. 3, 1987, 250, 252.

Table 3. Prior Occupational Profile of Italian Female Terrorists, January 1970–June 1984

Occupation Prior to Becoming a Terrorist	Number of Terrorists	Percentage of Total Terrorists
Clerk, secretary, nurse, technician	57	23.0
Criminal, subproletarian	5	2.0
Free professional (architect, lawyer, physician)	8	3.0
Housewife	11	5.0
Industrialist	5	2.0
Police, military	1	0.0
Small business proprietor, salesperson	3	1.0
Student	86	35.0
Teacher	50	20.0
Worker	18	7.0
TOTAL	244	100.0

Source: Based on information from Leonard Weinberg and William Lee Eubank, "Italian Women Terrorists," *Terrorism: An International Journal*, 9, No. 3, 1987, 250-52.

Table 4. Geographical Profile of Italian Female Terrorists, January 1970–June 1984

Place of Birth (Region)	Number of Terrorists	Percentage of Total Terrorists
North	96	45.0
Center	31	15.0
Rome	30	14.0
South	43	20.0
Foreign-born	12	6.0
TOTAL	212	100.0

Place of Birth (Size of Community)	Number of Terrorists	Percentage of Total Terrorists
Small community (under 100,000)	77	9.0
Medium-sized city (from 100,000 to 1 million)	71	29.0
Big City (more than 1 million)	81	34.0
Foreign-born	12	5.0
TOTAL	241	100.0

Place of Residence (Region)	Number of Terrorists	Percentage of Total Terrorists
North	246	56.0
Center	54	12.0
Rome	90	21.0
South	49	11.0
TOTAL	241	100.0

Place of Residence (Size of Community)	Number of Terrorists	Percentage of Total Terrorists
Small community (less than	37	8.0

Medium-sized community (100,000 to 1 million)	106	24.0
Big City (more than 1 million)	297	67.0
TOTAL	440	100.0

Source: Based on information from Leonard Weinberg and William Lee Eubank, "Italian Women Terrorists," *Terrorism: An International Journal*, 9, No. 3, 1987, 250-51.

Table 5. Age and Relationships Profile of Italian Female Terrorists, January 1970-June 1984

Time of Arrest	Number of Terrorists	Percentage of Total Terrorists
Before 1977	46	10.0
After 1977	405	90.0
TOTAL	451	100.0

Age at Time of Arrest	Number of Terrorists	Percentage of Total Terrorists
15 to 19	28	7.0
20 to 24	170	42.0
25 to 29	106	26.0
30 to 34	63	16.0
35 to 39	21	5.0
40 to 44	9	2.0
45 and over	5	1.0
TOTAL	402	100

Role in Organization	Number of Terrorists	Percentage of Total Terrorists
Supporter	120	27.0
Regular	298	66.0
Leader	33	7.0
TOTAL	451	100.0

Related to Other Terrorists	Number of Terrorists	Percentage of Total Terrorists
Yes	121	27.0
No	330	73.0
TOTAL	451	100.0

Nature of Relationship to Other Terrorists	Number of Terrorists	Percentage of Total Terrorists

Marital	81	67.0
Sibling	34	28.0
Parental	1	1.0
Other	5	4.0
TOTAL	121	100.0

Source: Based on information from Leonard Weinberg and William Lee Eubank, "Italian Women Terrorists," *Terrorism: An International Journal*, 9, No. 3, 1987, 250-52.

Table 6. Patterns of Weapons Use by the Revolutionary Organization 17 November, 1975-97		
Action	Date	Weapon(s) Used
A masked gunman assassinated U.S. Embassy official Richard Welch in front of his home in an Athens suburb.	December 23, 1975	Colt .45
Gunmen in a passing car shot and fatally wounded Petros Babalis, a former police officer, near his house in central Athens.	January 31, 1979	Colt .45
Gunmen riding on a motorcycle killed Pantalis Petrou, deputy chief of the antiriot police MAT (Units for the Restoration of Order), and seriously wounded his chauffeur in Pangrati, a suburb of Athens.	January 16, 1980	Colt .45
Two men on a motor scooter assassinated U.S. Navy Captain George Tsantes and fatally wounded his driver with the same Colt .45.	November 15, 1983	Colt .45
Two masked gunmen on a motorcycle shot and wounded U.S. Army Master Sergeant Robert Judd, who took evasive action, as he was driving to the Hellenikon base near Athens airport.	April 3, 1984	Colt .45
Two men on a motorcycle shot and wounded U.S. Master Sgt. Richard H. Judd, Jr., as he was driving in Athens.	April 3, 1984	Colt .45
Two men in a car intercepted conservative newspaper publisher Nikos Momferatos's Mercedes and shot to death him and seriously wounded his driver in Kolonaki in the most central part of Athens.	February 21, 1985	Colt .45 and .22-caliber pistol

A gunman riding on the back seat of a motor scooter opened fire on businessman Alexandros Athanasiadis when he stopped for a traffic light on Kifissia Avenue on his way to work, fatally wounding him.	March 1, 1988	Colt .45
Three gunmen ambushed New Democracy (ND) Party deputy Pavlos Bakoyannis, son-in-law of ND Chairman Konstandinos Mitsotakis, as he was waiting for the elevator to his office in Athens. One of the terrorists opened fire on the target from behind, hitting him five times, and then all three casually walked to their getaway car.	September 26, 1989	Colt .45
Three gunmen assassinated the Turkish Deputy Chief of Mission in Athens with seven bullets fired from at least one .45-caliber automatic, as he drove to work.	August(?) 1994	Colt .45
Murdered Cosfi Peraticos, scion of a Greek shipping family.	June 1997	Colt .45

Source: Compiled by the author from multiple sources.

GLOSSARY

Afghans—Term applied to veterans of the Afghan War. A number of the would-be mujahideen (*q.v.*), or Islamic resistance fighters, who flocked to Afghanistan in the 1980s and early 1990s later applied the skills and contacts acquired during the Afghan War and its aftermath to engage in terrorist activities elsewhere. The Afghans also transmitted the knowledge they acquired to a new generation of Muslim militants in countries as different as Algeria, Bosnia-Herzegovina, France, and the Philippines. This new breed of Afghan terrorists, who operate independently of state sponsors, draws on global funding, is savvy about modern weapons and explosives, and is able to take advantage of the most up-to-date means of communication and transportation. Whereas Muslim terrorists were cloistered by nationality prior to the Afghan War, after the war they began working together—Pakistanis, Egyptians, Algerians, and so forth. Al-Qaida's Afghan component is also known as the Armed Islamist Movement (AIM).

Assassins—From the eleventh through the thirteenth century, a sect of Shiite Muslims called the Assassins used assassination as a tool for purifying the Muslim religion. The Assassins' victims, who were generally officials, were killed in public to communicate the error of the targeted official. By carrying out the assassination in public, the Assassin would allow himself to be apprehended and killed in order to demonstrate the purity of his motives and to enter Heaven.

Baader-Meinhof Gang—Journalistic name for the Red Army Faction (Rote Armee Fraktion—RAF) (*q.v.*). Although the RAF had been reduced to fewer than 20 members by the early 1990s, it may still exist in an inactive status. If so, it would be in at least its second generation of leadership. The group's support network, reportedly involving hundreds of Germans, many of whom are well-educated professionals, helps to account for its possible survival.

fundamentalism—This term is used to refer to people who dedicate their lives to pursuing the fundamentals of their religion.

cult—A journalistic term for an unorthodox system of religious beliefs and ritual that scholars of religion refrain from using.

fight or flight—A theory developed by W.B. Cannon in 1929. When an individual is under stress, the heart rate increases, the lungs operate more efficiently, adrenalin and sugar are released into the bloodstream, and the muscles become infused with blood.

Frustration-Aggression Hypothesis—An hypothesis that every frustration leads to some form of aggression and every aggressive act results from some prior frustration. As defined by Ted Robert Gurr: "The necessary precondition for violent civil conflict is relative deprivation, defined as actors' perception of discrepancy between their value expectations and their environment's apparent value capabilities. This deprivation may be individual or collective."

Groupthink—As originally defined by I.L. Janis, "a mode of thinking that people engage in when the members' strivings for unanimity override the motivation to realistically appraise alternative courses of action."

guerrilla—A revolutionary who engages in insurgency as opposed to terrorism, although guerrillas also use terrorist methods. Usually operating relatively openly in less-developed countries, guerrillas attempt to hold territory and generally attack the state's infrastructure, whereas terrorists usually operate in urban areas and attack more symbolic targets. Guerrillas usually coerce or abduct civilians to join them, whereas terrorists are highly selective in whom they recruit.

international terrorism—Although the Central Intelligence Agency distinguishes between international and transnational terrorism (international being terrorism carried out by individuals or groups controlled by a sovereign state and transnational terrorism being terrorism carried out by autonomous nonstate actors), the distinction is not used in this paper. This is because the distinction is unnecessarily confusing, not self-evident, and lacking in usefulness, whereas the term "state-sponsored terrorism" is self-evident and unambiguous. Moreover, one would have to be extremely well informed to know which terrorist acts are state-sponsored. Thus, the term international terrorism is used here to refer to any act of terrorism affecting the national interests of more than one country. The WTC bombing, for example, was an act of international terrorism because its perpetrators included foreign nationals.

Intifada—The uprising by Palestinians begun in October 1987 against Israeli military occupation of the West Bank and the Gaza Strip. Also the name of the involved Liberation Army of Palestine, a loosely organized group of adult and teenage Palestinians active in 1987-93 in attacks on armed Israeli troops. Their campaign for self-determination included stone-throwing and petrol bombing. Some 1,300 Palestinians and 80 Israelis were killed in the uprising up to the end of 1991.

jihad—An Arabic verbal noun derived from *jahada* ("to struggle"). Although "holy war" is not a literal translation, it summarizes the essential idea of jihad. In the course of the revival of Islamic fundamentalism (*q.v.*), the doctrine of jihad has been invoked to justify resistance, including terrorist actions, to combat "un-Islamic" regimes, or perceived external enemies of Islam, such as Israel and the United States.

June Second Movement—An anarchistic leftist group formed in West Berlin in

1971 that sought to resist the liberal democratic establishment in West Berlin through bombings, bank robberies, kidnappings, and murders. The group was named after the anniversary of Benno Ohnejorg's death, who was killed in a demonstration against the visiting Shah of Iran in Berlin on June 2,1967. The group was closely associated with the Red Army Faction (*q.v.*) and after the majority of its members had been arrested by the end of the 1970s, the remainder joined the RAF.

mindset—A noun defined by *American Heritage Dictionary* as: "1. A fixed mental attitude or disposition that predetermines a person's response to and interpretation of situations; 2. an inclination or a habit." *Merriam Webster's Collegiate Dictionary* (10th ed.) defines it as 1. A mental attitude or inclination; 2. a fixed state of mind. The term dates from 1926 but apparently is not included in dictionaries of psychology.

mujahideen—A general designation for Muslim fighters engaged in jihad, as well as the name of various Muslim political and paramilitary groups, such as the Afghan (*q.v.*) Mujahideen.

personality—The distinctive and characteristic patterns of thought, emotion, and behavior that define an individual's personal style of interacting with the physical and social environment.

psychopath—A mentally ill or unstable person, especially one having a psychopathic personality (*q.v.*), according to *Webster's.*

psychopathy—A mental disorder, especially an extreme mental disorder marked usually by egocentric and antisocial activity, according to *Webster's.*

psychopathology—The study of psychological and behavioral dysfunction occurring in mental disorder or in social disorganization, according to *Webster's.*

psychotic—Of, relating to, or affected with psychosis, which is a fundamental mental derangement (as schizophrenia) characterized by defective or lost contact with reality, according to *Webster's.*

Red Army Faction—The RAF, formerly known as the Baader-Meinhof Gang, was a group of German anarchistic leftist terrorists active from May 11, 1972, to the early 1990s. (*q.v.*, Baader-Meinhof Gang)

sociopath—Basically synonymous with psychopath (*q.v.*). Sociopathic symptoms in the adult sociopath include an inability to tolerate delay or frustration, a lack of guilt feelings, a relative lack of anxiety, a lack of compassion for others, a hypersensitivity to personal ills, and a lack of responsibility. Many authors prefer the term *sociopath* because this type of person had defective socialization and a deficient childhood.

sociopathic—Of, relating to, or characterized by asocial or antisocial behavior or a psychopathic (*q.v.*) personality, according to *Webster's.*

terrorism—the calculated use of unexpected, shocking, and unlawful violence against noncombatants (including, in addition to civilians, off-duty military and security personnel in peaceful situations) and other symbolic targets perpetrated by a clandestine member(s) of a subnational group or a clandestine agent for the psychological purpose of publicizing a political or religious cause and/or intimidating or coercing a government(s) or civilian population into accepting demands on behalf of the cause.

BIBLIOGRAPHY

Alape, Arturo. *Las vidas de Pedro Antonio Marín/Manuel Marulanda Vélez: Tirofijo*. Bogotá: Planeta, 1989.

Alexander, Yonah, and John M. Gleason, eds. *Behavioral and Quantitative Perspectives on Terrorism*. New York: Pergamon, 1981.

Alexander, Yonah, and Lawrence Zelic Freedman, eds. *Perspectives on Terrorism*. Wilmington, Delaware: Scholarly Resources, 1983.

Amos II, John W. "Terrorism in the Middle East: The Diffusion of Violence." Pages 149–62 in David Partington, ed., *Middle East Annual*, 1984. London: G.K. Hall, 1985.

Anonymous. "The Psychology of Terrorism." In *Security Digest*, 18. Washington: Wilson Center Reports, 1987.

Anonymous. "Terrorism: Psyche or Psychos?," *TVI Journal*, 3, 1982, 3–11.

Aston, C.C. "Political Hostage—Taking in Western Europe." Pages 57–83 in W. Gutteridge, ed., *Contemporary Terrorism*. New York: Facts on File, 1986.

Bandura, Albert. "Mechanisms of Moral Disengagement." Pages 161–91 in Walter Reich, ed., *Origins of Terrorism: Psychologies, Ideologies, Theologies, States of Mind*. Cambridge: Cambridge University Press, 1990.

Barkey, Henri J., and Graham E. Fuller. *Turkey's Kurdish Question*. Carnegie Commission on Preventing Deadly Conflict Series. Lanham, Maryland, and Oxford, England: Rowman and Littlefield, 1998.

Becker, Julian. *Hitler's Children: The Story of the Baader-Meinhof Terrorist Gang*. Philadelphia: J.B. Lippincott, 1977.

Behar, Richard. "The Secret Life of Mahmud the Red," *Time*, October 4, 1993, 55–61.

Bell, J. Bowyer. "Old Trends and Future Realities," *Washington Quarterly*, Spring 1985.

Bell, J. Bowyer. "Psychology of Leaders of Terrorist Groups," *International Journal of Group Tensions*, 12, 1982, 84–104.

Benedek, E.P. *The Psychiatric Aspects of Terrorism*. Washington: American Psychiatric Association, 1980.

Benson, Mike, Mariah Evans, and Rita Simon. "Women as Political Terrorists," *Research in Law, Deviance, and Social Control*, 4, 1982, 121–30.

Berkowitz, B.J., et al. *Superviolence: The Threat of Mass Destruction Weapons*. Santa Barbara, California: ADCON Corporation, 1972.

Billig, Otto. "The Lawyer Terrorist and His Comrades," *Political Psychology*, 6, 1985, 29–46.

Bodansky, Yossef. *Bin Laden: The Man Who Declared War on America*. Rocklin, Georgia: Prima, 1999.

Bollinger, L. "Terrorist Conduct as a Result of a Psychological Process." In World Congress of Psychiatry, *Psychiatry: The State of the Art*, 6. New York: Plenum, 1985.

Brackett, D.W. *Holy Terror: Armageddon in Tokyo*. New York: Weatherhill, 1996.

Bruinessen, Martin van. "Kurdish Society, Ethnicity, Nationalism and Refugee Problems. Pages 33–67 in Philip G. Kreyenbroek and Stefan Sperl, eds., *The Kurds: A Contemporary Overview*. Routledge/SOAS Politics and Culture in the Middle East Series. London and New York: Routledge, 1992.

Bulloch, John, and Harvey Morris. *No Friends but the Mountains: The Tragic History of the Kurds*. New York and Oxford: Oxford University Press, 1992.

Ciment, James. *The Kurds: State and Minority in Turkey, Iraq and Iran*. Conflict and Crisis in the Post-Cold War World Series. New York: Facts on File, 1996.

Clark, R. "Patterns in the Lives of ETA Members," *Terrorism*, 6, No. 3, 1983, 423–54.

Cohen, G. *Women of Violence: Memoirs of a Young Terrorist*. Stanford, California: Stanford University Press, 1966.

Combs, Cindy C. *Terrorism in the Twenty-First Century*. Upper Saddle River, New Jersey: Prentice Hall, 1997.

Cooper, H.H.A. "Psychopath as Terrorist," *Legal Medical Quarterly*, 2, 1978, 253–62.

Cooper, H.H.A. "What Is a Terrorist? A Psychological Perspective," *Legal Medical Quarterly*, 1, 1977, 16–32.

Corrado, Raymond R. "A Critique of the Mental Disorder Perspective of Political Terrorism," *International Journal of Law and Psychiatry*, 4, 1981, 293–309.

Cordes, Bonnie. *When Terrorists Do the Talking: Reflections on Terrorist Literature*. Santa Monica, California: Rand, August 1987.

Corsun, Andrew. "Group Profile: The Revolutionary Organization 17 November in Greece (1975–91)." Pages 93–126 in Dennis A. Pluchinsky and Yonah Alexander, eds., *European Terrorism: Today & Tomorrow*. Washington: Brassey's 1992.

Crayton, John W. "Terrorism and the Psychology of the Self." Pages 33–41 in Lawrence Zelic Freedman and Yonah Alexander, eds., *Perspectives on Terrorism*. Wilmington, Delaware: Scholarly Resources, 1983.

Crenshaw, Martha. "The Causes of Terrorism," *Comparative Politics*, 13, July 1981, 379–99.

Crenshaw, Martha. "Current Research on Terrorism: The Academic Perspective," *Studies in Conflict and Terrorism*, 15, 1992, 1–11.

Crenshaw, Martha. "An Organization Approach to the Analysis of Political Terrorism," *Orbis,* 29, 1985, 465–89.

Crenshaw, Martha. "The Psychology of Political Terrorism." Pages 379–413 in Margaret Hermann, ed., *Handbook of Political Psychology*. San Francisco: Jossey-Bass, 1985.

Crenshaw, Martha. "Questions to Be Answered, Research to Be Done, Knowledge to Be Applied." Pages 247–60 in Walter Reich, ed., *Origins of Terrorism: Psychologies, Ideologies, Theologies, States of Mind*. Cambridge: Cambridge University Press, 1990.

Crenshaw, Martha. "Theories of Terrorism: Instrumental and Organizational Approaches." Pages 13–31 in David Rapoport, ed., *Inside Terrorist Organizations*. New York: Columbia University Press, 1988.

Cubert, Harold M. *The PFLP's Changing Role in the Middle East*. London and Portland, Oregon: Frank Cass, 1997.

Daly, L.N. "Terrorism: What Can the Psychiatrist Do?," *Journal of Forensic Sciences*, 26, 1981, 116–22.

Davies, T.R. "Aggression, Violence, Revolution and War." Pages 234–60 in Jeanne N. Knutson, ed., *Handbook of Political Psychology*. San Francisco: Jossey-Bass, 1973.

Dedman, Bill. "Secret Service Is Seeking Pattern for School Killers," *New York Times*, June 21, 1999, A10.

Della Porta, Donatella. "Political Socialization in Left-Wing Underground Organizations: Biographies of Italian and German Militants." In Donatella Della Porta, ed., *Social Movements and Violence: Participation in Underground Organizations*, 4. Greenwich, Connecticut: JAI Press, 1992.

Dobson, Christopher. *Black September: Its Short, Violent History*. London: Robert Hale, 1975.

Dowling, Joseph A. "A Prolegomena to a Psychohistorical Study of Terrorism." In Marius Livingston, ed., *International Terrorism in the Contemporary World*. Westwood, Connecticut: Greenwood, 1978.

Doyle, Leonard. "The Cold Killers of 17 November Who Always Go Free," *The Observer* [London], September 28, 1997.

Eckstein, Harry. "On the Etiology of Internal Wars." In Ivo K. Feierabend, Rosalind L. Feierabend, and Ted Robert Gurr, eds., *Anger, Violence and Politics:*

Theories and Research. Englewood Cliffs, New Jersey: Prentice-Hall, 1972.

Elliot, John D., and Leslie K. Gibson, eds. *Contemporary Terrorism: Selected Readings*. Gaithersburg, Maryland: International Association of Chiefs of Police, 1978.

Elliott, Paul. *Brotherhoods of Fear: A History of Violent Organizations*. London: Blandford, 1998.

Entessar, Nader. *Kurdish Ethnonationalism*. Boulder, Colorado: Lynne Rienner, 1992.

Falk, Richard. "The Terrorist Mind-Set: The Moral Universe of Revolutionaries and Functionaries." In Richard Falk, ed., *Revolutionaries and Functionaries: The Dual Face of Terrorism*. New York: E.P. Dutton, 1988.

Farrell, William R. *Blood and Rage: The Story of the Japanese Red Army*. Lexington, Massachusetts: Lexington Books, 1990.

Ferracuti, Franco. "Ideology and Repentance: Terrorism in Italy." Pages 59–64 in Walter Reich, ed., *Origins of Terrorism: Psychologies, Ideologies, Theologies, States of Mind*. Cambridge, England: Cambridge University Press, 1990.

Ferracuti, Franco. "Psychiatric Aspects of Terrorism in Italy." In I.L. Barak-Glantz and U.R. Huff, eds., *The Mad, the Bad, and the Different*. Lexington, Massachusetts: Lexington, 1981.

Ferracuti, Franco. "A Psychiatric Comparative—Analysis of Left and Right Terrorism in Italy." In World Congress of Psychiatry, *Psychiatry: The State of the Art*, 6. New York: Plenum, 1985.

Ferracuti, Franco. "A Sociopsychiatric Interpretation of Terrorism," *The Annals of the American Academy of Political and Social Science*, 463, September 1982, 129–41.

Ferracuti, Franco, and F. Bruno. "Psychiatric Aspects of Terrorism in Italy." Pages 199–213 in I.L. Barak-Glantz and C.R. Huff, eds., *The Mad, the Bad and the Different: Essays in Honor of Simon Dinhz*. Lexington, Massachusetts: Lexington Books, 1981.

Fields, Rona M. "Child Terror Victims and Adult Terrorists," *Journal of Psychohistory*, 7, No. 1, Summer 1979, 71–76.

Flemming, Peter A., Michael Stohl, and Alex P. Schmid. "The Theoretical Utility of Typologies of Terrorism: Lessons and Opportunities." Pages 153–95 in Michael Stohl, ed., *The Politics of Terrorism*. 3d ed. New York: Marcel Dekker, 1988.

Freedman. Lawrence Zelic. "Terrorism: Problems of the Polistaraxic." Pages 3–18 in Yonah Alexander and L.Z. Freedman, eds., *Perspectives on Terrorism*. Wilmington, Delaware: Scholarly Resources, 1983.

Freedman, Lawrence Zelic, and Yonah Alexander, eds. *Perspectives on Terrorism*. Wilmington, Delaware: Scholarly Resources, 1983.

Fried, Risto. "The Psychology of the Terrorist."Pages 119–24 in Brian M. Jenkins, ed., *Terrorism and Beyond: An International Conference on Terrorism and Low-Level Conflict*. Santa Monica, California: Rand, 1982.

Friedlander, Robert A. "The Psychology of Terrorism: Contemporary Views." In Patrick J. Montana and George S. Roukis, eds., *Managing Terrorism: Strategies for the Corporate Executive*. Westport, Connecticut: Quorum, 1983.

Foote, Donna. "A Shadow Government: An Insider Describes the Workings of the IRA, Europe's Most Potent Guerrilla Organization," *Newsweek*, September 12, 1988, 37–38.

Galvin, Deborah M. "The Female Terrorist: A Socio-Psychological Perspective," *Behavioral Science and the Law*, 1, 1983, 19–32.

Georges-Abeyie, Daniel E. "Women as Terrorists." In Lawrence Zelic Freedman and Yonah Alexander, eds., *Perspectives on Terrorism*. Wilmington, Delaware: Scholarly Resources, 1983.

Goltz, Thomas. "Ankara Dispatch: Just How Authentic Was Abdullah Ocalan's Claim to Represent the Dispossessed of Turkey?," *The New Republic*, March 15, 1999, 14–16.

Greaves, Douglas. "The Definition and Motivation of Terrorism," *Australian Journal of Forensic Science*, 13, 1981, 160–66.

Gunaratna, Rohan. "LTTE Child Combatants," *Jane's Intelligence Review*, July 1998.

Gurr, Ted Robert. "Psychological Factors in Civil Violence," *World Politics*, 20, No. 32, January 1968, 245–78.

Gurr, Ted Robert. *Why Men Rebel*. Princeton, New Jersey: Princeton University Press, 1970.

Gutteridge, W., ed. *Contemporary Terrorism*. New York: Facts on File, 1986.

Guttman, D. "Killers and Consumers: The Terrorist and His Audience," *Social Research*, 46, 1979, 517–26.

Hacker, Frederick J. *Crusaders, Criminals, Crazies: Terror and Terrorism in Our Time*. New York: W.W. Norton, 1996.

Hacker, Frederick J. "Dialectical Interrelationships of Personal and Political Factors in Terrorism." Pages 19–32 in Lawrence Zelic Freedman and Yonah Alexander, eds., *Perspectives on Terrorism*. Wilmington, Delaware: Scholarly Resources, 1983.

Hamilton, L.C., and J.D. Hamilton. "Dynamics of Terrorism," *International Studies Quarterly*, 27, 1983, 39–54;

Harris, Jonathan. "The Mind of the Terrorist." In Jonathan Harris, ed., *The New Terrorism: Politics of Violence*. New York: Julian Messner, 1983.

Haynal, André, Miklos Molnar, and Gérard de Puymège. *Fanaticism: A Historical and Psychoanalytical Study*. New York: Schocken Books, 1983.

Heskin, Ken. "The Psychology of Terrorism in Ireland." Pages 88–105 in Yonah Alexander and Alan O'Day, eds., *Terrorism in Ireland*. New York: St. Martin's Press, 1984.

Heyman, E. "The Diffusion of Transnational Terrorism." Pages 190–244 in R. Shultz and S. Sloan, eds., *Responding to the Terrorist Threat: Security and Crisis Management*. New York: Pergamon, 1980.

Heyman, E., and E. Mickolus. "Imitation by Terrorists: Quantitative Approaches to the Study of Diffusion Patterns in Transnational Terrorism." Pages 175–228 in Yonah Alexander and J.M. Gleason, eds., *Behavioral and Quantitative Perspectives on Terrorism*. New York: Pergamon, 1980.

Heyman, E., and E. Mickolus. "Observations on Why Violence Spreads," *International Studies Quarterly*, 24, 1980, 299–305.

Hoffman-Ladd, V.J. "Muslim Fundamentalism: Psychological Profiles." Paper presented at the Fundamentalist Project, M.E. Marty and S.R. Appleby, eds., 1993.

Holmes, Ronald M., and Stephen T. Holmes. *Profiling Violent Crimes: An Investigative Tool*. Thousand Oaks, California: SAGE, 1996.

Holloway, Harry C., and Anne E. Norwood. "Forensic Psychiatric Aspects of Terrorism." Pages 409–451 in R. Gregory Lande, and David T. Armitage, eds., *Principles and Practice of Military Forensic Psychiatry*. Springfield, Illinois: Charles C. Thomas, 1997.

Hubbard, David G. "The Psychodynamics of Terrorism." Pages 45–53 in Yonah Alexander, T. Adeniran, and R.A. Kilmarx, eds., *International Violence*. New York: Praeger, 1983.

Hubbard, David G. *The Skyjacker: His Flights of Fantasy*. New York: Macmillan, 1971.

Jaber, Hela. *Hezbollah: Born with a Vengeance*. New York: Columbia University Press, 1977.

Janis, I.L. "Group Identification under Conditions of External Danger." Pages 80–90 in D. Cartwright and A. Zander, eds., *Group Dynamics*. New York: Free Press, 1968.

Janis, I.L. *Victims of Groupthink*. Boston: Houghton-Mifflin, 1972.

Jenkins, Brian M. *High Technology Terrorism and Surrogate Warfare: The Impact of New Technology on Low-Level Violence*. Santa Monica, California: Rand, 1975.

Jenkins, Brian M. "International Terrorism: A New Mode of Conflict." In David Carlton and Carolo Schaerf, eds., *International Terrorism and World Security*. London: Croom Helm, 1975.

Jenkins, Brian M. "Terrorists at the Threshold." In E. Nobles Lowe and Harry D. Shargel, eds., *Legal and Other Aspects of Terrorism*. New York: 1979.

Jenkins, Brian M., ed. *Terrorism and Beyond: An International Conference on Terrorism and Low-Level Conflict*. Santa Monica, California: Rand, 1982.

Jerome, Richard. "Japan's Mad Messiah: Jailed in Tokyo's Subway Gassing, A Guru is Alone with His Grand Delusions," *People Weekly*, 43, No. 23, June 12, 1995, 48 .

Johnson, Chalmers. "Perspectives on Terrorism." Reprinted in Walter Laqueur, ed., *The Terrorism Reader*. New York: New American Library, 1978.

Joshi, Monoj. "On the Razor's Edge: The Liberation Tigers of Tamil Eelam," *Studies in Conflict and Terrorism*, 19, No. 1, 1996, 19–42.

Juergensmeyer, Mark. *Terror in the Mind of God: The Global Rise of Religious Violence*. Berkeley: University of California Press, 2000.

Kallen, K. *Terrorists—What Are They Like? How Some Terrorists Describe Their World and Actions*. Santa Monica, California: Rand, 1979.

Kaplan, Abraham. "The Psychodynamics of Terrorism," *Terrorism*, 1, 1978, 237–57.

Kaplan, David, and Andrew Marshall. *The Cult at the End of the World: The Terrifying Story of the Aum Doomsday Cult, from the Subways of Tokyo to the Nuclear Arsenals of Russia*. New York: Crown, 1996.

Karan, Vijay. *War by Stealth: Terrorism in India*. New Delhi: Viking (Penguin Books India), 1997.

Kellen, Konrad. "Ideology and Rebellion: Terrorism in West Germany." Pages 43–58 in Walter Reich, ed., *Origins of Terrorism: Psychologies, Ideologies, Theologies, States of Mind*. Washington: Woodrow Wilson Center, 1998.

Kellen, Konrad. "Terrorists—What Are They Like? How Some Terrorists Describe Their World and Actions." Pages 125–73 in Brian M. Jenkins, ed., *Terrorism and Beyond: An International Conference on Terrorism and Low-Level Conflict*. Santa Monica, California: Rand, 1980.

Kent, I., and W. Nicholls. "The Psychodynamics of Terrorism," *Mental Health and Society*, 4, 1977, 1–8.

Khaled, Leila. *My People Shall Live: The Autobiography of a Revolutionary*. George Hajjar, ed.. London: Hodder and Stoughton, 1973.

Kifner, John. "Alms and Arms: Tactics in a Holy War," *New York Times*, March 15, 1996, A1, A8.

Kim, Hyun Hee. *The Tears of My Soul*. New York: Morrow, 1994.

Knutson, Jeanne N. "Social and Psychodynamic Pressures Toward a Negative Identity. Pages 105–52 in Yonah Alexander and John M. Gleason, eds., *Behavioral and Quantitative Perspectives on Terrorism*. New York: Pergamon, 1981.

Knutson, Jeanne N. "The Terrorists' Dilemmas: Some Implicit Rules of the Game," *Terrorism*, 4, 1980, 195–222.

Knutson, Jeanne N. "Toward a United States Policy on Terrorism," *Political Psychology*, 5, No. 2, June 1984, 287–94.

Knutson, Jeanne N., ed. *Handbook of Political Psychology*. San Francisco: Jossey-Bass, 1973.

Kolinsky, Eva. "Terrorism in West Germany. Pages 75–76 in Juliet Lodge, ed., *The Threat of Terrorism*. Boulder, Colorado: Westview Press, 1988.

Kovaleski, Serge F. "Rebel Movement on the Rise: Leftist Guerrillas Use Military Force, Not Ideology, to Hold Power," *Washington Post*, February 5, 1999, A27–28.

Kramer, Martin. "The Structure of Shi'ite Terrorism." Pages 43–52 in Anat Kurz, ed., *Contemporary Trends in World Terrorism*. New York: Praeger, 1987.

Kreyenbroek, Philip G., and Stefan Sperl, eds. *The Kurds: A Contemporary Overview*. Routledge/SOAS Politics and Culture in the Middle East Series. London and New York: Routledge, 1992.

Kross, Peter. *Spies, Traitors, and Moles: An Espionage and Intelligence Quiz Book*. Lilburn, Georgia: IllumiNet Press, 1998.

Kurz, Anat, ed. *Contemporary Trends in World Terrorism*. New York: Praeger, 1987.

Kurz, Anat, with Nahman Tal. *Hamas: Radical Islam in a National Struggle*. Tel Aviv: Jaffee Center for Strategic Studies, Tel Aviv University, 1997.

Kushner, Harvey W. "Suicide Bombers: Business as Usual," *Studies in Conflict and Terrorism*, 19, No. 4, 1996, 329–37.

Kushner, Harvey W. *Terrorism in America: A Structural Approach to Understanding the Terrorist Threat*. Springfield, Illinois: Charles C. Thomas, 1998.

Labeviere, Richard. *Les dollars de la terreur: Les États-Unis et les Islamistes*. Paris: Grasset, 1999.

Laqueur, Walter. *The Age of Terrorism*. Boston: Little, Brown, 1987.

Laqueur, Walter. *Terrorism*. Boston: Little, Brown, 1977.

Lewis, Bernard. "License to Kill: Usama bin Ladin's Declaration of Jihad," *Foreign Affairs*, 77, No. 6, November/December 1998, 14–19.

Lodge, Juliet, ed. *The Threat of Terrorism*. Boulder, Colorado: Westview Press, 1988.

MacDonald, Eileen. *Shoot the Women First*. New York: Random House, 1992.

Margolin, Joseph. "Psychological Perspectives in Terrorism." Pages 273–74 in Yonah Alexander and Seymour Maxwell Finger, eds., *Terrorism: Interdisciplinary Perspectives*. New York: John Jay, 1977.

Mathiu, Mutuma. "The Kurds Against the World: Why Abdullah Ocalan Is a Hero to Kurds," *World Press Review*, 46, No. 5, May 1999.

McCauley, C.R., and M.E. Segal. "Social Psychology of Terrorist Groups." In C. Hendrick, ed., *Group Processes and Intergroup Relations*, Vol. 9 of *Annual Review of Social and Personality Psychology*. Beverly Hills: Sage, 1987.

McKnight, Gerald. *The Mind of the Terrorist*. London: Michael Joseph, 1974.

Melman, Yossi. *The Master Terrorist: The True Story Behind Abu Nidal*. New York: Adama, 1986.

Merari, Ariel. "Problems Related to the Symptomatic Treatment of Terrorism," *Terrorism*, 3, 1980, 279–83.

Merari, Ariel, and N. Friedland. "Social Psychological Aspects of Political Terrorism." in S. Oskamp, ed., *Applied Social Psychology Annual*. Beverly Hills, California: Sage, 1985.

Mickolus, Edward F., with Susan L. Simmons. *Terrorism, 1992–1995: A Chronology of Events and A Selectively Annotated Bibliography*. Westport, Connecticut: Greenwood Press, 1997.

Middendorf, Wolf. "The Personality of the Terrorist." In M. Kravitz, ed., *International Summaries: A Collection of Selected Translations in Law Enforcement and Criminal Justice*, 3. Rockville, Maryland: National Criminal Justice Reference Service, 1979.

Midlarsky, M.I., Martha Crenshaw, and F. Yoshida. "Why Violence Spreads: The Contagion of International Terrorism," *International Studies Quarterly*, 24, 1980, 262–98.

Milbank, D.L. *International and Transnational Terrorism: Diagnosis and Prognosis*. Washington: Central Intelligence Agency, 1976.

Mishal, Shaul, and Avraham Sela. *Hamas: A Behavioral Profile*. Tel Aviv: The Tami Steinmetz Center for Peace Research, Tel Aviv University, 1997.

Monroe, Kristen Renwick, and Lina Haddad Kreidie. "The Perspective of Islamic Fundamentalists and the Limits of Rational Choice Theory," *Political Psychology*, 18, No. 1, 1997, 19–43.

Mullen, R.K. "Mass Destruction and Terrorism," *Journal of International Affairs*, 32, No. 1, 1978, 62–89.

Mylroie, Laurie. "The World Trade Center Bomb: Who Is Ramzi Yousef? And Why It Matters," *U.S. News and World Report*, 118, No. 7, February 20, 1995, 50–54.

Neuburger, Luisella de Cataldo, and Tiziana Valentini. *Women and Terrorism*. New York: St. Martin's Press, 1996.

Neuhauser, P. "The Mind of a German Terrorist: Interview with M.C. Baumann," *Encounter*, September 1978, 81–88.

Oberst, Robert C. "Sri Lanka's Tamil Tigers," *Conflict*, 8, No. 2/3, 1988, 185–202.

O'Ballance, Edgar. *The Kurdish Struggle, 1920–94*. London: Macmillan Press, 1996.

O'Ballance, Edgar. *The Language of Violence: The Blood Politics of Terrorism*. San Rafael, California: Presidio Press, 1979.

Oots, Kent Layne, and Thomas C. Wiegele. "Terrorist and Victim: Psychiatric and Physiological Approaches from a Social Science Perspective," *Terrorism: An International Journal*, 8, No. 1, 1985, 1–32.

Paine, L. *The Terrorists*. London: Robert Hale, 1975.

Pearlstein, Richard M. *The Mind of the Political Terrorist*. Wilmington, Delaware: Scholarly Resources, 1991.

Post, Jerrold. "Current Understanding of Terrorist Motivation and Psychology: Implications for a Differentiated Antiterrorist Policy," *Terrorism*, 13, No. 1, 1990, 65–71.

Post, Jerrold M. "'Hostilité, Conformité, Fraternité': The Group Dynamics of Terrorist Behavior," *International Journal of Group Psychotherapy*, 36, No. 2, 1986, 211–24.

Post, Jerrold M. "Individual and Group Dynamics of Terrorist Behavior." In World Congress of Psychiatry, *Psychiatry: The State of the Art*, 6. New York: Plenum, 1985.

Post, Jerrold M. "Notes on a Psychodynamic Theory of Terrorist Behavior," *Terrorism: An International Journal*, 7, No. 3, 1984, 242–56.

Post, Jerrold M. "Rewarding Fire with Fire? Effects of Retaliation on Terrorist Group Dynamics." Pages 103–115 in Anat Kurz, ed., *Contemporary Trends in World Terrorism*. New York: Praeger, 1987.

Post, Jerrold M. "Terrorist Psycho-Logic: Terrorist Behavior as a Product of Psychological Forces." Pages 25–40 in Walter Reich, ed., *Origins of Terrorism: Psychologies, Ideologies, Theologies, States of Mind*. Cambridge, England: Cambridge University Press, 1990.

Prunckun, Jr., Henry W. *Shadow of Death: An Analytic Bibliography on Political Violence, Terrorism, and Low-Intensity Conflict.* Lanham, Maryland, and London: Scarecrow Press, 1995.

Rapoport, David C. *Assassination and Terrorism.* Toronto: CBC Merchandising, 1971.

Rapoport, David C. "Fear and Trembling: Terrorism in Three Religious Traditions," *American Political Science Review*, 78, No. 3, 1984, 655–77.

Rapoport, David C. "Sacred Terror: A Contemporary Example from Islam." Pages 103–30 in Walter Reich, ed., *Origins of Terrorism: Psychologies, Ideologies, Theologies, States of Mind.* Cambridge, England: Cambridge University Press, 1990.

Rasch, W. "Psychological Dimensions of Political Terrorism in the Federal Republic of Germany," *International Journal of Law and Psychiatry*, 2, 1979, 79–85.

Reeve, Simon. *The New Jackals: Ramzi Yousef, Osama bin Laden and the Future of Terrorism.* Boston: Simon Reeve/Northeastern University Press, 1999.

Reich, Walter, ed. *Origins of Terrorism: Psychologies, Ideologies, Theologies, States of Mind.* Cambridge, England: Cambridge University Press, 1990.

Robins, Robert S., and Jerrold M. Post. *Political Paranoia: The Psychopolitics of Hatred.* New Haven, Connecticut: Yale University Press, 1997.

Rogers, John D., Jonathan Spencer, and Jayadeva Uyangoda. "Sri Lanka: Political Violence and Ethnic Conflict," *American Psychologist*, 58, No. 7, July 1998, 771–77.

Ronfeldt, David, and William Sater. "The Mindsets of High-Technology Terrorists: Future Implication from an Historical Analog." Pages 15–38 in Yonah Alexander and Charles K. Ebinger, eds., *Political Terrorism and Energy: The Threat and the Response.* New York: Praeger, 1982.

Rosenberg, Tina. *Children of Cain: Violence and the Violent in Latin America.* New York: Morrow, 1991.

Russell, Charles A., and Bowman H. Miller. "Profile of a Terrorist." Pages 81–95 in John D. Elliott and Leslie K. Gibson, eds., *Contemporary Terrorism: Selected Readings.* Gaithersburg, Maryland: International Association of Chiefs of Police, 1978.

Russell, Charles A., and Bowman H. Miller. "Profile of a Terrorist," *Terrorism: An International Journal*, 1, No. 1, 1977, 17–34.

Salewski, Wolfgang D. "The Latest Theory Recognized by Sociological Research in Terrorism and Violence," *Terrorism*, 3, 1980, 297–301.

Samaranayake, Gamini. "Political Violence in Sri Lanka: A Diagnostic Approach," *Terrorism and Political Violence*, 9, No. 2, Summer 1997, 99–119.

Schalk, P. "Resistance and Martyrdom in the Process of State Formation of Tamililam." Pages 61–83 in J. Pettigrew, ed., *Martyrdom and Political Resistance: Essays From Asia and Europe*. Amsterdam: VU University Press, 1997.

Schalk, P. "Women Fighters of the Liberation Tigers in Tamil Ilam: The Martial Feminism of Atel Palancinkam," *South Asia Research*, 14, 1994, 163–83.

Schmid, Alex P., and Albert J. Jongman. *Political Terrorism: A New Guide to Actors, Authors, Concepts, Data Bases, Theories, and Literature*. New Brunswick, New Jersey: Transaction Books, 1988.

Schweitzer, Yoram. "Terrorism: A Weapon in the Shi'ite Arsenal." Pages 66–74 in Anat Kurz, ed., *Contemporary Trends in World Terrorism*. New York: Praeger, 1987.

Shaw, Eric D. "Political Terrorists: Dangers of Diagnosis and an Alternative to the Psychopathology Model," *International Journal of Law and Psychiatry*, 8, 1986, 359–68.

Shifter, Michael. "Colombia on the Brink: There Goes the Neighborhood," *Foreign Affairs*, 78, No. 4, July/August 1999, 14–20.

Silj, Alessandro. *Never Again Without a Rifle: The Origins of Italian Terrorism*. New York: Karz, 1979.

Spaeth, Anthony. "Engineer of Doom: Cult Leader Shoko Asahara Didn't Just Forecast Armageddon, He Planned It (Japan's Aum Shinrikyo Guru Planned to Precipitate World War)," *Time*, 145, No. 24, June 12, 1995, 57.

Sprinzak, Ehud. "The Psychopolitical Formation of Extreme Left Terrorism in a Democracy: The Case of the Weathermen." Pages 65–85 in Walter Reich, ed., *Origins of Terrorism: Psychologies, Ideologies, Theologies, States of Mind*. Cambridge, England: Cambridge University Press, 1990.

Steinhoff, Patricia G. "Portrait of a Terrorist: An Interview with Kozo Okamoto," *Asian Survey*, 16, No. 9, September 1976, 830–45.

Stern, Jessica. *The Ultimate Terrorists*. Cambridge, Massachusetts: Harvard University Press, 1999.

Stohl, Michael, ed. *The Politics of Terrorism*. 3d ed. New York: Marcel Dekker, 1988.

Strentz, Thomas. "The Terrorist Organizational Profile: A Psychological Role Model." Pages 86–104 in Yonah Alexander and John M. Gleason, eds., *Behavioral and Quantitative Perspectives on Terrorism*. New York: Pergamon, 1981.

Strentz, Thomas. "A Terrorist Psychosocial Profile: Past and Present," *Law Enforcement Bulletin*, 57, No. 4, 1988, 11–18.

Sullwold, Lilo. "Biographical Features of Terrorists." In World Congress of Psychiatry, *Psychiatry: The State of the Art*, 6. New York: Plenum, 1985.

Taheri, Amir. *Holy Terror: Inside the World of Islamic Terrorism*. Bethesda, Maryland: Adler and Adler, 1987.

Tanter, Raymond. *Rogue Regimes: Terrorism and Proliferation*. New York: St. Martin's Griffin, 1999.

Taylor, Maxwell. *The Terrorist*. London: Brassey's, 1988.

Taylor, Maxwell, and Ethel Quayle. *Terrorist Lives*. London and Washington: Brassey's, 1994.

Taylor, Maxwell, and Helen Ryan. "Fanaticism, Political Suicide and Terrorism," *Terrorism*, 11, No. 2, 1988, 91–111.

Thiranagama, Rajani, Rajan Hoole, Daya Somasundaram, and K. Sritharan. *The Broken Palmyra: The Tamil Crisis in Sri Lanka: An Inside Account*. Claremont, California: Sri Lankan Studies Institute, 1990.

"TVI Profile Report: Fatah Revolutionary Council (FRC)," *TVI Profile*, 8, No. 3, 1989, 5–8.

"TVI Profile Report: Hizbollah (Party of God)," *TVI Profile*, 9, No. 3, 1990, 1–6.

"TVI Profile Report: Provisional Irish Republican Army (PIRA)," *TVI Profile*, 8, No. 2, 1988, 13–15.

United States. Department of State. *Patterns of Global Terrorism*, 1998. Washington, D.C.: 1999.

Wagenlehner, Gunther. "Motivation for Political Terrorism in West Germany." Pages 195–203 in Marius H. Livingston, ed., *International Terrorism in the Contemporary World*. Westport, Connecticut: Greenwood Press, 1978.

Warren, Ward W., ed. "1996 AFIO Convention on Changing Trends in Terrorism," *Periscope: Newsletter of the Association of Former Intelligence Officers*, 22, No. 1, 1997.

Wasmund, Klaus. "The Political Socialization of West German Terrorists." In Peter H. Merkl, ed., *Political Violence and Terror: Motifs and Motivations*. Berkeley: University of California Press, 1986.

Watanabe, Manabu. "Religion and Violence in Japan Today: A Chronological and Doctrinal Analysis of Aum Shinrikyo," *Terrorism and Political Violence* [London], 10, No. 4, Winter 1998, 80–100.

Wege, Carl Anthony. "The Abu Nidal Organization," *Terrorism*, 14, January–March 1991, 59–66.

Weinberg, Leonard, and William Lee Eubank. "Italian Women Terrorists," *Terrorism: An International Journal*, 9, No. 3, 1987, 241–62.

Wickham-Crowley, Timothy P. *Guerrillas and Revolution in Latin America: A Comparative Study of Insurgents and Regimes since 1956*. Princeton, New Jersey: Princeton University Press, 1992.

Wijesekera, Daya. "The Cult of Suicide and the Liberation Tigers of Tamil Eelam," *Low Intensity Conflict & Law Enforcement*, 5, No. 1, Summer 1996, 18–28.

Wijesekera, Daya. "The Liberation Tigers of Tamil Eelam (LTTE): The Asian Mafia," *Low Intensity Conflict & Law Enforcement*, 2, No. 2, Autumn 1993, 308–17.

Wilkinson, Paul. "Hamas—An Assessment," *Jane's Intelligence Review*, 5, No. 7, July 1993, 31–32.

Wilkinson, Paul. *Political Terrorism*. London: Macmillan, 1974.

Wilkinson, Paul. "Terrorism: International Dimensions." Pages 29–56 in *Contemporary Terrorism*. New York: Facts on File, 1986.

Wolman, Benjamin B. "Psychology of Followers of Terrorist Groups," *International Journal of Group Tensions*, 12, 1982, 105–21.

Wright, Robin. *Sacred Rage: The Wrath of Militant Islam*. New York: Linden Press/Simon and Schuster, 1985.

Zawodny, J.K. "Internal Organizational Problems and the Sources of Tension of Terrorist Movements as Catalysts of Violence," *Terrorism*, 1, No. 3/4, 1978, 277–85.

Zisser, Eyal. "Hizballah in Lebanon—At the Crossroads," *Terrorism and Political Violence*, 8, No. 2, Summer 1996, 90–110.

CPSIA information can be obtained at www.ICGtesting.com
Printed in the USA
LVOW090816311012

305182LV00001B/43/A

9 781410 212771

Theory: CST is based in Western anatomy and physiology, and osteopathic science. The craniosacral system (i.e., cranium, spine, and sacrum) is connected by a fascial membrane called the dura mater that houses the brain and central nervous system. Cerebralspinal fluid is pumped throughout the system, creating a pulse or craniosacral rhythm (CSR). CST techniques aim to balance the CSR so that cerebralspinal fluid flows freely through the system. Once this is achieved, the body's own healing mechanism can function properly.

Websites: The Upledger Institute (www.upledger.com)
Craniosacral Therapy Association of North America
    (www.craniosacraltherapy.org)

6. Esalen Massage

Origin: Esalen massage was developed at the Esalen Institute in Big Sur, California, in the 1970s. Its development grew out of the Human Potential Movement and counterculture of the 1960s. Esalen massage was popularized in the classic *The Massage Book* by George Downing, published in 1972.

Technique: Esalen massage is a form of Western massage loosely based in Swedish massage. It emphasizes the sensual qualities of massage, and is associated with scented oils, incense, and New Age music. It initially was performed without draping, but accepted draping standards are now observed in most settings.

Theory: Esalen massage is applied to help the recipient get in touch with his or her senses and inner self, and is considered a meditative and personal growth experience. General health benefits of Swedish massage apply to Esalen massage.

Reference: *The Massage Book* by George Downing (New York: Random House Trade Paperbacks, 1998) (1st edition, 1972).

Website: Esalen Institute (www.esalen.org)

7. Feldenkrais Method®

Origin: The Feldenkrais Method was developed by Moshe Feldenkrais (1904–1984), who was an engineer, physicist, judo master, and mathematician. In efforts to heal himself of a knee injury, Feldenkrais developed a system of movement reeducation. The Feldenkrais Method came to light during the human potential movement of the 1970s–1980s.

Technique: Feldenkrais Method is a form of contemporary bodywork consisting of Functional Integration (i.e., hands-on table work in which the practitioner uses her hands to communicate new sensory movement patterns to the recipient through passive movements). In Awareness Through Movement, a teacher leads a group through structured movement experiences performed on the floor.

Theory: Feldenkrais Method is based in Western anatomy and physiology. Integrated movement patterns are established by reeducating the sensory-motor nervous system through repeated movements.

Websites: Feldenkrais Guild® of North America (www.feldenkrais.com)
International Feldenkrais Federation (www.feldenkrais-method.org)

8. Infant Massage

Origin: Massage has been given to infants from time immemorial by their mothers, grandmothers, and other caregivers. Instances of infant massage are found among native tribes in Africa, South Sea Islands, and North America, in ancient and modern India, and folk cultures of Europe. Recent interest in infant massage was revived by Vimala Schneider in the 1980s, and by the research of Dr. Tiffany Fields at the University of Miami in the 1990s.

Technique: Infant massage is a specialty within Western massage and consists of simple techniques like stroking, kneading, twisting, and pressing performed with gentle pressure. Some passive joint movements are incorporated. Eye contact and communication with the infant are emphasized.

Theory: Infant massage is based in Western anatomy, physiology, and theories of child development. It aims to help the infant relax, improve circulation and other body functions, improve immune function, and promote neurological development. Research confirms the necessity of touch and movement for healthy human development, and the benefits of massage for premature infants.

Reference: *Infant Massage: A Handbook for Loving Parents* by Vimala Schneider McClure, revised edition (New York: Bantam Doubleday Dell, 2000).

Websites: International Institute of Infant Massage
    (www.infantmassageinstitute.com)
Loving Touch Foundation (www.lovingtouch.com)
Touch Research Institute (www.miami.edu/touch-research)

9. Lomi-Lomi

Origin: Lomi-lomi is a traditional massage of the natives of the Hawaiian Islands practiced for centuries. Different styles of lomi-lomi were developed within families. Typically a tutu (i.e., grandmother), or other respected family member was the keeper of the tradition. Its modern form was popularized by Aunty Margaret Machado of Kona, Hawaii in the 1970s–1980s.

Technique: Lomi-lomi is a form of traditional native massage consisting of pressing and squeezing techniques performed with the fingers, palm and elbow. Kukui nut, macadamia, or coconut oil may be used. The recipient lies on a mat, or in modern times a massage table, to receive lomi-lomi. Associated methods include baths, bone adjusting techniques, and prayer.

Theory: Lomi-lomi is based in traditional Hawaiian culture, and emphasizes letting go of stress, offering unconditional love, and opening the heart to harmony, acceptance, and healing.

Reference: *Hawaiian Lomi-Lomi: Big Island Massage* by Nancy S. Kahalewai (Hilo, HI: Island Massage Publishing, 2000).

Website: Aunty Margaret Homepage
    (www.hawaiian.net/~kea/aunty. html)

10. Lymphatic Massage

Origin: Manual techniques applied to enhance lymphatic system function and treat lymphedema were developed as early as the 1880s. Emil and Astid Vodder developed their Manual Lymph Drainage (MLD), or Vodder Method, in the 1930s in France. In the 1970s, Hungarians Michael and Ethel Foldi combined Vodder's MLD with other modalities to create a treatment for lymphedema called Complete Decongestive Therapy (CDT).

Technique: Lymphatic massage is a specialized form of Western massage consisting of gentle techniques applied to the superficial skin layers to stretch the tissue and open the superficial lymphatic vessels so that lymph fluid can enter the vessels more easily. Classic Vodder techniques include stationary circles, scoop, pump, rotary, and light effleurage applied rhythmically and in specific directions.

Theory: Lymphatic massage is based on Western anatomy and physiology, and knowledge of the lymphatic system. Techniques are applied in a way to enhance the movement of lymph fluid into superficial vessels and through the system. Lymphatic massage improves immune function, reduces areas of edema, and aids injury healing.

Websites: Academy of Lymphatic Studies (www.acols.com)
Dr. Vodder School North America (www.vodderschool.com)

11. Medical Massage

Origin: Massage has been used to treat ailments from time immemorial all over the globe. Historically in Western medicine, it has been called medical rubbing, frictions, massage, massotherapeutics, and physiotherapy. Medical massage is emerging in the 21st century as a specialty within the broader field of therapeutic massage and bodywork. It is sometimes called *clinical massage.*

Technique: Medical massage is a specialty of Western massage in which soft tissue manipulation and related techniques are applied in the treatment of pathological conditions. A subspecialty is the treatment of musculoskeletal dysfunction.

Theory: Medical massage is based in Western anatomy, physiology, kinesiology, and pathology. Traditional and contemporary massage techniques are used as appropriate in treatment plans.

References: *Basic Clinical Massage Therapy: Integrating Anatomy and Treatment* by James H. Clay and David M. Pounds (Philadelphia: Lippincott Williams & Wilkins, 2003).

Clinical Massage Therapy: Understanding, Assessing and Treating over 70 Conditions by Fiona Rattray and Linda Ludwig (Toronto: Talus Incorporated, 2000).
Massage for Orthopedic Conditions by Thomas Hendrickson (Philadelphia: Lippincott Williams & Wilkins, 2003).
Medical Massage by Ross Turchaninov and Connie Cox (Scottsdale, AZ: Stress Less Publishing, 1998).

12. Myofascial Massage

Origin: Manual techniques that target the myofascial tissues were developed in the 1950s by Ida Rolf (1896–1979) in her system of Rolfing®, and by osteopath Robert Ward as myofascial release technique in the 1960s. Since then several systems of bodywork that treat myofascial tissues have been developed.

Technique: Myofascial massage techniques apply traction to the skin and underlying tissues to slowly and gently push, pull, and stretch fascial tissues and break fascial adhesions. They are applied without oil so that restrictions can be palpated and techniques applied without slipping.

Theory: Myofascial massage is based in Western anatomy and physiology. It focuses on connective or myofascial tissues that surround muscles, nerves, blood vessels, and all organs of the body. Restrictions in fascial tissues can cause a variety of dysfunctions, including limited mobility, postural distortion, poor cellular nutrition, and pain. Myofascial massage produces a softening of tissues and freeing of fascial restrictions.

Reference: *The Myofascial Release Manual,* 3rd edition, by Carol J. Manheim (Thorofare, NJ: Slack, Inc., 2001).

13. Neuromuscular Therapy (NMT)

Origin: A precursor to today's NMT was developed by a natural healer named Stanley Lief in the 1920s. Trigger Point Therapy was brought to public attention through the work of Janet Travell, MD (1901–1997), an expert in myofascial pain, and her treatment of Presidents Kennedy and Johnson in the 1960s. Fitness expert Bonnie Prudden developed a popular system of NMT called Myotherapy® in the 1970s.

Technique: Neuromuscular Therapy is a form of contemporary Western massage in which trigger points, i.e., hyperirritable taut bands in the myofascial tissues, are located and deactivitated using ischematic compression. Pressure is applied to trigger points for about 30 seconds using the thumb, fingers, or small hand tool. A stretch of the affected muscle follows application of pressure on trigger points.

Theory: A trigger point is a taut band or irritable spot in myofascial tissue that causes muscle pain at the trigger point and in its referral zones. It also causes muscle shortening, and decreased strength. Under a microscope, trigger points appear to be bands of contracted muscle tissue.

References: *Myofascial Pain and Dysfunction: The Trigger Point Manual, Volume 1—Upper Half of the Body,* 2nd editon by J. G. Travell and D. G. Simons. (Baltimore: Williams & Wilkins, 1999).

Myofascial Pain and Dysfunction: The Trigger Point Manual, Volume 2—The Lower Extremities by J. G. Travell and D. G. Simons. (Baltimore: Williams & Wilkins, 1992).

Website: Bonnie Prudden Myotherapy (www.bonnieprudden.com)

14. Polarity Therapy

Origin: Polarity Therapy was developed by Randolph Stone (1890–1981) in the 1930–1950s. Stone combined Western knowledge with theories from Chinese and Ayurvedic medicine, particularly regarding energy balancing. Upon his retirement in 1973, Stone's successors taught Polarity Therapy throughout the United States. The American Polarity Therapy Association was founded in 1984.

Technique: Polarity Therapy is an eclectic form of energy bodywork. Most Polarity Therapy techniques consist of placing the hands in different positions on the body to affect the free flow of energy. Other techniques include pressing, gentle rocking, and brushing.

Theory: Polarity Therapy techniques aim to remove obstructions to the free flow of energy in the body. Stone developed his own esoteric theories of energy flow after studying Chinese and Ayurvedic medicine.

Website: American Polarity Therapy Association (www.polaritytherapy.org)

15. Reflexology

Origin: Modern reflexology was developed by Eunice Ingham Stopfel (1889–1974), who combined the theory of Zone Therapy with compression massage of the feet and hands. She mapped the feet for their corresponding zones of reference and developed pressure techniques for stimulating points on the feet to affect specific organs and structures of the body. She started her work in the 1930s and taught throughout the United States in the 1950s–1960s.

Technique: Reflexology is performed primarily on the feet. Pressure is applied to areas of the feet to stimulate other parts of the body. Reflexology techniques include thumb walking, finger walking, hook and backup, along with Western massage and joint movements applied to the feet.

Theory: Reflexology is based in Zone Therapy, which postulates that 10 longitudinal zones of the body end in the feet and the hands. Pressure to a zone in the feet causes stimulation of the entire zone. Reflexology charts map out which specific organs or body structures will be affected by pressure on specific areas of the feet. Reflexology is thought to normalize function, improve circulation, and promote relaxation. Knowledge of Western anatomy, physiology, and pathology are important in reflexology.

Websites: Home of Reflexology (www.reflexology.org)

International Institute of Reflexology (www.reflexology-usa.net)

16. Rolfing® Structural Integration

Origin: Rolfing was developed by Ida P. Rolf (1896–1979), and brought to public recognition during the 1970s within the human potential movement. The Rolf Institute® of Structural Integration was founded in 1971 and provides training and certification for Rolfing practitioners.

Technique: Rolfing is a form of contemporary Western bodywork, also called Structural Integration. It includes soft tissue manipulation and movement education. In Rolfing, myofascial tissues are manipulated so that they lengthen and glide, to balance the body around its vertical axis, achieving proper alignment or posture. In the process of working with deep myofascial tissues, past emotional trauma is also released.

Theory: Rolfing is based in Western anatomy and physiology, especially of fascial tissues, and psychology.

Website: The Rolf Institute for Structural Integration (www.rolf.org)

17. Shiatsu—Namikoshi

Origin: Shiatsu evolved from traditional Japanese massage called Amma. Tokujiro Namikoshi (1905–2000) developed a system of finger pressure to treat various ailments. He founded the first Shiatsu Institute of Therapy on Hokkaido in 1925, and the Japan Shiatsu Institute in Tokyo in 1940. His son, Toru Namikoshi (1931–), popularized Shiatsu in Japan and throughout the world in the 1950s–1970s.

Technique: Shiatsu is a form of Asian Bodywork Therapy. Shiatsu literally means finger pressure (shi-atsu) in Japanese. Pressure is applied along energy (ki) meridians and to acupoints with the thumbs, fingers, or elbows. The recipient is either lying on a mat on the floor or on a bodywork table.

Theory: Shiatsu, as developed by Namikoshi, combines traditional Chinese medicine and Western anatomy and physiology. Important acupoints are pressed to elicit desired results, and to enhance the balance and flow of ki, or energy.

Website: American Organization of Bodywork Therapies of Asia (www. aobta.org)

18. Sports Massage

Origin: Sports massage can be traced to ancient Greece and Rome where massage was given in the gymnasia and public baths. Massage prepared athletes for exercises and helped in recovery from competition. In the late 19th century, rubbers and athletic masseurs used massage in the training of athletes. Sports massage was revived in the 1970s within the context of Western massage.

Technique: Sports massage is a specialty within Western massage. Western massage techniques are applied to enhance athletic performance, prevent injuries, prepare for and recover from competition, and in rehabilitation of injuries. Modern sports massage given at events emphasizes the technique of compression and other forms of petrissage. Individual practitioners may add other bodywork approaches to achieve the goals of the athlete.

Theory: Sports massage is based in Western anatomy, physiology, kinesiology, pathology, and sports science.

Reference: *Understanding Sports Massage* (2nd ed.) by Patricia J. Benjamin & Scott Lamp (Champaign, IL: Human Kinetics, 2005).

19. Stone Massage

Origin: Stones have been used in healing practices all over the world, including Asia. Healing or hot stone massage is a treatment that gained popularity in North American spas in the 1990s–2000s.

Technique: Stone massage is a form of contemporary bodywork and spa treatment. Stones of various sizes, shapes and textures are used as massage tools and as a form of thermal therapy. As massage tools, stones are used instead of the hands to apply pressure during techniques such as effleurage. As thermal therapy, stones may be heated and placed on the body over certain anatomical structures or in patterns over energy centers and meridians; or cooled and used as cryotherapy to reduce swelling and cool tissues.

Theory: Stone massage is practiced as an eclectic form of bodywork incorporating Western anatomy and physiology with traditional Asian medicine. Geological properties of various kinds of stones are considered. Hot stones applied to the body impart weight and heat that promotes relaxation, normal body function, and energy balancing.

References: *Healing Stone Massage.* Video with Carollanne Crichton (Real Bodywork, 2001).

Japanese Hot Stone Massage by Mark Hess and Shogo Mochizuki (Kotobuki Publications, 2002).

20. Swedish Massage

Origin: Swedish massage and related techniques were developed in Europe in the early 1800s and brought to North America in the 1860s. It can be traced historically to the work of two men, Pehr Henrick Ling (1776–1839) of Sweden, and Johann Mezger (1838–1909) of Amsterdam. The heyday of Swedish massage in the United States was the 1930s–1950s, when it was offered in health clubs, salons, and as part of physiotherapy.

Technique: Swedish massage is a form of traditional Western massage. The five classic technique categories of Swedish massage soft tissue manipulation are effleurage (stroking, sliding), petrissage (kneading, compression), tapotement (percussion), friction, and vibration. Joint movements and hydrotherapy are also within the scope of Swedish massage.

Theory: Swedish massage is based in Western anatomy, physiology, and pathology. It is applied to support the normal function of the human body and its systems, as well as enhance its innate healing capacity.

See Western Massage.

21. Thai Massage

Origin: Nuad bo-Rarn means *ancient massage* in the language of Thailand. It has been practiced for over 2500 years. At the Temple of the Reclining Buddha in Bangkok, 200-year-old stone engravings illustrate the energy lines and points, and techniques of this ancient practice. Thai massage is passed down in families and also taught at schools of Traditional Thai Medicine.

Technique: In Thai massage, the practitioner uses passive movement, yoga-like stretching, and pressure techniques to stimulate energy channels called *sen lines,* and release tension in the body. Application is gentle and rhythmic. Recipients lie on floor mats to receive Thai Massage.

Theory: Thai massage is based on Ayurvedic (India) and Chinese medicine, and was influenced by yoga, as it evolved in ancient Thailand. Techniques stimulate the free flow of energy through channels.

Website: Institute of Thai Massage (www.thai-massage.org)

22. Therapeutic Touch (TT)

Origin: Therapeutic Touch was developed by Delores Krieger, a professor of nursing, and her teacher, Dora Kunz in the 1960s–1970s. It is a modification of the ancient practice of laying on of the hands.

Technique: Therapeutic Touch is a system of energy bodywork performed in five steps: (1) centering of the practitioner, (2) assessment of the energy field of the recipient with the palms of the hands, (3) clearing blockages, imbalances or congestion of energy with sweeping hand movements, (4) establishing harmony in the energy field using the mind, and (5) smoothing out the energy field by sweeping the hands outward toward the periphery of the field.

Theory: Therapeutic Touch is based in theories of bioelectricity and electromagnetic energy fields. The sweeping hand movements of TT move energy to create balance and harmony in a person's energy field. Imbalances, blockages, and congestion in the energy field are thought to result in disease and dysfunction. TT is used in the treatment of many different ailments.

Website: Nurse Healers–Professional Associates International (www.therapeutictouch.org)

23. Trager® Approach

Origin: Trager Approach, also known as Psychophysical Integration, was developed by Milton Trager, MD (1908–1997). After earning a medical degree after World War II, Trager opened a practice in Hawaii in 1959 and gave a public demonstration of his work in 1973.

Technique: The Trager Approach is a system of contemporary Western bodywork that combines tissue and joint mobilization, relaxation and movement re-education. The practitioner applies continuous rhythmic movement to different joints in the body with the recipient lying on a table. Recipients recreate the easy, light, free movements of the table work in a system of active exercise called Mentastics.

Theory: Trager focuses on creating the sensations of lighter, easier, and freer movement through affecting neurological mechanisms of the body. It imparts an experience of deep relaxation, and greater joint mobility.

Website: Trager International (www.trager.com)

24. Tuina

Origin: The origin of Tuina, or Chinese medical massage, is clouded in the mists of time. It developed from the same roots as acupuncture in Chinese medicine. Tuina is written about in several ancient medical texts, and a Tuina department was set up in the Imperial Health Administration in the Tang Dynasty (618–907 CE). Tuina for infants and children became popular in the Qing Dynasty (1644–1911 CE).

Technique: Tuina is a form of Chinese medical massage, i.e., Asian Bodywork Therapy. Techniques of Tuina include stroking, pushing, grasping, pressing, palm-rubbing, twisting, pinching, rubbing, rolling, tapping, stretching, kneading, lifting, and holding. Techniques are applied to stimulate acupoints and affect blood circulation. Tuina also includes joint manipulation, herbal remedies, and therapeutic exercise.

Theory: Tuina is based in theory of Chinese medicine including *qi* or energy, energy channels, and yin-yang. Modern Tuina incorporates knowledge of Western anatomy, physiology, and pathology. Tuina is used to treat ailments recognized by Chinese medicine, as well as Western pathology.

Reference: *Chinese Tuina Therapy* by Wang Fu (Bejing, China: Foreign Languages Press, 1994).

25. Western Massage

Origin: Western massage can be traced to health and healing practices of ancient Greece and Rome. Techniques of soft tissue manipulation were further developed through the centuries in Europe and North America. Western massage today is an outgrowth of Swedish massage, massage used in Western medicine, and various contemporary systems of massage and bodywork.

Description: Western massage techniques include classic Swedish massage techniques, plus various forms of contemporary massage (e.g., neuromuscular therapy, myofascial massage, lymphatic drainage massage, and other forms of massage therapy based in Western anatomy, physiology, and pathology). Western massage practitioners tend to be eclectic, incorporating various techniques, including energy approaches, with classic Swedish massage.

Theory: Western massage is based in Western anatomy, physiology, and pathology. It aims to enhance the normal functioning of the body and its systems, including the innate healing power in each person.

Websites: American Massage Therapy Association (www.amtamassage.org) Associated Bodywork and Massage Professionals (www.abmp.com)

Personal Care and Health Professionals

This is a guide to personal care and health professionals who interact with massage therapists in typical work settings. Licensing of these occupations varies from state to state in the United States and from country to country throughout the world.

PERSONAL CARE PROVIDERS

Barbers specialize in men's grooming (e.g., cutting hair and beards, shaving facial hair).

Cosmetologists specialize in women's grooming (e.g., styling hair; giving facials, manicures, and pedicures; and applying cosmetics); sometimes called beauticians, hairstylists.

Estheticians specialize in nonmedical skin care.

SPORTS, FITNESS, AND RECREATION PROFESSIONALS

Athletic trainers (ATs) focus on prevention and treatment of injuries common in sports; typically they have college degrees, have completed an internship, and have professional certification. *See* National Athletic Trainers' Association (www.nata.org).

Coaches organize sports teams and train individual athletes; responsibilities include teaching sports skills, organizing practices, developing strategies, and directing play during competitions.

Personal trainers are health and fitness specialists hired by individuals to develop exercise programs, and supervise and motivate them to achieve their fitness goals; different levels of training for personal trainers range from workshops to college degrees, usually in exercise physiology; professional certification from different organizations. *See* National Strength and Conditioning Association (www.nsca-cc.org) and National Council on Strength and Fitness (www.ncsf.org/certexam).

HEALTH CARE PROFESSIONALS

Conventional

Medical doctors (MDs) are trained in conventional medicine; diagnose and treat diseases of the human body/mind primarily with drugs, surgery, and referral to therapists.

Nurses (RNs, LPNs) specialize in direct patient care including treatment, education, record keeping, and providing emotional support for patients and their families; *RN* means registered nurse and *LPN* means licensed practical nurse; RN and LPN represent different levels of training and licensure. *See* American Nurses Association (www.nursingworld.org).

Osteopaths (DOs) historically traced disease to imbalances in the musculoskeletal structure of the human body and rejected use of drugs and surgery; in many places today, including the United States, they have expanded their scope of practice to conventional medicine; different philosophies prevail in different countries. *See* American Osteopathic Association (www.osteopathic.org).

Physiatrists are physicians who specialize in physical medicine and rehabilitation and focus on restoring musculoskeletal function; typically have 8 years of graduate and postdoctorate medical training. *See* American Academy of Physical Medicine and Rehabilitation (www.aapmr.org).

Psychologists study the human mind including behavior and thinking; clinical psychologists provide mental health care to clients. *See* American Psychological Association (www.aps.org).

Therapists*

Occupational therapists (OTs) help clients who have disabilities to better perform activities of daily living and work tasks; teach people with permanent disabilities to use adaptive equipment; typically have college degrees. *See* American Occupational Therapy Association (www.aota.org).

Physical therapists (PTs) use exercise, hydrotherapy, and other modalities to restore function and reduce pain from injury and illness; typically have college degrees; in some places called *physiotherapists*. *See* American Physical Therapy Association (www.apta.org).

Physical therapist aides or assistants (PTAs) help administer physical therapy treatments to patients under the direction of a physical therapist and perform some clerical tasks; trained on the job or in associate/vocational degree programs. *See* American Physical Therapy Association (www.apta.org).

Respiratory therapists (RTs) evaluate, treat, and care for patients with respiratory disorders; use oxygen, respiratory physiotherapy, and other modalities. *See* American Association for Respiratory Care (www.aarc.org).

Complementary and Alternative (CAM)

Acupuncturists provide treatment based in Chinese medicine (Oriental medicine); use needles, pressure, and other methods to stimulate traditional energy points. *See* American Association of Oriental Medicine (www.aaom.org).

Chiropractors (DCs) or chiropractic physicians address misalignment of the musculoskeletal structure to affect the nervous system and treat diseases

---

*These practitioners focus on the application of specific modalities for rehabilitation and in the treatment of diseases and injuries. A doctor's prescription must be obtained for treatment by these professionals in most cases. Licenses are required to practice in most states.

and improve health; primary treatment is spinal adjustments. *See* American Chiropractic Association (www.amerchiro.org).

Homeopaths or homeopathic physicians treat medical conditions using homeopathic preparations; based on the Law of Similars; not regulated in the United States. *See* National Center for Homeopathy (www.homeopathic.org).

Naturopaths or naturopathic physicians (NDs) use natural remedies such as herbs, nutritional supplements, and other natural modalities to treat human diseases; licensed in 14 states. *See* American Association of Naturopathic Physicians (www.naturopathic.org).

Osteopaths (DOs) *See* Conventional health care professionals.

Therapists**

Aromatherapists use essential oils from plants to evoke good health and healing.

Art therapists are mental health professionals that use the creative processes of art to improve physical, mental, and emotional well-being.

Bodywork practitioners or bodyworkers apply manual techniques and movement therapy for holistic well-being; includes massage therapists.

Equine therapists or equitherapists use horses and the movement of horses in treatment of a variety of physical and mental conditions.

Hypnotherapists use the mental therapy of hypnosis in treating a variety of conditions.

Massage therapists apply soft tissue manipulation and related therapies to improve health and promote healing.

Music therapists use music in the treatment of a variety of human ills.

Recreation therapists or therapeutic recreation specialists plan, organize, and conduct recreation programs for special populations, and teach people with various disabilities to participate in leisure activities for social, physical, and mental health.

Further information may be found in the U.S. Department of Labor, *Occupational Outlook Handbook*, which lists the nature of the work, typical work conditions, training necessary, earnings, and additional sources of information. The website for the Bureau of Labor Statistics is www.bls.gov. Another resource is the National Center for Complementary and Alternative Medicine (NCCAM) at the National Institutes of Health at www.nccam.nih.gov.

**These practitioners focus on the application of specific modalities in the treatment of diseases and injuries and to improve health. Several of these occupations are off-shoots of more established professions, and some require board certification and licenses to practice in certain jurisdictions. All are holistic and are considered complementary or alternative therapies.

Competent massage therapists have acquired the following knowledge and skills.

1. Plan and organize an effective massage and bodywork session.
- ▶ Knowledge of the structure and function of the human body and its systems in health and disease
- ▶ Knowledge of the effects of massage and bodywork techniques
- ▶ Understanding and using appropriate terminology
- ▶ Knowledge of the components of a therapeutic environment
- ▶ Knowledge of a wellness model and its relationship to massage therapy and bodywork practice
- ▶ Performance of assessment and data collection for the purpose of determining contraindications and formulating a treatment strategy
- ▶ Formulation and documentation of a treatment strategy based on assessment findings and client response to previous application of massage and bodywork techniques
- ▶ For Asian bodywork: knowledge of Asian anatomy, physiology, pathology; knowledge of general Asian philosophy and cosmology; ability to apply concepts of yin/yang

2. Perform massage and bodywork for therapeutic benefit.
- ▶ Effective organization and management of the client session
- ▶ Application of appropriate techniques utilizing hands, fingers, thumbs, elbows, forearms, and feet as applicable
- ▶ Application and use of appropriate equipment and supplies
- ▶ Application and use of hydrotherapy, thermal agents, and complementary therapies

3. Develop and implement a self-care strategy.
- ▶ Identify methods of self-assessment and stress management
- ▶ Identify strategies to prevent self-injury and enhance the efficacy of techniques through the use of proper body mechanics, centering, focusing, and breathing

4. Develop successful and ethical therapeutic relationships with clients.

► Use effective communication in the therapist–client relationship
► Establish and maintain safe and respectful boundaries with clients
► Identify and discuss the implementation of ethical principles in the practice of massage therapy and bodywork

5. Develop a strategy for a successful practice, business, or employment situation.

► Identify and describe basic business practices relevant to the practice of massage therapy/bodywork
► Demonstrate knowledge of effective communication related to business and marketing
► Identify strategies to develop and maintain a client base
► Identify strategies for effective communication with other professionals regarding client care and referrals
► Identify strategies for effective management of the work environment
► Discuss the process for establishing and maintaining professional boundaries and relationships with peers, in the workplace, and with other professionals
► Identify strategies of conflict resolution skills in relationships with other professionals

6. Identify strategies to participate in professional activities and pursue personal professional development.

► Identify characteristics of effective interaction in groups/organizations
► Identify strategies to attain new knowledge
► Demonstrate the ability to read and evaluate technical information found in articles in health-related journals and determine biases and limitations in the findings or premises on which the articles are based

Adapted from Curriculum Standards of the Commission on Massage Therapy Accreditation, effective March 2003. The COMTA Accreditation Standards, of which curriculum and competencies are a part, can be found on their website at www.comta.org.

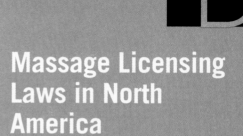

The following list contains information about state (United States) and provincial (Canada) licensing for massage therapists. It is current up to the time of publication of this text. Please check one of the following websites for more current information: www.amtamassage.org, www.abmp. com, www.massagemag.com, or for the most current information, contact the government agency responsible for licensing.

Education required lists only massage therapy education, however, CPR or other education may also be required. Most states require graduation from a state-approved or accredited school or program. Check state laws for most complete information about requirements. NCETMB refers to the National Certification Examination for Therapeutic Massage and Bodywork (www.ncbtmb.org).

UNITED STATES

Alabama Massage Therapy Board
610 S. McDonough Street
Montgomery, AL 36104
Phone: (334) 269-9990
Website: almtbd.state.al.us
Education required: 650 hours
Exam: NCETMB
Continuing education: 16 hours biennially

Arizona Board of Massage Therapy
1400 West Washington, Suite 230
Phoenix, AZ 85007
Phone: (602) 542-8604
Website: massageboard.az.gov
Education required: 500 hours
Exam: NCETMB
Continuing education: 25 hours biennially

Arkansas State Board of Massage Therapy
P.O. Box 20739
Hot Springs, AR 71903
Phone: (501) 520-0555
Website: www.arkansasmassagetherapy.com
Education required: 500 hours
Exam: NCETMB or state exam (written and practical)
Continuing education: 3 hours annually

Connecticut – Massage Therapy Licensure
Department of Public Health & Addiction Services
150 Washington Street
Hartford, CT 06106
Phone: (860) 509-7603
Website: www.dph.state.ct.us
Education required: 500 hours
Exam: NCETMB
Continuing education: 6 hours annually

Delaware Board of Massage and Bodywork

Cannon Building
861 Silver Lake Boulevard, #203
Dover, DE 19904
Phone: (302) 744-4537
Website: www.dpr.delaware.gov/boards/
     massagebodyworks
Education required: 500 hours, massage therapist; 300
     hours, certified massage technician
Exam: NCETMB for massage therapist; none for certified
     technician
Continuing education: 24 hours biennially for massage
     therapists; 12 hours biennially for certified technicians

District of Columbia Board of Massage Therapy

Department of Health
717 14th Street, N.W.
Washington, D.C. 20005
Phone: (877) 672-2174
Website: www.dchealth.dc.gov
Education required: 500 hours
Exam: NCETMB
Continuing education: 12 hours biennially

Florida Board of Massage Therapy

Department of Health, Medical Quality Assurance
4052 Bald Cypress Way
Tallahassee, FL 32399
Phone: (850) 245-4161
Website:www.doh.state.fl.us/mqa/massage/
     ma_lic_req.html
Education required: 500 hours
Exam: NCETMB
Continuing education: 25 hours biennially

Georgia Board of Massage Therapy

237 Coliseum Drive
Macon, GA 31217
Phone: (478) 207-1300
Website: http://sos.georgia.gov/plb/massage
Requirements to be determined

Hawaii State Board of Massage Therapy

Department of Commerce and Consumer Affairs
P.O. Box 3469
1010 Richards Street
Honolulu, HI 96801
Phone: (808) 587-3222
Website: www.hawaii.gov/dcca/areas/pvl/boards/massage
Education required: 570 hours
Exam: state exam
Continuing education: none

Illinois Department of Financial and Professional Regulation

320 West Washington Street, 3rd Floor
Springfield, IL 62686
Phone: (217) 782-8556
Website: www.idfpr.com
Education required: 500 hours
Exam: NCETMB or other approved certifying exam
Continuing education: 24 hours biennially

Indiana Professional Licensing Agency

State Board of Massage Therapy
402 West Washington Street, Room W072
Indianapolis, IN 46204
Website: www.in.gov/pla/bandc/massage/index.html
Education required: 500 hours
Exam: State board-approved certification exam (exam to
     be determined)
Continuing education: To be determined
*(After January 1, 2009, all massage therapists will need to be state
     certified)*

Iowa Board of Massage Therapy Examiners

Lucas State Office Building, 5th Floor
321 E. 12th Street
Des Moines, IA 50319
Phone: (515) 281-6959
Website: www.idph.state.ia.us/licensure
Education required: 500 hours
Exam: NCETMB
Continuing education: 24 hours biennially

Kentucky Board of Licensure for Massage Therapy

P.O. Box 1360
Frankfort, KY 40602
Phone: (502) 564-3296
Website: www.finance.ky.gov/ourcabinet/caboff/OAS/
     op/massth
Education required: 600 hours
Exam: NCETMB or NCCA-approved certifying exam
Continuing education: 24 hours biennially

Louisiana Board of Massage Therapy

12022 Plank Road
Zachary, LA 70811
Phone: (225) 771- 4090
Website: www.lsbmt.org
Education required: 600 hours
Exam: NCETMB or written and oral exam
Continuing education: 12 hours annually

Maine Massage Therapy
Department of Professional and Financial Regulation
Office of Licensing and Registration
35 State House Station
Augusta, ME 04333
Phone: (207) 624-8613
Website: www.maine.gov/professionallicensing
Education required: 500 hours
Exam: NCETMB
Continuing education: none

Maryland Massage Therapy Advisory Committee
Board of Chiropractic Examiners
4201 Patterson Avenue, 5th Floor
Baltimore, MD 21215
Phone: (410) 764-4738
Website: www.mdmassage.org
Education required: 500 hours + 60 hours college credit
   and NCETMB for Certified Massage Therapist; or 500
   hours + NCETMB for Registered Massage Practitioner
Exam: NCETMB
Continuing education: 24 hours biennially

Massachusetts Board of Registration of Massage Therapy
239 Causeway Street, Suite 500
Boston, MA 02114
Phone: (617) 727-5369
Website: www.mass.gov/dpl/boards
Education required: 500 hours
Exam: TBD
Continuing education: TBD

Mississippi State Board of Massage Therapy
P.O. Box 12489
Jackson, MS 39236
Phone: (601) 856-6127
Website: www.msbmt.state.ms.us
Education required: 700 hours
Exam: NCETMB
Continuing education: 12 hours annually

Missouri State Board of Therapeutic Massage
Division of Professional Regulation
3605 Missouri Boulevard
P.O. Box 1335
Jefferson City, MO 65102
Phone: (573) 522-6277
Website: www.pr.mo.gov/massage.asp
Education required: 500 hours
Exam: NCETMB
Continuing education: 12 hours biennially

Nebraska Massage Therapy Board
Health and Human Services
Credentialing Division
Lincoln, NE 68509
Phone: (402) 471-2115
Website: www.hhs.state.ne.us/crl/mhcs/mass/
   massage.htm
Education required: 1,000 hours
Exam: NCETMB
Continuing education: 24 hours biennially

Nevada Board of Massage Therapy
111 West Telegraph, Suite 200
Carson City, NV 89703
Phone: (775) 688-1888
Website: www.massagetherapy.nv.gov
Education required: TBD
Exam: NCETMB
Continuing education: TBD

New Hampshire Office of Program Support
Licensing and Regulatory Services
Board of Massage Therapy
129 Pleasant Avenue
Concord, NH 03301
Phone: (603) 271-4814
Website: www.dhhs.state.nh.us/DHHS/LRS/eligibility/
   massage-license.htm
Education required: 750 hours
Exam: NCETMB
Continuing education: 12 hours biennially

New Jersey Board of Nursing
Massage, Bodywork & Somatic Therapy Examining
   Committee
124 Halsey Street
Newark, NJ 07102
Phone: (973) 504-6430
Website: www.state.nj.us/lps/ca/medical/nursing.
   htm#massage
License required: 500 hours *or* NCETMB
Continuing education: none

New Mexico Massage Therapy Board
2550 Cerrillos Road
Santa Fe, NM 87505
Phone: (505) 476-4870
Website: www.rld.state.nm.us/massage/index.html
Education required: 650 hours
Exam: NCETMB
Continuing education: 16 hours biennially

New York State Board of Massage Therapy

Office of Professions, Division of Professional Licensing
Services
89 Washington Avenue
Albany, NY 12234
Phone: (518) 474-3817 ext. 150
Website: www.op.nysed.gov/mtlic.htm
Education required: 1,000 hours
Exam: State exam
Continuing education: none

North Carolina Board of Massage and Bodywork Therapy

P.O. Box 2539
Raleigh, NC 27602
Phone: (919) 546-0050
Website: www.bmbt.org
Education required: 500 hours
Exam: NCETMB
Continuing education: 25 hours biennially

North Dakota State Board of Massage

P.O. Box 218
Beach, ND 58621
Phone: (701) 872-4895
Website: www.ndboardofmassage.com
Education required: 750 hours
Exam: State exam, NCETMB
Continuing education: 18 hours annually

Ohio State Medical Board

Massage Licensing Division
77 South High Street, 17th Floor
Columbus, OH 43266
Phone: (614) 466-3934
Website: www.med.ohio.gov/mtsubwebindex.htm
Education required: 600 hours
Exam: State exam
Continuing education: none

Oregon Board of Massage

748 Hawthorne Avenue, NE
Salem, OR 97301
Phone: (503) 365-8657
Website: www.oregonmassage.org
Education required: 500 hours
Exam: NCETMB + practical exam
Continuing education: 25 hours biennially + current CPR

Rhode Island Department of Health

Office of Health Professionals Regulation
3 Capitol Hill, Room 104
Providence, RI 02908
Phone: (401) 222-2827
Website: www.health.state.ri.us/hsr/professions/
massage.php
Education required: 500 hours from COMTA-accredited
school/program
Exam: NCETMB
Continuing education: none

South Carolina Division of Professional Regulation

110 Center View
Columbia, SC 29210
Phone: (803) 896-4490
Website: www.llr.state.sc.us/POL/massagetherapy
Education required: 500 hours
Exam: NCETMB
Continuing education: 12 hours biennially

Tennessee Massage Licensure Board

Cordell Hull Building
227 French Landing, Suite 300
Heritage Place Metro Center
Nashville, TN 37243
Phone: (615) 532-3202 ext. 3211
Website: http://health.state.tn.us/Boards/Massage
Education required: 500 hours
Exam: NCETMB
Continuing education: 25 hours biennially

Texas Department of State Health Services

Massage Therapy Licensing Program
1100 West 49th Street
Austin, TX 78756
Phone: (512) 834-6616
Website: www.dshs.state.tx.us/massage/default.shtm
Education required: 500 hours
Exam: state written and practical exam
Continuing education: 12 hours biennially

Utah Division of Occupational and Professional Licensing

Board of Massage Therapy
160 East 300 South
Salt Lake City, UT 84145
Phone: (801) 530-6628
Website: www.dopl.utah.gov/licensing/massage_therapy.
html
Education required: 600 hours
Exam: NCETMB
Continuing education: none

Virginia Board of Nursing

Department of Health Professions
6606 W. Broadway Street, 5th Floor
Richmond, VA 23230
Phone: (804) 662-9909
Website: www.dhp.virginia.gov/Nursing/
    nursing_forms.htm#Massage%20Therapist
Education required: 500 hours
Exam: NCETMB
Continuing education: 16 hours biennially

Washington State Department of Health

Massage Therapy Program
P.O. Box 47867
Olympia, WA 98504
Phone: (360) 236-4700
Website:fortress.wa.gov/doh/hpqa1/hps3/
    Massage_Therapy/newlicense.htm
Education required: 500 hours
Exam: NCETMB
Continuing education: 16 hours biennially

State of West Virginia

Massage Therapy Licensure Board
200 Davis Street, #1
Princeton, WV 24740
Phone: (304) 487-1400
Website: www.wvmassage.org
Education required: 500 hours
Exam: NCETMB
Continuing education: 25 hours biennially

Wisconsin Department of Regulation and Licensing

Massage Therapy Board
1400 East Washington Avenue
Madison, WI 53703
Phone: (608) 266-2112
Website: drl.wi.gov/prof/mass/def.htm
Education required: 600 hours
Exam: state exam *and* NCETMB
Continuing education: none

CANADA

British Columbia

College of Massage Therapists of British Columbia
103–1089 West Broadway
Vancouver, BC V6H 1E5
Phone: (604) 736-3404
Website: www.cmtbc.bc.ca
Education required: 3,000 hours
Exam: written and practical exams
Continuing education: 24 hours biennially

Newfoundland and Labrador

College of Massage Therapists of Newfoundland and
    Labrador
P.O. Box 23204
Churchill Square
St. John's, NL A1B 4J9
Phone: (709) 739-7181
Website: www.cmtnl.ca
Education required: 2,200 hours
Exam: written and practical exam
Continuing education: 30 hours every 3 years

Ontario

College of Massage Therapists of Ontario
1867 Yonge Stree, Suite 810
Toronto, ON M4S 1Y5
Website: www.cmto.com
Education required: 2- to 3-year full-time program
Exam: written and practical exam
Continuing education: 30 hours every 3 years

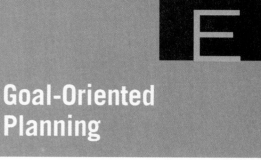

LONG-TERM PLANNING—INITIAL SESSION AND ONGOING EVALUATION

Step 1. **Gather information from the client.**
- ▶ Review intake form
- ▶ Review health history form
- ▶ Conduct interview

Step 2. **Collect information through observation and measurement.**
- ▶ Observe client (e.g., general posture, motion, expression, stress level)
- ▶ Conduct tests and measurements related to stated goals or complaint

Step 3. **Assess the overall situation and establish long-term goals.**
- ▶ Identify wellness goals that can be addressed with massage
- ▶ Identify problems for which massage is indicated
- ▶ Identify contraindications and cautions
- ▶ Prioritize goals together with the client

Step 4. **Develop an action plan to achieve long-term goals.**
- ▶ Suggest frequency and length of massage sessions
- ▶ Determine general massage approaches to use
- ▶ Set a date for evaluating progress on specific goals
- ▶ Suggest home care to help achieve goals (e.g., self-massage, hot and cold applications, stretching, exercises, relaxation techniques)

Step 5. **Implement the long-term plan.**
- ▶ Make appointments
- ▶ Provide client with information or tools for home care

Step 6. **Evaluate progress toward long-term goals.**
- ▶ Write SOAP notes to document the long-term plan
- ▶ Adjust the long-term plan as needed to achieve original client goals and/or set new or modified goals
- ▶ Set date for evaluating progress toward long-term goals

INDIVIDUAL SESSION PLANNING

Step 1. **Gather information from the client, and review previous documentation.**
- ▶ Review intake and health history forms
- ▶ Review notes from previous sessions
- ▶ Pre-session interview
  - Ask about changes in health status or medications
  - Ask about progress or regression since last session

Step 2. **Collect information through observation and measurement.**
- ▶ Observe the client (e.g., general posture, motion, expression)
- ▶ Palpation and simple measurements during the session

Step 3. **Assess the situation and set session goals.**
- ▶ Identify current client state and next step to reach long-term goals
- ▶ Prioritize goals for the session
- ▶ Determine cautions and contraindications for this session

Step 4. **Develop a general plan for the session.**
- ▶ Plan session organization including body areas to be addressed, and in what order to apply massage
- ▶ Choose general approach to use in the session (e.g., relaxation massage, trigger points, myofascial massage, lymph drainage massage, polarity therapy, etc.)
- ▶ Determine use of adjunct methods (e.g., hot or cold applications, aromatherapy, electronic vibration device)

Step 5. **Implement the session plan.**
- ▶ Apply massage and related techniques

Step 6. **Evaluate progress toward the session goals.**
- ▶ Ongoing evaluation during session
- ▶ Post-session evaluation (e.g., post-session observations, post-session client interview)
- ▶ Ongoing adjustments during the massage session
- ▶ Write SOAP notes to document the session

TREATMENT PLANNING—FOR TREATMENT AND RECOVERY FROM ILLNESS OR INJURY

Step 1. **Gather information from client related to the illness, injury, or complaint.**
- ▶ Review intake form
- ▶ Review medical history
- ▶ Review medical diagnosis if available
- ▶ Conduct initial interview
  - Onset of condition
  - Symptoms
  - Degree of pain
  - Functional limitations
  - Activities of daily living (ADL) affected
  - First aid or home remedies applied
  - What seems to make it better or worse

Step 2. **Collect information related to the illness or injury through observation and measurement.**
- ▶ Observe general state of client (e.g., facial expression, voice quality, energy level)
- ▶ Take measurements relative to the complaint or diagnosed condition (e.g., standing posture, sitting posture, walking gait, body mechanics, range of motion at specific joints)
- ▶ Visual observation of skin (e.g., color, bruises, swelling, pitting, scars, moles, wounds, rashes)
- ▶ Palpation of soft tissues in specific areas (e.g., texture [degree of oiliness or dryness], temperature, pliability, firmness, adhesion, fibrosis, puffiness, springiness)
- ▶ Palpation of muscle and tendon structures (e.g., firmness, shape, tension, atrophy or wasting, taut bands in muscle tissue, trigger points, taut tendons)
- ▶ Palpation of movement (e.g., ease of movement, crepitations)
- ▶ Orthopedic tests for specific pathologies

Step 3. **Assess the situation and set treatment goals.**
- ▶ Determine the condition of tissues
- ▶ Determine function or loss of function
- ▶ Identify contraindications and cautions for massage therapy
- ▶ Determine how massage can alleviate symptoms or facilitate healing
- ▶ Set anatomical, physiological, and/or functional treatment goals

Step 4. **Develop a treatment action plan.**
- ▶ Suggest the frequency and length of massage sessions
- ▶ Choose a general approach to reach goals (e.g., Western massage, myofascial massage, neuromuscular therapy, lymphatic massage, foot reflexology, polarity therapy)
- ▶ Set a date for evaluating progress on specific goals
- ▶ Suggest home care (e.g., self-massage, hot and cold applications, stretching, exercises, relaxation techniques)

Step 5. **Implement the treatment plan.**
- ▶ Make appointments
- ▶ Provide client with information or tools for home care

Step 6. **Evaluate progress toward healing and recovery.**
- ▶ Adjust the treatment plan as needed to achieve goals for healing and recovery
- ▶ Write SOAP notes to document the treatment plan

Intake and Health History Forms

NEW CLIENT INFORMATION FORM

Date _____

Name _____ Gender: ☐ male ☐ female

Address _____

City _____ State _____ Zip _____

Home Phone _____ Cell Phone _____

Work Phone _____ E-Mail Address _____

Age _____ Date of Birth _____ Occupation _____

Primary Health Care Provider _____

Address _____ City _____ State _____ Zip _____

Phone _____

Insurance Company _____ Policy # _____

ID # _____ Group # _____ Claim # _____

Phone Number _____

Emergency Contacts:

1st Name _____ Relationship _____

Phone Number(s) _____

2nd Name _____ Relationship _____

Phone Number(s) _____

(1 of 3)

327

Policies, Privacy, and Consent Form

General Policies

1. Massage sessions are available by appointment only from 9:00 AM – 6:00 PM, Tuesday–Saturday.

2. Payment is due at the time of the massage appointment.

3. Fees are $65 for a 60-minute appointment, $90 for a 90-minute appointment.

4. Payments must be in cash or check. Credit cards are not accepted.

5. Appointments are reserved for the time slot chosen. Clients arriving late for their appointments will receive massage as possible during the remainder of their reserved time.

6. There is a 24-hour cancellation policy. Clients will be charged for missed appointments.

7. Client records are kept secure and confidential (see Privacy Policy, below).

8. Clients are expected to exhibit good hygiene and are asked to minimize the use of perfume, cologne, and heavily scented personal products.

9. The use of cell phones or beepers is not allowed during the massage session, except in special circumstances agreed upon beforehand by the massage therapist.

10. Massage sessions may be terminated at any time the massage therapist has reason to believe that a client is sexualizing the massage, or uses inappropriate or threatening language or behavior.

11. This office follows the Code of Ethics and Standards of Practice of the American Massage Therapy Association (www.amtamassage.org).

Privacy Policy

Your massage therapy records are kept in the strictest confidence by this office. All client records are kept in a secure place, and only those who need to see a client's file for legitimate business or professional purposes have access to them. Your records will not be released to third parties, including health care providers and insurance companies, without your written consent. Records may be surrendered if required by law.

General Agreement and Consent

I, _____, understand that the massage therapy given
to me by _____ is for the purpose of general health
and wellness, relaxation, improved circulation, pain management, and other
effects supported by experience and research. Massage therapy is performed
here within the scope of practice of massage therapists in this state.

I understand that massage therapists do not diagnosis medical conditions, nor
do they prescribe medical treatments or medications, nor do they perform
spinal manipulation or chiropractic adjustments.

I understand that massage therapy is not a substitute for examination by a
medical provider, and that it is recommended that I seek medical attention
first for any illness, injury, or disorder that I might have.

I understand that massage therapy can be a valuable complement to health
care provided by medical doctors, chiropractic physicians, naturopathic physicians, practitioners of traditional Chinese medicine, and psychiatrists and psychologists. I agree to keep my massage therapist informed of any medical
treatment I am receiving with the understanding that it may impact the massage therapy I receive.

I have stated all my known medical conditions, treatments, and medications,
and I agree to keep the massage therapist updated on any changes.

My signature below confirms my agreement to the general policies, privacy policy, and consent statements above.

Name _____ Date _____

Witness _____ Date _____

(3 of 3)

Health History for Massage Therapy—Wellness

Name _____ Date of initial visit _____
Address _____ Phone _____
Occupation _____ Date of birth _____
Sports/physical activities/hobbies _____

The following information will be used to help plan safe and effective massage sessions. Please answer the questions to the best of your knowledge.

1. Have you had professional massage before?   Yes   No

2. Do you have any difficulty lying on your front, back, or side?   Yes   No
   If yes, please explain _____

3. Do you have allergic reactions to oils, lotions, ointments, liniments, or other substances put on your skin?   Yes   No
   If yes, please explain _____

4. Do you wear contact lenses ( ) dentures ( ) a hearing aid ( )?

5. Do you sit for long hours at a workstation, computer, or driving?   Yes   No
   If yes, please describe _____

6. Do you perform any repetitive movement in your work, sports, or hobby?   Yes   No
   If yes, please describe _____

7. Do you experience stress in your work, family, or other aspect of your life?
   Yes   No
   If yes, how do you think it has affected your health?
   muscle tension ( ) anxiety ( ) insomnia ( ) irritability
   ( ) other _____

8. Is there a particular area of the body where you are experiencing tension, stiffness, or other discomfort?   Yes   No
   If yes, please identify _____

9. Do you have any particular goals in mind for this massage session?   Yes   No

   If yes, please explain _____

In order to plan a massage session that is safe and effective, we need some general information about your medical history.

10. Are you currently under medical supervision?   Yes   No
    If yes, please explain _____

11. Are you currently taking any medication?   Yes   No
    If yes, please list _____

(1 of 2)

12. Please check any condition listed below that applies to you:

_____ contagious skin condition	_____ joint disorder
_____ open sores or wounds	rheumatoid arthritis
_____ easy bruising	_____ osteoporosis
_____ recent accident or injury	_____ epilepsy
_____ current fever	_____ headaches
_____ swollen glands	_____ cancer
_____ allergies	_____ epilepsy
_____ heart condition	_____ diabetes
_____ high or low blood pressure	_____ decreased sensation
_____ circulatory disorder	_____ recent surgery
_____ non-contagious skin condition	_____ joint disorder
varicose veins	_____ artificial joint
atherosclerosis	
phlebitis	

Comments:

_____

_____

_____

13. For women: Are you pregnant?   Yes   No
    If yes, how many months? _____

14. Is there anything else about your health history that you think would be useful for your massage practitioner to know to plan a safe and effective massage session for you?

_____

_____

_____

_____

I understand that these massage sessions are for general wellness purposes and that I should see a doctor or other appropriate health care provider for diagnosis and treatment of any suspected medical problem. Also, that it is my responsibility to keep my massage practitioner informed of any changes in my health, and any medications that I may begin to take in the future.

Signature _____ Date _____

(2 of 2)

Health History for Massage Therapy Treatment

Name _____ Date of initial visit _____

Address _____ Phone _____

Occupation _____ Date of birth _____

Name of physician _____ Phone _____

Other health care provider _____

Referred by _____

1. Have you had massage therapy before?   Yes   No

2. For women: Are you pregnant?   Yes   No
   If yes, how many months? _____

3. Do you have any difficulty lying on your front, back, or side?   Yes   No
   If yes, please explain _____

4. Do you have allergic reactions to oils, lotions, ointments, liniments, or other substances put on your skin?   Yes   No
   If yes, please explain _____

5. Do you wear contact lenses ( ) dentures ( ) a hearing aid ( )?

6. Do you sit for long hours at a workstation, computer, or driving?
   Yes   No
   If yes, please describe _____

7. Do you perform any repetitive movement in your work, sports, or hobby?
   Yes   No
   If yes, please describe _____

8. Do you experience stress in your work, family, or other aspect of your life?   Yes   No

   How would you describe your stress level?
   Low   Medium   High   Very high

   If high, how do you think stress has effected your health?
   muscle tension ( ) anxiety ( ) insomnia ( ) irritability
   ( ) other _____

9. Is there a particular area of the body where you are experiencing tension, stiffness, or other discomfort?   Yes   No
   If yes, please identify _____

In order to plan a massage session that is safe and effective, we need some general information about your medical history.

10. Are you currently under medical supervision?   Yes   No
    If yes, please explain _____

11. Are you currently taking any medication?   Yes   No
    If yes, please list _____

12. Please check any condition listed below that applies to you:

_____ Skin condition (e.g., acne, rash, skin cancer, allergy, easy bruising, contagious condition)

_____ Allergies

_____ Recent accident, injury, or surgery (e.g., whiplash, sprain, broken bone, deep bruise)

_____ Muscular problems (e.g., tension, cramping, chronic soreness)

_____ Joint problems (e.g., osteoarthritis, rheumatoid arthritis, gout, hypermobile joints, recent dislocation)

_____ Lymphatic condition (e.g., swollen glands, nodes removed, lymphoma, lymphedema)

_____ Circulatory or blood conditions (e.g., atherosclerosis, varicose veins, phlebitis, arrhythmias, high or low blood pressure, heart disease, recent heart attack or stroke, anemia)

_____ Neurologic condition (e.g., numbness or tingling in any area of the body, sciatica, damage from stroke, epilepsy, multiple sclerosis, cerebral palsy)

_____ Digestive conditions (e.g., ulcers)

_____ Immune system conditions (e.g., chronic fatigue, HIV/AIDS)

_____ Skeletal conditions (e.g., osteoporosis, bone cancer, spinal injury)

_____ Headaches (e.g., tension, PMS, migraines)

_____ Cancer

_____ Emotional difficulties (e.g., depression, anxiety, panic attacks, eating disorder, psychotic episodes). Are you currently seeing a psychotherapist for this condition?   Yes   No

_____ Previous surgery, disease, or other medical condition that may be affecting you now (e.g., polio, previous heart attack or stroke, previously broken bones)

Comments:

_____

_____

_____

13. Is there anything else about your health history that you think would be useful for your massage practitioner to know to plan a safe and effective massage session for you?

_____

_____

_____

14. Has your physician or other health care provider recommended massage for any of the conditions listed above?   Yes   No
If yes, please explain _____

15. Do you have any particular goals in mind for this massage session related to any of the conditions mentioned above?   Yes   No
If yes, please explain _____

I understand that I should see a doctor or other appropriate health care provider for diagnosis and treatment of any suspected medical problem. It may be beneficial for my massage practitioner to speak to my doctor about my medical condition to determine how massage may help the healing process, and to avoid worsening the condition. I will be asked for permission to contact my doctor, if the massage practitioner thinks that it might be useful. I also understand that it is my responsibility to keep my massage practitioner informed of any changes in my health, and any medications that I may begin to take in the future.

Signature _____ Date _____

Intake Form for Outreach Events

Massage Therapist _____ Date _____

WELCOME! To ensure a safe and healthy experience of massage therapy, please tell your massage therapist the following:

▶ If you have a medical condition that may be adversely affected by massage
▶ If you are taking medication that affects circulation or ability to sense pain
▶ If you have had a serious illness or injury recently
▶ If you are pregnant
▶ Any areas the massage therapist should avoid

Your signature below indicates that you have given the massage therapist the information requested and give your consent to receive massage. The massage therapist and the sponsoring organization are not responsible for unforeseeable adverse reactions to the massage received.

Name   Time

1. _____   _____
    print   signature

2. _____   _____
    print   signature

3. _____   _____
    print   signature

4. _____   _____
    print   signature

5. _____   _____
    print   signature

6. _____   _____
    print   signature

7. _____   _____
    print   signature

8. _____   _____
    print   signature

9. _____   _____
    print   signature

10. _____   _____
    print   signature

Form # _____ MT Initials _____

NATIONAL CERTIFICATION BOARD FOR THERAPEUTIC MASSAGE AND BODYWORK CODE OF ETHICS

(as approved Dec. 5, 2005)

Massage and Bodywork Therapists shall act in a manner that justifies public trust and confidence, enhances the reputation of the profession, and safeguards the interest of individual clients. To this end, massage and bodywork therapists in the exercise of accountability will:

I. Have a sincere commitment to provide the highest quality of care to those who seek their professional services.

II. Represent their qualifications honestly, including education and professional affiliations, and provide only those services that they are qualified to perform.

III. Accurately inform clients, other health care practitioners, and the public of the scope and limitations of their discipline.

IV. Acknowledge the limitations of and contraindications for massage and bodywork and refer clients to appropriate health professionals.

V. Provide treatment only where there is reasonable expectation that it will be advantageous to the client.

VI. Consistently maintain and improve professional knowledge and competence, striving for professional excellence through regular assessment of personal and professional strengths and weaknesses and through continued education training.

VII. Conduct their business and professional activities with honesty and integrity, and respect the inherent worth of all persons.

VIII. Refuse to unjustly discriminate against clients or health professionals.

IX. Safeguard the confidentiality of all client information, unless disclosure is required by law or necessary for the protection of the public.

X. Respect the client's right to treatment with informed and voluntary consent. The certified practitioner will obtain and record the informed consent of the client, or client's advocate, before providing treatment. This consent may be written or verbal.

XI. Respect the client's right to refuse, modify, or terminate treatment regardless of prior consent given.

XII. Provide draping and treatment in a way that ensures the safety, comfort, and privacy of the client.

XIII. Exercise the right to refuse to treat any person or part of the body for just and reasonable cause.

XIV. Refrain, under all circumstances, from initiating or engaging in any sexual conduct, sexual activities, or sexualizing behavior involving a client, even if the client attempts to sexualize the relationship.

XV. Avoid any interest, activity, or influence which might be in conflict with the practitioner's obligation to act in the best interests of the client or the profession.

XVI. Respect the client's boundaries with regard to privacy, disclosure, exposure, emotional expression, beliefs, and the client's reasonable expectations of professional behavior. Practitioners will respect the client's autonomy.

XVII. Refuse any gifts or benefits that are intended to influence a referral, decision, or treatment, or that are purely for personal gain and not for the good of the client.

XVIII. Follow all policies, procedures, guidelines, regulations, codes, and requirements promulgated by the National Certification Board for Therapeutic Massage and Bodywork.

NATIONAL CERTIFICATION BOARD FOR THERAPEUTIC MASSAGE AND BODYWORK STANDARDS OF PRACTICE

Adopted February 6, 2000; Implemented September 15, 2000; Updated November 4, 2006

Background

The mission of the National Certification Board for Therapeutic Massage and Bodywork (NCBTMB) is to foster high standards of ethical and professional practice in the delivery of services through a recognized credible certification program that assures the competency of practitioners of therapeutic massage and bodywork.

The NCBTMB developed the Standards of Practice to ensure that practitioners who have attained the credential Nationally Certified in Therapeutic Massage and Bodywork or Nationally Certified in Therapeutic Massage are aware of the existence of high standards of practice for the profession and are committed to upholding those standards. Also, the Standards of Practice are meant to assist members of the general public, including consumers, other health care professionals, and State and Municipal Regulatory Agencies or Boards with understanding the duties and responsibilities of NCBTMB certificants and applicants for certification.

The NCBTMB developed and adopted the Standards of Practice to provide certificants and applicants for certification with a clear statement of the expectations of professional conduct and level of practice afforded the public in, among other things, the following areas: Professionalism, Legal and Ethical Requirements, Confidentiality, Business Practices, Roles and Boundaries, and Prevention of Sexual Misconduct. Before the NCBTMB Board of Directors granted final approval of the document, representatives of the certificant population and key stakeholders of the NCBTMB ratified the Standards of Practice.

Copyright © 2005 NCBTMB National Certification Board for Therapeutic Massage and Bodywork

Preamble

These Standards of Practice for the touch therapies profession are the guiding principles by which certificants and applicants for certification conduct their day-to-day responsibilities within their scope of practice. These principles help to assure that all professional behaviors are conducted in the most ethical, compassionate, and responsible manner. Through these Standards of Practice, NCBTMB seeks to establish and uphold the highest standards, traditions, and principles of the practices that constitute the profession of therapeutic massage and bodywork. The Standards are statements of enforceable guidelines for professional conduct. The Standards are stated in observable and measurable terms and are intended as minimum levels of practice to which each certificant and applicant for certification is held accountable. Upon submission of the application for the National Certification Examinations (NCETMB and/or NCETM), each applicant must agree to uphold and abide by the NCBTMB Code of Ethics, Standards of Practice, and applicable policies. An applicant's or certificant's failure to comply with the Code of Ethics and the Standards of Practice as provided herein constitutes professional misconduct and may result in sanctions, or other appropriate disciplinary actions, including the suspension or revocation of certification.

NCBTMB certificants and applicants for certification are obligated to report unethical behavior and violations of the Code of Ethics and the Standards of Practice, performed by other NCBTMB certificants and applicants for certification to NCBTMB.

These Standards of Practice reflect NCBTMB's clear commitment to assuring that NCBTMB certificants provide an optimal level of service and strive for excellence in their practice. This includes remaining in good standing with NCBTMB, making a commitment, without limitation, to continued personal and professional growth through self-assessment and continuing education, seeking support from peers and experienced professionals to provide optimal service to themselves and others, serving as a mentor, and understanding and accepting that personal and professional actions reflect on the integrity of the therapeutic massage and bodywork profession and NCBTMB. Each certificant and applicant for certification is responsible for showing and maintaining professional compliance with the Standards of Practice. As the therapeutic massage and bodywork profession evolves, so, too, will the Standards of Practice. The Standards of Practice are, therefore, a live and dynamic document and subject to revision in keeping with the changing demands and expectations of the therapeutic massage and bodywork profession.

Standards of Practice

Standard I: Professionalism

The certificant or applicant must provide optimal levels of professional therapeutic massage and bodywork services and demonstrate excellence in practice by promoting healing and well-being through responsible, compassionate, and respectful touch. In his/her professional role the certificant or applicant shall:

  a. adhere to the NCBTMB Code of Ethics, Standards of Practice, policies, and procedures
  b. comply with the peer review process conducted by the NCBTMB Ethics and Standards Committee regarding any alleged violations of the NCBTMB Code of Ethics and Standards of Practice

   c. conduct him/herself in a manner in all settings meriting the respect of the public and other professionals

   d. treat each client with respect, dignity, and worth

   e. use professional verbal, nonverbal, and written communications

   f. provide an environment that is safe and comfortable for the client and which, at a minimum, meets all legal requirements for health and safety

   g. use standard precautions to ensure professional hygienic practices and maintain a level of personal hygiene appropriate for practitioners in the therapeutic setting

   h. wear clothing that is clean, modest, and professional

   i. obtain voluntary and informed consent from the client prior to initiating the session

   j. if applicable, conduct an accurate needs assessment, develop a plan of care with the client, and update the plan as needed

   k. use appropriate draping to protect the client's physical and emotional privacy

   l. be knowledgeable of his/her scope of practice and practice only within these limitations

   m. refer to other professionals when in the best interest of the client and practitioner

   n. seek other professional advice when needed

   o. respect the traditions and practices of other professionals and foster collegial relationships

   p. not falsely impugn the reputation of any colleague

   q. use the initials NCBTMB to designate his/her professional ability and competency to practice therapeutic massage and bodywork, or the initials NCTM to designate his/her professional ability and competency to practice therapeutic massage only

   r. remain in good standing with NCBTMB and maintain NCBTMB certification

   s. understand that the NCBTMB certificate may be displayed prominently in the certificant's principal place of practice

   t. use the NCBTMB logo and certification number on business cards, brochures, advertisements, and stationery only in a manner that is within established NCBTMB guidelines

   u. not duplicate the NCBTMB certificate for purposes other than verification of the practitioner's credentials

   v. immediately return the certificate to NCBTMB if certification is revoked

   w. inform NCBTMB of any changes or additions to information included in his/her application for NCBTMB certification or recertification.

Standard II: Legal and Ethical Requirements

The certificant or applicant must comply with all the legal requirements in applicable jurisdictions regulating the profession of therapeutic massage and bodywork. In his/her professional role the certificant or applicant shall:

   a. obey all applicable local, state, and federal laws

   b. refrain from any behavior that results in illegal, discriminatory, or unethical actions

   c. accept responsibility for his/her own actions

   d. report to the proper authorities any alleged violations of the law by other certificants or applicants for certification

   e. maintain accurate and truthful records

f. report to NCBTMB any criminal conviction of, or plea of guilty, nolo contendere, or no contest to, a crime in any jurisdiction (other than a minor traffic offense) by him/herself and by other certificants or applicants for certification

g. report to NCBTMB any pending civil litigation in which the basis of the complaint against him/herself or another certificant or applicant is alleged negligence, malpractice, lack of professional competence, or sexual misconduct and the resulting resolution of such litigation

h. report to NCBTMB any pending complaints in any state or jurisdiction against his/her professional conduct or competence, or that of another certificant, and the resulting resolution of such complaint

i. respect existing publishing rights and copyright laws, including, but not limited to, those that apply to NCBTMB's copyright-protected examinations.

Standard III: Confidentiality

The certificant or applicant shall respect the confidentiality of client information and safeguard all records. In his/her professional role the certificant or applicant shall:

a. protect the confidentiality of the client's identity in social conversations, all advertisements, and any and all other matters unless disclosure of identifiable information is requested by the client in writing, is medically necessary, or is required by law

b. protect the interests of clients who are minors or who are unable to give voluntary consent by securing permission from an appropriate third party or guardian

c. solicit only information that is relevant to the professional client/therapist relationship

d. share pertinent information about the client with third parties when required by law

e. maintain the client files for a minimum period of four years

f. store and dispose of client files in a secure manner.

Standard IV: Business Practices

The certificant or applicant shall practice with honesty, integrity, and lawfulness in the business of therapeutic massage and bodywork. In his/her professional role the certificant or applicant shall:

a. provide a physical setting that is safe and meets all applicable legal requirements for health and safety

b. maintain adequate and customary liability insurance

c. maintain adequate progress notes for each client session, if applicable

d. accurately and truthfully inform the public of services provided

e. honestly represent all professional qualifications and affiliations

f. promote his/her business with integrity and avoid potential and actual conflicts of interest

g. advertise in a manner that is honest, dignified, and representative of services that can be delivered and remains consistent with the NCBTMB Code of Ethics and Standards of Practice

h. advertise in a manner that is not misleading to the public by, among other things, the use of sensational, sexual, or provocative language and pictures to promote business

    i. comply with all laws regarding sexual harassment

    j. not exploit the trust and dependency of others, including clients and employees/co-workers

    k. display/discuss a schedule of fees in advance of the session that is clearly understood by the client or potential client

    l. make financial arrangements in advance that are clearly understood by and safeguard the best interests of the client or consumer

    m. follow acceptable accounting practices

    n. file all applicable municipal, state, and federal taxes

    o. maintain accurate financial records, contracts and legal obligations, appointment records, tax reports, and receipts for at least four years.

Standard V: Roles and Boundaries

The certificant or applicant shall adhere to ethical boundaries and perform the professional roles designed to protect both the client and the practitioner, and safeguard the therapeutic value of the relationship. In his/her professional role the certificant or applicant shall:

    a. recognize his/her personal limitations and practice only within these limitations

    b. recognize his/her influential position with the client and not exploit the relationship for personal or other gain

    c. recognize and limit the impact of transference and counter-transference between the client and the certificant

    d. avoid dual or multidimensional relationships that could impair professional judgment or result in exploitation of the client or employees and/or coworkers

    e. not engage in any sexual activity with a client

    f. acknowledge and respect the client's freedom of choice in the therapeutic session

    g. respect the client's right to refuse the therapeutic session

    h. refrain from practicing under the influence of alcohol, drugs, or any illegal substances (with the exception of a prescribed dosage of prescription medication which does not significantly impair the certificant)

    i. have the right to refuse and/or terminate the service to a client who is abusive or under the influence of alcohol, drugs, or any illegal substance.

Standard VI: Prevention of Sexual Misconduct

The certificant or applicant shall refrain from any behavior that sexualizes, or appears to sexualize, the client/therapist relationship. The certificant or applicant recognizes the intimacy of the therapeutic relationship may activate practitioner and/or client needs and/or desires that weaken objectivity and may lead to sexualizing the therapeutic relationship. In his/her professional role the certificant or applicant shall:

    a. refrain from participating in a sexual relationship or sexual conduct with the client, whether consensual or otherwise, from the beginning of the client/therapist relationship and for a minimum of six months after the termination of the client/therapist relationship

    b. in the event that the client initiates sexual behavior, clarify the purpose of the therapeutic session, and, if such conduct does not cease, terminate or refuse the session

    c. recognize that sexual activity with clients, students, employees, supervisors, or trainees is prohibited even if consensual

d. not touch the genitalia

e. only perform therapeutic treatments beyond the normal narrowing of the ear canal and normal narrowing of the nasal passages as indicated in the plan of care and only after receiving informed voluntary written consent

f. only perform therapeutic treatments in the oropharynx as indicated in the plan of care and only after receiving informed voluntary consent

g. only perform therapeutic treatments into the anal canal as indicated in the plan of care and only after receiving informed voluntary written consent

h. only provide therapeutic breast massage as indicated in the plan of care and only after receiving informed voluntary consent from the client.

Glossary of Terms Used in This Document

Acceptable Accounting Procedures: Rules, conventions, standards, and procedures that are widely accepted among financial accountants.

Boundary: A boundary is a limit that separates one person from another. Its function is to protect the integrity of each person.

Competency: Study and development of a particular professional knowledge base and skills associated with and applied in practice within that knowledge base.

Counter-transference: A practitioner's unresolved feelings and issues which are unconsciously transferred to the client.

Dignity: The quality or state of being worthy, honored or esteemed.

Dual Relationships: An alliance in addition to the client/therapist relationship, such as social, familial, business, or any other relationship that is outside the therapeutic relationship.

Genitalia, Female: Labia majora, labia minora, clitoris, and vaginal orifice.

Genitalia, Male: Testes, penis, and scrotum.

Impugn: To assail by words or arguments, oppose or attack as false.

Integrity: Honesty. Firm adherence to a code of values.

Multidimensional Relationships: Overlapping relationships in which therapist and client share an alliance, in addition to the therapeutic relationship. Multidimensional relationships suggest a more complex interweaving of roles.

Progress Notes: Notes written, by a practitioner certified by NCBTMB, and kept in a separate client file that indicates the date of the session, areas of complaint as stated by client, and observations made and actions taken by the practitioner.

Scope of Practice: The minimum standards necessary for safe and effective practice and the parameters of practice determined by the certificant's professional training and education, and, when applicable, regulatory bodies.

Sexual Activity: Any verbal and/or nonverbal behavior for the purpose of soliciting, receiving, or giving sexual gratification.

Sexual Harassment: Sexual harassment consists of unwelcome sexual advances, requests for sexual favors, and other verbal or physical conduct of a sexual nature when: 1. Submission to such conduct is made either explicitly or implicitly a term or condition of an individual's employment; 2. Submission to, or rejection of, such conduct by an individual is used as the basis for employment decisions affecting such individuals; or 3. Such conduct has the purpose or effect of unreasonably interfering with an individual's work performance or creating an intimidating, hostile, or offensive working environment.

Transference: The displacement or transfer of feelings, thoughts, and behaviors originally related to a significant person, such as a parent, onto someone else, such as a massage therapist (or doctor, psychotherapist, teacher, spiritual advisor).

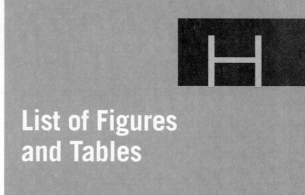

List of Figures and Tables

CHAPTER 1: A CAREER IN MASSAGE THERAPY

Figures

Table

CHAPTER 2: THE MASSAGE THERAPY PROFESSION

Figures

Tables

CHAPTER 3: A HISTORY OF MASSAGE AS A VOCATION

Figures

CHAPTER 4: PERSONAL DEVELOPMENT AND PROFESSIONALISM

Figures

Table

CHAPTER 5: SOCIAL AND COMMUNICATION SKILLS

Figures

References are the sources of quotes and specific content in the chapters and **Additional Resources** are valuable sources for further information.

CHAPTER 1

References

American Massage Therapy Association. (2004). *Consumer fact sheet*. Evanston, IL.

American Massage Therapy Association. (2004, May/June). Study shows massage ranks first among spa treatments. *Hands-On*, p. 1.

Barnes, P.M., Powell-Griner, E., McFann, K., & Nahin, R. (2004, May 27). *Complementary and alternative medicine use among adults: United States, 2002*. (Advance Data *Report No. 343*). Hyattsville, MD: U.S. Department of Health and Human Services, Centers for Disease Control and Prevention.

Huitt, W.G. (2002). *Maslow's hierarchy of needs*. Retrieved March 2007 from http://chiron.valdosta.edu/whuitt/col/regsys/maslow.html

McPherson, F., & Schwenka, M.A. (2004). Use of complementary and alternative therapies among active duty soldiers, military retirees, and family members at a military hospital. *Military Medicine, 169,* 354–357.

National Center for Complementary and Alternative Medicine. (2004). *NCCAM Newsletter, 11*(3).

White House Commission on Complementary and Alternative Medicine Policy. (2002). *Final report*. Washington, DC: Department of Health and Human Services. Available at www.whccamp.hhs.gov

Additional Resources

American Massage Therapy Association (www.amtamassage.org)
Associated Bodywork and Massage Professionals (www.abmp.com)
Hospital-Based Massage Network (www.hbmn.com)
International SPA Association (ISPA) (www.experienceispa.com)

CHAPTER 2

Additional Resources

American Hospital Association (www.aha.org)
American Massage Therapy Association (www.amtamassage.org)
American Organization of Bodywork Therapies of Asia (www.aobta.org)
American Polarity Therapy Association (www.polaritytherapy.org)
Associated Bodywork and Massage Professionals (www.abmp.com)
Bonnie Prudden Myotherapy® (www.bonnieprudden.com)
Collaboration for Healthcare Renewal Foundation (www.thecollaboration.org)
Commission on Massage Therapy Accreditation (www.comta.org)
Hospital-Based Massage Network (www.hbmn.com)
Integrated Healthcare Policy Consortium (http://ihpc.info)
International Association of Infant Massage (www.iaim.net)
International Institute of Reflexology (www.reflexology-usa.net)
International Spa Association (www.experienceispa.com)
Jin Shin Do® Foundation (www.jinshindo.org)
Massage Therapy Foundation (www.amtafoundation.org)
National Association of Nurse Massage Therapists (www.nanmt.org)
National Certification Board for Therapeutic Massage and Bodywork (www.ncbtmb.org).
National Certification Commission for Acupuncture and Oriental Medicine (www.nccaom.org)
National Commission for Certifying Agencies (www.noca.org/ncca)
Rolf Institute for Structural Integration (www.rolf.org)
Touch Research Institute (www.miami.edu/touch-research.html)
United States Department of Education (www.ed.gov)
White House Commission on Complementary and Alternative Medicine Policy (www.whccamp.hhs.gov)

CHAPTER 3

References

AMTA National Historian's Report. (1987, Fall). AMTA membership 1943–1987. *Massage Therapy Journal*, pp. 12–15.

Armstrong, D., & Armstong, E.M. (1991). *The great American medicine show: Being an illustrated history of hucksters, healers, health evangelists, and heroes from Plymouth Rock to the present.* New York: Prentice Hall.

Baumgartner, A.J. (1947). *Massage in athletics.* Minneapolis, MN: Burgess.

Benjamin, P.J. (2002). Breast massage: Old becomes new again. *Massage Therapy Journal, 41* (1), 154–158.

Benjamin, P.J. (2001). Genuine Swedish massage applied to slim down. *Massage Therapy Journal, 40* (2), 152–154.

Benjamin, P.J. (1986, Fall). National historian's report: Annual convention programs. *Massage Therapy Journal*, pp. 8–9.

Calvert, R. (2002). *The history of massage: An illustrated survey from around the world.* Rochester, VT: Healing Arts Press.

Johnson, W. (1866). *The anatriptic art: A history of the art termed anatripsis by Hippocrates, tripsis by Galen, frictio by Celsus, manipulation by Beveridge, and medical rubbing in ordinary language, from earliest times to the present day.* London: Simpkin, Marshall & Co.

Ellison, M.A. (1909). *A manual for students of massage* (3rd ed.). London: Baillere, Tindall and Cox.

Erz, A.A. (c. 1924). Ad for book *The medical question: The truth about official medicine and why we must have medical freedom*. Butler, NJ: Nature Cure Publishing.

Frierwood, H.T. (1953, September–October). The place of health service in the total YMCA program. *Journal of Physical Education*.

Graham, D. (1902). *A treatise on massage: Its history, mode of application and effects* (3rd ed.). Philadelphia: Lippincott.

Haggard, H.W. (1932). *The lame, the halt, and the blind: The vital role of medicine in the history of civilization*. New York: Blue Ribbon Books.

Joya, M. (1958). *Mock Joya's things Japanese*. Tokyo: Tokyo News Service.

Kellogg, J.H. (1895). *The art of massage: Its physiological effects and therapeutic applications*. Battle Creek, MI: Modern Medicine Publishing.

Livingston, H., & Maroni, A. (1945). *Everyday beauty culture*. Bloomington, IL: McKnight & McKnight.

McKenzie, R.T. (1915). *Exercise in education and medicine* (2nd ed.). Philadelphia: Saunders.

Mitchell, S.W. (1877). *Fat and blood and how to make them*. Philadelphia: J. B. Lippincott & Co.

M'Lean, T. (1914). *Picturesque representations of the dress and manners of the Chinese*. London: Howlett & Brimmer.

Murphy, M.C. (1914). *Athletic training*. New York: Scribner's.

Nissen, H. (1889). *A manual of instruction for giving Swedish movement and massage treatment*. Philadelphia: F.A. Davis.

Perrone, B., Stockel, H. H., & Krueger, V. (1989). *Medicine women, curanderas, and women doctors*. Norman: University of Oklahoma Press.

Pollard, D.W. (1902). *Massage in training*. Unpublished thesis, International Young Men's Christian Association Training School, Springfield, MA.

Puderbach, P. (1925). *The massage operator*. Butler, NJ: Dr. Benedict Lust.

Roth, M. (1851). *The prevention and cure of many chronic diseases by movements*. London: John Churchhill.

Taylor, G. (1900). *Health by exercise ... showing what exercises to take ... including the process of massage*. New York: The Improved Movement Cure Institute. (Original work published 1860)

Thomas, N. (2003). *Cook: The extraordinary voyages of Captain James Cook*. New York: Walker & Company.

Williams, R.J. (1943). Second annual national YMCA health service clinic. *Journal of Physical Education, 41*.

Zhang, Y. (Director). (2000). *Shower* [Film]. Sony Pictures Entertainment, Inc.

CHAPTER 4

References

American heritage dictionary of the English language (4th ed.). (2000). New York: Houghton Mifflin.

Bloom, B. (Ed.). (1956). *Taxonomy of educational objectives: Handbook I. Cognitive domain*. New York: Longman.

Chuckrow, R. (1998). *The tai chi book: Refining and enjoying a lifetime of practice*. Boston: YMAA Publication Center.

Chuen, L.K. (1991). *The way of energy: Mastering the Chinese art of internal strength with chi kung exercise*. New York: Simon & Schuster.

Csikszentmihalyi, M. (1997). *Finding flow: The psychology of engagement with everyday life*. New York: Basic Books.

Goleman, D. (1995). *Emotional intelligence: Why it can matter more than IQ*. New York: Bantam Books.

Greene, E., & Goodrich-Dunn, B. (2004). *The psychology of the body*. Philadelphia: Lippincott Williams & Wilkins.

Hall, S. (1991). *Basic biomechanics*. St. Louis, MO: Mosby.

Heckler, R.S. (1997). *Holding the center: Sanctuary in a time of confusion*. Berkeley, CA: Frog.

Kagan, J., Snidman, N., Arcus, D., & Reznick, J.S. (1998). *Galen's prophecy: Temperament in human nature*. Boulder, CO: Westview Press.

Levine, M. (2002). *A mind at a time*. New York: Simon & Schuster.

Makely, S. (2005). *Professionalism in health care: A primer for career success* (2nd ed.). Upper Saddle River, NJ: Prentice Hall.

McCormick, A.R., & McCormick, M.D. (1997). *Horse sense and the human heart: What horses can teach us about trust, bonding, creativity and spirituality*. Deerfield Beach, FL: Health Communications.

Mipham, S. (2003). *Turning the mind into an ally*. New York: Penguin Putnam.

Schlosberg, S. (2005). *The ultimate workout log*. Boston: Houghton Mifflin Company.

Simpkins, C.A., & Simpkins, A. (2000). *Simple Confucianism: A guide to living virtuously*. Boston: Tuttle.

Additional Resources

National Heart, Lung, and Blood Institute (www.nhlbisupport.com/bmi/bmicalc.htm)

CHAPTER 5

References

Benjamin, B. E., & Sohnen-Moe, C. (2003) *The ethics of touch*. Tucson, AZ: SMA.

Bixler, S., & Dugan L. S. (2001). *5 steps to professional presence: How to project confidence, competence, and credibility at work*. Avon, MA: Adams Media Corporation.

Booher, D. (1994). *Communicate with confidence: How to say it right the first time and every time*. New York: McGraw-Hill

Cole, K. (2002). *The complete idiot's guide to clear communication*. Indianapolis, IN: Alpha.

Hahn, P. R. (2003). *The everything writing well book: Master the written word and communicate clearly*. Avon, MA: Adams Media Corporation.

McIntosh, N. (1999). *The educated heart: Professional guidelines for massage therapists, bodyworkers and movement teachers*. Memphis, TN: Decatur Bainbridge Press.

CHAPTER 6

References

Associated Bodywork and Massage Professionals. (2001). *Successful business handbook*. Evergreen, CO: Author.

American Massage Therapy Association. (2002). *The business of massage*. Evanston, IL: Author.

Benjamin, P.J. (2008). *Tappan's handbook of healing massage techniques*. Upper Saddle River, NJ: Prentice Hall.

Biel, A. (2005). *Trail guide to the body: How to locate muscles, bones, and more* (3rd ed.). Boulder, CO: Books of Discovery.

Chaitow, L. (1997). *Palpation skills: Assessment and diagnosis through touch*. New York: Churchill Livingston.

Greenman, P. (1989). *Principles of manual medicine*. Baltimore: Williams & Wilkins.

Holey, E., & Cook, E. (2003). *Evidence-based therapeutic massage: A practical guide for therapists*. London: Churchill Livingston.

Hoppenfeld, S. (1976). *Physical examination of the spine and extremities*. Upper Saddle River, NJ: Prentice Hall.

Lowe, W. (2001). *Functional assessment in massage therapy* (3rd ed.). Sisters, OR: Orthopedic Massage Education & Research Institute (www.omeri.com).

Lowe, W. (2004). *Orthopedic massage: Theory and technique*. St. Louis, MO, Mosby.

Rattray, L., & Ludwig, L. (2000). *Clinical massage therapy: Understanding, assessing, and treating over 70 conditions*. Toronto: Talus Incorporated.

Sohnen-Moe, C.M. (1997). *Business mastery* (3rd ed.). Tucson, AZ: Sohnen-Moe Associates.

Thompson, D.L. (2002). *Hands heal: Communication, documentation, and insurance billing for manual therapists* (2nd ed.). Philadelphia: Lippincott Williams & Wilkins.

Yates, J. (2004). *A physician's guide to therapeutic massage* (3rd ed.). Toronto: Curties-Overzet.

CHAPTER 7

References

Associated Bodywork and Massage Professionals. (2001). *Successful business handbook*. Evergreen, CO: Author.

American Massage Therapy Association. (2002). *The business of massage*. Evanston, IL: Author.

Sohnen-Moe, C. M. (1997). *Business mastery* (3rd ed.). Tucson, AZ: Sohnen-Moe Associates.

Thompson, D. L. (2005). *Hands heal: Communication, documentation, and insurance billing for manual therapists* (3rd ed.). Philadelphia: Lippincott Williams & Wilkins.

Additional Resources

U.S. Department of Health and Human Services, HIPAA Privacy Rules (www.hhs.gov/ocr/hipaa)

CHAPTER 8

References

Benjamin, B. E., & Sohnen-Moe C. (2003). *The ethics of touch*. Tucson, AZ: SMA.

Purtilo, R. (1993). *Ethical dimensions in the health professions* (2nd ed.). Philadelphia: W. B. Saunders.

Taylor, K. (1995). *The ethics of caring*. Santa Cruz, CA: Hanford Mead.

Additional Resources

American Massage Therapy Association (www.amtamassage.org)

American Organization of Bodywork Therapies of Asia (www.aobta.org)

Associated Bodywork & Massage Professionals (www.abmp.com)

National Certification Board for Therapeutic Massage & Bodywork (www.ncbtmb.org)

National Certification Commission for Acupuncture and Oriental Medicine (www.nccaom.org)

CHAPTER 9

References

Benjamin, B. E., & Sohnen-Moe, C. (2003). *The ethics of touch*. Tucson, AZ: SMA.

Greene, E., & Goodrich-Dunn B. (2004). *The psychology of the body*. Philadelphia: Lippincott Williams & Wilkins.

Kisch, R. M. (1998). *Beyond technique: The hidden dimensions of bodywork*. Dayton, OH: BLHY Growth Publications.

McIntosh, N. (1999). *The educated heart: Professional guidelines for massage therapists, bodyworkers, and movement teachers*. Memphis, TN: Decatur Bainbridge Press.

Additional Resources

HIPAA Guidelines (www.hhs.gov/ocr/hipaa)

National Certification Board for Therapeutic Massage and Bodywork (www.ncbtmb.org)

CHAPTER 10

References

Benjamin, B.E., & Sohnen-Moe, C. (2003). *The ethics of touch*. Tucson, AZ: SMA.

Federal Trade Commission. (1980). *FTC guides concerning use of endorsements and testimonials in advertising*. Retrieved December 2, 2005 from www.ftc.gov/bcp/guides/ensorse.htm.

Federal Trade Commission. (1983). *FTC statement on deception*. Retrieved January 2, 2006 from www.ftc.gov/bcp/policystmt/ad-decept. htm

Federal Trade Commission. (1984). *FTC policy statement regarding advertising substantiation*. Retrieved January 3, 2006 from www. ftc. gov/bcp/ guides/ ad3subst. htm

Federal Trade Commission. (2000). *Guides against bait advertising*. Retrieved January 2, 2006 from www. ftc. gov/ bcp/ guides/ baitads-gd. htm

National Certification Board for Therapeutic Massage and Bodywork. (2001). Code of ethics. Retrieved January 5, 2006 from www.ncbtmb.com/handbooks/2002/code_of_ethics.htm

U. S. Copyright Office. (2000). *Circular 1: Copyright basics*. Retrieved January 9, 2006 from www.copyright.gov/circs/circ1.html

Additional Resources

Better Business Bureau (www.bbb.org)

Federal Trade Commission (www.ftc.gov)

Internal Revenue Service (www.irs.gov)

National Certification Board for Therapeutic Massage and Bodywork (www.ncbtmb.com)

U.S. Copyright Office (www.copyright.gov)

U.S. Patent and Trademark Office (www.uspto.gov)

CHAPTER 11

References

Makely, S. (2005). *Professionalism in health care: A primer for career success* (2nd ed.). Upper Saddle River, NJ: Prentice Hall.

Mariotti, S. (2007). *Entrepreneurship: Starting and operating a small business.* Upper Saddle River, NJ: Prentice Hall.

Additional Resources

U.S. Equal Employment Opportunity Commission (www.eeoc.gov)
Internal Revenue Service (www.irs.gov)
National Employers Association (neasa-sa.com)
National Labor Relations Board (www.nlrb.gov)

CHAPTER 12

References

American Massage Therapy Association. (2005). *Massage therapy consumer survey fact sheet.* Evanston, IL: Author.
Internal Revenue Service. (2005). *Business Expenses*, IRS Publication 535.
Internal Revenue Service. (2006). *Self-Employment Tax*, Schedule SE (Form 1040).
Internal Revenue Service. (2006). *Starting a Business and Keeping Records,* IRS Publication 583.
Internal Revenue Service. (2006). *Tax Withholding and Estimated Tax*, IRS Publication 505.
Internal Revenue Service. (2005). *Your Federal Income Tax—For Individuals*, IRS Publication 17.
Kamoroff, B. B. (2003). *Small time operator: How to start your own business, keep your books, pay your taxes, and stay out of trouble.* Laytonville, CA: Bell Springs Publishing.
Mariotti, S. (2007). *Entrepreneurship: Starting and operating a small business.* Upper Saddle River, NJ: Prentice Hall.

Additional Resources

American Massage Therapy Association (www.amtamassage.org)
Internal Revenue Service (www.irs.gov)
QuickBooks® (www.quickbooks.intuit.com)
U.S. Small Business Administration (www.sba.gov)

Interactive Glossary

This interactive glossary defines terms used in the text and also suggests relationships among terms. Look for the words **See, Compare to,** and **Contrast with,** which designate relationships between certain terms.

Accountability A trait in which individuals accept responsibility for their actions, do not make excuses for repeated mistakes, and apologize sincerely for and correct mistakes that they have made. See *Work ethic.*

Accreditation Recognition awarded to institutions or education programs by a nongovernmental organization that sets standards of excellence; accredited schools have undergone a peer evaluation to confirm that the accreditation standards are met.

Active listening A communication skill that involves reflecting back to the speaker what the listener thinks was said; accomplished by paraphrasing or restating the words to clarify their meaning. Contrast with *Affirmative listening.*

Active range of motion (AROM) Refers to the evaluation of motion at a joint while a person actively moves that joint through its range; observations include degree of motion possible, restrictions or shortening, and any discomfort experienced; used to collect objective information for *goal-oriented planning.* Contrast with *Passive range of motion.*

Advertising A paid public announcement providing information about a product or service to potential customers; ads may be in print or electronic media, or may appear in various places like the side of a pen or a billboard. Contrast with *Promotions.*

Affirmative listening A communication skill that involves letting the speaker know that you are paying attention; accomplished by occasional verbal cues and body language. Contrast with *Active listening.*

Aleiptes A historical term used in ancient Greece to describe the people in a gymnasium who rubbed athletes with oil.

Ammashi A historical term for a practitioner of traditional Japanese massage; occupation for the blind in 19th- and 20th-century Japan.

Assertive behavior A confident, authoritative manner that demands obedience or attention. See *Intervention model.*

Assessment Refers to the practitioner's conclusions from the subjective and objective information gathered during goal-oriented planning; for primary health care providers it includes a diagnosis of the problem; from a wellness perspective it may identify long- and short-term goals for the client; written in the A section of *SOAP notes.*

Athletic masseur A historical term used in the mid-20th century for a trained massage practitioner who worked primarily with athletes; indicates a higher level of training and knowledge than the rubbers of the past. See *Rubbers.*

Attendance An aspect of work ethic reflected in showing up when expected or when scheduled for work. See *Work ethic.*

Bait advertising An attractive but insincere offer to sell a product or service that the advertiser does not intend or want to actually sell; purpose is to generate leads to potential customers, or to sell something else at a higher price, an illegal practice called bait and switch. See *Business ethics.*

Barbershop A personal care business catering to consumers' needs related to grooming hair and nails, and skin care; typically focused on services to men. See *Personal care.*

Bath attendant A historical term used in late 19th and early 20th century Europe and North America describing persons who assisted patrons of public baths and natural healing resorts; included giving a superficial rubdown after a bath.

Beauty salon A personal care business catering to consumers' needs related to grooming hair and nails, and skin care; typically focused on services to women. See *Personal care.*

Biomechanical analysis The examination of the body in motion; takes into account principles of motion and the structure and function of the human body, especially the muscle and skeletal systems; a branch of kinesiology and an important aspect of sports medicine; used to collect objective information for goal-oriented planning. Compare to *Gait analysis.*

Body awareness The ability to sense where your body is in space while at rest and in motion and to coordinate movement with mind; entails an integration of body and mind so that a person exists as an embodied being.

Body charts A diagram of the human figure that is marked by the client to locate problem areas and to indicate the nature of a complaint; offers a visual and kinesthetic way to give subjective information. See *Interview skills.*

Body language Communication through physical presence; includes posture, hand gestures, eye contact, and facial expression.

Body–mind practices Physical exercises useful for improving various aspects of physical fitness with the added benefit of developing coordination, body awareness, concentration, and relaxation; examples are yoga, tai chi, qi gong, and pilates. See *Self-care.*

Bodywork A term coined in the late 20th century to encompass a wide variety of manual therapies including massage, movement integration, structural integration, and energy balancing; the terms massage and bodywork are often used together to describe the occupational field of massage therapy.

Boundaries Borders or limits that define personal and professional space; fences placed around ourselves to preserve our integrity as individuals; good boundaries allow two individuals to meet with integrity without violation of the other's space, but close enough to make a connection. See *Personal boundaries* and *Professional boundaries*.

Boundary crossing A transgression of personal or professional boundaries that may or may not be experienced as harmful. See *Personal boundaries* and *Professional boundaries*.

Boundary violation A transgression of personal or professional boundaries that causes harm; leaves a sense of being violated, which is stronger than feeling annoyed or uncomfortable; personal or professional integrity is compromised in some way. Contrast with *Boundary crossing*.

Business ethics The study of moral behavior relative to commerce and consumers. Contrast with *Professional ethics*.

Business license A document that grants permission to operate a commercial enterprise in a certain legal jurisdiction; allows government agencies to know who is doing business in their area, and can ensure that they are complying with all related laws. Compare to *Massage establishment license*.

Business plan A document that spells out the details of putting a business or practice vision into operation; four major parts: a description of the business, marketing, management, and finances.

CAM An acronym for complementary and alternative medicine.

Cash reserve Money set aside to cover emergencies and deficits in income at certain time periods; recommended to have at least 3 months' fixed costs in reserve when starting a massage practice; should be figured in startup costs. See *Startup costs* and *First-year budget*.

Centered Refers to finding your focal point or point of organization from which being and movement occur and to staying there; has a physical and psychological dimension; opposite is being scattered, off balance, and moving from the periphery. Compare to being *Grounded*.

Certificate program A course of study in a particular subject for which a certificate of completion is awarded. Contrast with *Certification*.

Certification A type of credential given after extensive education in a specific subject and may also include examinations, continuing education, and renewal. Contrast with *Certificate program*.

Chinese medicine clinic A health care facility offering traditional Asian (Chinese) medicine for example, acupuncture, herbal remedies, tuina (Chinese massage), and other therapies based in traditional Chinese medicine. See *Complementary and alternative medicine*.

Chiropractic office A health care facility offering chiropractic medicine. See *Complementary and alternative medicine*.

Clinical reasoning The cognitive process used to plan treatment for a health problem or medical condition; involves problem definition, information collection, data analysis, therapeutic application planning and implementation, and outcomes evaluation. See *Goal-oriented planning*.

Clinical supervision Formal consultation with a specially trained supervisor about problems and ethical issues that come up in the therapeutic relationship; an opportunity for massage therapists to process what is happening in their practices and their experiences with clients.

Club spa A day spa within a fitness facility like a health club. See *Spa* and *Day spa*.

Code of ethics A document listing the acceptable and encouraged moral behavior of members of a profession. Contrast with *Standards of practice*.

Communication skills The means of information exchange among people; includes verbal (i.e., speech and writing) and nonverbal (i.e., body language, facial expression, touch) methods. Compare to *Social skills*.

Compassion The awareness of the suffering of others coupled with the wish to relieve it; combines empathy with a dedication to service to others. See *Empathy* and *Emotional intelligence*.

Competencies An educational term referring to applications of knowledge and skills essential to the practice of a profession; define education in terms of what a practitioner can actually do, rather than just having completed a number of hours in certain subjects. See *Accreditation*.

Competitive advantage A marketing concept that identifies the reasons customers would come to someone for a service or product instead of going elsewhere; competitive advantage factors for massage therapists include quality, expertise, price, location, selection or variety, level of service, convenience, and environment. See *Marketing*.

Complementary and alternative medicine CAM therapies are healing systems or modalities considered outside of mainstream allopathic medicine, for example, herbal remedies, acupuncture, naturopathic medicine, biofeedback, chiropractic, and massage therapy.

Concentration The ability to sustain attention on something for a period of time; length of time for concentration before being distracted is called attention span; can be improved with practice. See *Meditation*.

Confidentiality A principle based on the understanding and trust that one person will not divulge private information about others without their permission; based on a person's right to privacy; enforced by law for health professionals. See *HIPAA*.

Conflict resolution A social skill used in solving problems or differences between two people or groups; options for resolution include collaboration, accommodation, compromise, avoidance, and force. See *Social skills*.

Consumer Someone who pays money for goods or services for his or her own use; also called customer.

Continuing education Education beyond entry-level training in an occupation or profession; often needed for license or certification renewal.

Continuing notes A form of documentation that records the session-by-session history of a client's visits. See *SOAP notes*.

Contract A legal agreement between two or more people; may be verbal or written; the terms of a contract may be upheld in court if one party breaches or violates the agreement; lawsuits arise when agreements are either not clear or have not been kept.

Copyright Laws that protect written, musical, and artistic works from unauthorized use; designated by the symbol ©; copyrights are administered in the United States by the U.S. Copyright Office at the Library of Congress in Washington, D.C. Compare to *Patent* and *Trademark*.

Countertransference A psychological phenomenon that occurs when a therapist transfers negative or positive feelings toward someone in his or her past into the therapeutic relationship; can lead to misunderstanding and unethical behavior. Contrast with *Transference*.

Courtesy Polite behavior that is expected in social situations; shows respect for others and exhibits thoughtfulness about their feelings, comfort, and safety; good manners.

CPT codes Medical codes used to process insurance claims; acronym for current procedural terminology.

Credential Refers to a title, certificate, or other form of recognition that testifies to the accomplishments of the person holding it; allows others to evaluate a person's background in a given field; is awarded by a school, organization, or government agency to a person meeting their criteria for the credential.

Critical thinking A higher-level thinking process that aims to discover the truth about something; weighs reasons to believe against reasons to doubt; looks for objective evidence, confirmation of claims, errors, distortions, false information, and exaggerations; looks beneath the surface for authenticity and honesty; takes into consideration the thinker's own prejudices and beliefs. See *Intellectual skills*.

Cruise ship spa A type of day spa located on a cruise ship; caters to vacationers. See *Spa* and *Day spa*.

Day spa A type of spa in which patrons come for one or more services, staying a short time or an entire day. See *Spa*.

Deceptive advertising Advertising that misleads the public about the nature of goods or services offered for sale and their benefits, prices, or credentials; violates values of honesty and integrity; violates consumer protections laws.

Defamation A legal term for injury to a person or an organization's reputation; known as libel if written and as slander if spoken.

Defense mechanisms Behaviors or thoughts that help people cope with unwanted feelings like fear, anxiety, guilt, and anger; common types are projection, denial, repression, displacement, and resistance; often unconscious.

Demonstrations A method of presentation that shows an audience how something is done or how something works by actually performing the action while giving a verbal description or explanation. Contrast with *Explanation* and *Persuasion*.

Destination spa A type of spa with overnight accommodations that immerses guests in a healthy environment, including fitness activities, nutritious meals, lifestyle education, and day spa services. See *Spa*. Contrast with *Day spa*.

Diploma A document that states that a specific person has successfully completed a course of study; also called certificate of completion; typically designates the school name, location, course of study, number of hours completed, and date of graduation, and is signed by school officials. Contrast with *Transcript*.

Discharge notes A form of documentation containing a final summary of a client's progress, and any comments about the course of treatment. See *Documentation*.

Documentation The process of writing session records for future reference; also called note-taking or charting; may refer to the documents themselves; kept on paper or in electronic form. Compare to *SOAP notes*.

Dual relationship Refers to the existence of other social or professional connections between a client and a massage therapist in addition to the therapeutic relationship; examples are clients who are also family members, friends, coworkers, neighbors, fellow club members, service providers, or any other additional relationship. See *Therapeutic relationship*.

Duties Obligations to act in a particular way; responsibilities that arise out of being in a certain position in relationship to others, or as the result of some action. Compare to *Rights*.

Emerging profession A profession in which some of the hallmarks of a mature profession are still in development. See *Profession*.

Emotional intelligence Defined by a set of skills related to five domains: knowing one's emotions, managing emotions, motivating oneself, recognizing emotions in others, and handling relationships; works with intellectual and physical skills for full maturity and success as a professional.

Empathy Recognizing emotions in others; the basis for creating rapport and the root of caring. Compare to *Compassion*.

Employee A person who works for an employer who controls when, where, and how the employee performs the work; defined by IRS and U.S. Labor Laws. Contrast with *Self-employment* and *Independent contractor*.

Endorsements Anecdotes from others besides the advertiser about how well a product or service worked for them; reflects the opinions, beliefs, findings, or experience of parties other than the sponsoring advertiser; also called *testimonials*.

Enthusiasm An aspect of the work ethic that means having a positive attitude and exhibiting keen interest and eagerness for your work and studies. See *Work ethic*.

Estimated tax Payments paid to the IRS quarterly (four times a year) based on the amount of income tax expected to be owed at the end of the year; similar to withholding for employment income; estimated tax payments should appear on the annual budget as an expense. See *Income tax*.

Ethical decision-making model A step-by-step process of thinking through an ethical question or ethical dilemma; involves critical thinking and problem solving; takes into consideration both external and internal standards in making an ethical choice of action.

Ethical dilemmas A type of ethical question in which two or more principles are in conflict and where something of value will be compromised regardless of the choice of action; involves selecting the lesser harm or greater good. See *Ethical questions*.

Ethical judgment Consistency in making good ethical decisions; strengthened by awareness, learning, and experience; improves with critical thinking and evaluating results.

Ethical questions Problems related to the morality of certain actions; require judgment to determine the most ethical choice. See *Ethical decision-making model*.

Ethical standards Statements designating the generally accepted and encouraged moral behavior of members of a profession; appear as codes of ethics and standards of practice documents developed by professional associations.

Ethics The study of the nature of moral behavior, of right and wrong; based on values, duties, and rights; examines choices for behavior, and uses a decision-making process to determine the degree of morality of certain actions. See *Professional ethics* and *Business ethics*.

Explanations A method of presentation using verbal descriptions to tell the what, how, and/or why of something. Contrast with *Demonstration* and *Persuasion*.

Explicit agreements Understandings between people that are spoken or written; agreements that are in the open and can be verified. Contrast with *Implicit agreements*.

Fiduciary A legal term used to describe a relationship in which person A has placed a special trust in person B, who is then obligated to watch out for person A's best interests.

First impressions The thoughts, beliefs, and feelings about others formed immediately upon meeting them for the first time.

First-year budget A document that forecasts income and expenses for the initial 12 months of operation of a business or practice. See *Startup costs*.

Fixed costs Expenses incurred whether a massage therapist sees clients or not, for example, rent and utilities; sometimes called overhead. See *First-year budget*. Contrast with *Variable costs*.

Form 1040 An IRS form used to file U.S. income taxes for individuals; covers both employment and self-employment; a summary form to which other forms and schedules are attached; must be filed annually by April 15.

Full time Work earning most or all of your income in one job or occupation; for massage therapists full time is 15–20 clients per week or working 4–5 days in employment, or some comparable combination. Contrast with *Part time*.

Gait analysis The examination of biomechanics while walking or running; looks at normal gait and deviations from normal; used to collect information for goal-oriented planning. See *Biomechanics*.

General membership organization An organization that welcomes practitioners of different forms of massage and bodywork; can be further categorized into *professional associations* and *member services organizations*. Contrast with *Specialty association*.

Goal-oriented planning A type of session planning that focuses on meeting specific client needs, rather than giving a standardized massage routine; client goals provide the focal point for organizing massage sessions and choosing appropriate techniques. See *Session planning*.

Graduate masseuse and **graduate masseur** Historical titles used in early 20th century Europe and North America for massage practitioners trained in a school, as opposed to someone who learned massage by apprenticeship or on the job; served as a kind of credential.

Grounded Refers to having a connection or being rooted to the earth through the legs and feet; the meaning can be extended to having a stable base and connection to a foundation whether standing or sitting. Compare to *Centered*.

Guarantee A promise that something will work as stated, usually with the implication that the money charged will be refunded if it does not. Contrast with *Endorsement*.

Health care settings Places where patients are treated for illnesses and injuries.

Health service operator A historical term used in early to mid-20th century North America in the YMCA for practitioners trained in physical therapeutics or physiotherapy; included massage, hydrotherapy, electrotherapy, light, relaxation techniques, and exercise; goals focused on health, fitness, and general well-being.

HIPAA An acronym for Health Information Portability and Accountability Act of 1996; outlines privacy rules for accessibility and security of client medical records. See *Confidentiality*.

Home visit practice Refers to a massage therapy business in which the massage therapist travels to clients' homes to provide massage; convenient for clients.

Hospital-based massage A specialty in which massage is integrated into the regular hospital setting such as in the pediatric ward, cancer unit, or cardiac care.

Implicit agreements Understandings between people that may be unspoken and unwritten; agreements assumed or taken for granted. Contrast with *Explicit agreements*.

Income goal Part of a business plan that specifies the desired net income for a projected annual budget. See *Business plan*.

Income tax A tax paid to a government based on income from employment and/or profits from a business; taxable income from a private practice equals gross income minus qualified business expenses; tips are considered taxable income; U.S. income tax is filed annually with the Internal Revenue Service on form 1040. See *Self-employment tax*.

Independent contractor A form of self-employment in which a person performs services for another person or business, but is not an employee; is contracted to accomplish a certain result, but is not under the direct control of an employer. See *Self-employment*. Contrast with *Employee*.

Informed voluntary consent A process used to get the client's permission to touch areas of the body that may have sexual associations or areas out of the scope of general care; involves permission by the client who exercises his or her right to self-determination. See *Rights*.

Intake The process of gathering relevant information from a new client. See *Interview skills*.

Intake note A type of documentation that includes the client's stated reason for massage or complaint, related subjective and objective information, agreed-upon long-term goals, and a general plan. See *Long-term planning* and *Documentation*.

Integrative medicine center A health-care facility that offers a team approach to the treatment of illness and injury; includes a variety of Western medical health care providers, traditional and indigenous healers, and CAM practitioners in a collaborative effort.

Intellectual skills Thinking or cognitive abilities; six levels identified by educators include knowledge, comprehension, application, analysis, synthesis, and evaluation.

Intervention model A process used to address sexual misconduct or suspected misconduct by clients; steps include stopping the session, describing the behavior of concern, asking for clarification, restating professional boundaries, evaluating the client's response, deciding whether to proceed or not, and documenting the situation. See *Sexual misconduct*.

Interview skills Communication skills used to elicit useful information from clients; used in initial client interviews and taking health histories. See *Intake note*.

Introduction A social process in which one person presents another person to a third person giving some basic information like name and other relevant facts; also self-introduction to another person. See *Social skills*.

Intuition A direct perception of the truth, independent of any rational process; lets us respond to our environment without calling rational problem solving into play; related to instinct.

Laws Rules of conduct established by governmental bodies at the local, state, and federal levels to protect the public from harm or to ensure fair practices; violations of law are determined by a judge or by trial, and are punishable by fines, community service, or time in jail.

Listening Making a conscious effort to hear what someone is trying to communicate; allows you to gather information, understand others better, and take in new ideas; helps build good relationships. See *Active listening* and *Affirmative listening*.

Logo A symbol or graphic that identifies a person or business at a glance; can be original artwork or clip art in the public domain; if original, can be registered as a trademark for protection of use. See *Trademarks*.

Long-term planning A form of goal-oriented planning in which the goal is to accomplish a client's specific health objectives over a series of massage sessions; long term refers to more than one massage session, or the interval between an initial session and a progress session to check the extent to which goals have been reached. See *Goal-oriented planning*.

Manipulator A historical term for massage practitioner used in the early 20th century in the United States.

Manual therapy Refers to healing methods applied with the therapist's hands touching or moving the recipient's body.

Market research The process of collecting relevant information for identifying and reaching potential customers. See *Marketing*.

Marketing The process of identifying potential customers or clients, and meeting their needs and wants. See *Market research*.

Massage The intentional and systematic manipulation of the soft tissues of the body to enhance health and healing; joint movements and stretching are commonly performed as part of massage; adjunct modalities within the scope of massage include the use of hot and cold packs, and hydrotherapy in the form of whirlpool bath, sauna, and steam room.

Massage and bodywork Terms often used together to describe the occupational field of massage therapy.

Massage establishment license A business license to operate a commercial space where customers come for massage; typically requires revealing the owner(s) identities, detailing hygiene and safety standards, posting services and prices, and affirming that all practitioners in the establishment have the required occupational licenses. Contrast with *Business license*.

Massage operator A historical term for massage practitioner in the early 20th century United States.

Massage therapy A general term used to refer to all of the different systems of soft tissue manipulation, and for all health and healing practices based on touch and movement; sometimes used synonymously with the term *bodywork*.

Masseur The historical French term used in 20th century Europe and North America for a male massage therapist.

Masseuse The historical French term used in 20th century Europe and North America for a woman massage therapist; corrupted in mid-20th century United States by association with prostitution.

Mechanotherapy A historical term used in early 20th century Europe and North America for a tradition of bodywork also known as medical gymnastics and physical therapeutics; cure of diseases through movement including active and passive exercises; sometimes used machines to perform movements.

Medical gymnast A historical term used in late 19th and early 20th century Europe and North America for a practitioner trained in medical gymnastics or Swedish movement cure; used active and passive movements to treat disease.

Medical spa A type of spa that integrates spa services with conventional and complementary therapies for healing mind and body. See *Spa*.

Meditation A practice designed to improve the ability to concentrate or pay focused attention; basic meditation technique involves choosing something like a word or object to place attention on, and when the mind wanders, bringing it back to the object of attention. See *Concentration*.

Member services organization A general membership organization whose major mission is to provide benefits like professional liability insurance, group health insurance, publications, information of interest to their members, and may also promote the interests of members related to licensing and legislation; may be non-profit or for-profit corporation. Contrast with *Professional association*.

Mineral spring spa A type of spa located at a natural mineral or hot springs site that uses the spring water in treatments offered. See *Spa*.

Mission statement A part of the vision outlined in a business plan that defines the purpose of the business and the main strategy for achieving competitive advantage; states the focus of the business. See *Vision* and *Competitive advantage*.

Multiple-choice questions Inquiries that give clients a choice of descriptors in answer to a question; gives clients choices that they might not have thought of themselves and have meaning for the interviewer. See *Interview skills*. Contrast with *Open-ended questions* and *Rating scale*.

National certification Refers to a credential given by a non-governmental nonprofit organization that attests to a person's competency in a given profession; usually involves qualifying by education and/or experience, passing a written examination and/or performance evaluation, and abiding by a code of ethics; is renewed periodically and usually requires a certain amount of continuing education; sometimes referred to as *board certification*.

Naturopathic physician's office A health care facility offering naturopathic medicine. See *Complementary and alternative medicine*.

Objective information Refers to what the practitioner observes about the client during goal-oriented planning; includes observations, qualitative and quantitative measurements, and results of orthopedic tests; written in O section of *SOAP notes*.

Observation The act of noticing a client's condition using the eyes, ears, nose, and hands; used to collect information for goal-oriented planning. See *Objective information*.

Occupational licensing Permission granted to qualified practitioners to accept compensation for massage in a specific governmental jurisdiction; is awarded by the government agency that regulates professions in the jurisdiction; is required to practice.

On-site massage practice Refers to a massage therapy business in which the massage therapist goes to a workplace or public location outside of his or her office to provide massage to clients; convenient for clients; often seated or chair massage. Contrast with *Home visit practice*.

Open-ended questions Inquiries that steer clients to specific topics, but leave space for them to answer in their own words; rather than dictating the form of response, the inter-

viewer listens to what the client has to say in answer to a simple question. See *Interview skills*. Contrast with *Multiple-choice questions* and *Rating scales*.

Optimism An aspect of emotional intelligence that means expecting that things will turn out all right in the end, despite setbacks and difficulties; an optimistic attitude helps a person when the going gets rough; opposite of pessimism or expecting failure. See *Emotional intelligence*.

Orthopedic tests Methods of assessing pathology in musculoskeletal structures, movement and locomotor disorders, and sources of soft tissue pain and dysfunction; used to gather objective information in treatment planning. See *Objective information*.

Paidotribe A historical term for the trainers in the ancient Greek gymnasium; served in many capacities including coach, nutritionist, masseur, physiotherapist, and hygienist.

Palpation The act of sensing information about the client through touch; is about the "feel" of tissues and of movement at joints; used to collect objective information for goal-oriented planning. See *Objective information*.

Part time Earning a portion of your income from a particular job or occupation; for a massage therapist, part time ranges anywhere from 1–10 clients per week, or one or two days or nights at place of employment, or some comparable combination.

Passive range of motion (PROM) Refers to the evaluation of motion at a joint while it is passively moved through its range by a therapist; observations include degree of motion possible, restrictions or shortening, and any discomfort experienced; used to collect objective information for *goal-oriented planning*. Contrast with *Active range of motion*.

Patents Legal protections for inventions, and include utility and design patents; administered by the U.S. Patent and Trademark Office; patented inventions may not be copied by others for sale. Compare to *Copyright* and *Trademark*.

Peer-reviewed publications Professional journals in which a panel of experts in the subject evaluates each article for accuracy, reviews any research for validity, and approves each article for publication; more rigorous process than editorial review.

Personal boundary A limit established by a person to maintain his or her own integrity, comfort, or well-being. See *Boundary, Boundary crossing,* and *Boundary violation*.

Personal care settings Provide personal grooming, relaxation, and rejuvenation services to patrons. Compare to *Spa*.

Personal temptation An attraction to unethical actions. Contrast with *Ethical dilemma* and *Ethical question*.

Persuasion A method of presentation in which the goal is to convince an audience to behave a certain way, take a specific course of action, agree on a particular solution to a problem, or accept a certain fact or belief. Contrast with *Explanation* and *Demonstration*.

Physical fitness Refers to optimal function of the physical body; elements include cardiovascular fitness, muscular strength and endurance, flexibility, and body composition.

Physcultopathist A historical term used in the early 20th century United States for a medical gymnast trained in Bernarr Macfadden's School of Physical Culture.

Plan Refers to the activities and applications chosen to achieve results for meeting client goals; a final step in goal-oriented planning; written in P section of *SOAP notes*.

Policies Rules set down to guide the operation of a business or practice; practice policies for massage therapists include pricing, late arrivals, missed appointments, conduct, and confidentiality.

Posture analysis The evaluation of body alignment; evaluation of standing, sitting, and sleeping postures; used to collect information for goal-oriented planning. Contrast with *Gait analysis*.

Power differential Refers to the difference in authority between a massage therapist and a client in the therapeutic relationship; massage therapists have more power in the relationship by virtue of training, experience, and perception of greater authority. See *Therapeutic relationship*.

Practice clients Family and friends of students who agree to allow students of massage to practice techniques on them; a type of dual relationship; special type of client for whom professional boundaries and ethical considerations apply.

Practice identity The part of a business plan that creates the image you project to the world; includes business name and logo, credentials, résumé, business cards and stationary, website, dress, and office decoration.

Private practice Refers to self-employment as a heath care practitioner; combines both the business and professional sides of being a practitioner. See *Self-employment*.

Problem solving A systematic approach to finding a solution to a problem using critical thinking skills; starting point is some issue, question, or dilemma for which there are choices for responding; time and effort are taken to gather information needed to make an informed choice or formulate a solution; information gathered is analyzed and evaluated, and finally a solution is determined. See *Intellectual skills*.

Profession Refers to an occupation with a higher level of organization, standards, and ethical conduct; sometimes refers to any highly skilled occupation or trade.

Professional associations Nonprofit organizations run by elected leadership, whose mission is to promote their profession, to represent their members and the profession in the larger world, to offer services to members, and to set standards; typically have an IRS designation as 501(c)(6) corporations (United States) (i.e., nonprofit professional association). Contrast with *Member services organization*.

Professional boundaries Limits that clarify the nature of the therapeutic relationship and the roles of massage therapist and client; five types of professional boundaries are physical, emotional, intellectual, sexual, and energetic. Compare to *Personal boundaries*.

Professional ethics The study of moral behavior relative to a specific occupation. Contrast with *Busness ethics*.

Professional image Projecting a professional presence in dress, grooming, posture, and language; identifies a person as someone clients can have confidence in and trust; should be clean, neat, modest, and appropriate for the work setting.

Professionalism A state of mind, a way of being, knowing, and doing that reflects a sense of being individuals who value their work and hold themselves to the highest standards of their occupations. See *Professional image*.

Progress notes A form of documentation used for special sessions that reevaluate a client's progress related to his or her long-term goals; contain more assessment information than regular session notes, and may identify new goals and plans. See *Goal-oriented planning* and *SOAP notes*.

Promotions Methods to encourage people to act to buy goods or services; includes discounts, specials, and gift certificates. Contrast with *Advertising*.

PSOAP A variation of a SOAP note that separates the problem, complaint, or referral diagnosis into the first P section; recommended if one routinely accepts referrals from health care providers. See *SOAP notes*.

Psychotherapy A health profession that treats problems and disorders related to the mind and emotions; sometimes referred to as "talk therapy"; outside of the scope of practice of massage therapists.

Punctuality An aspect of work ethic that means showing up for work on time or early. See *Work ethic*.

Qualifying statements Explanations that accompany claims for a product or service and identify the source of information for the claim; sources may include reading, logic, experience, hearsay, or scientific research. See *Business ethics*.

Rating scales Rough measurements of things from the client's subjective view; use numbers to measure the degree or level of the client's experience of some factor related to their goals; example: a scale from 1 to 10. See *Interview skills*. Contrast with *Multiple-choice questions* and *Open-ended questions*.

Reconstruction aide A historical term for a practitioner trained to help rehabilitate wounded soldiers using corrective exercise and massage; antecedent of physical therapists; active in early 20th century during and after World War I.

Reliability An aspect of a work ethic that means people can depend on you to do what you say you are going to do, when you are supposed to do it; if you are reliable, people will have trust and confidence in you. See *Work ethic*.

Resort/hotel spa A type of spa located within a resort or hotel facility; caters to business and vacation travelers. See *Spa*.

Résumé A document that provides a summary of training, experience, and credentials in an occupation or profession; used to present qualifications for a job, volunteer position, or whenever a summary of past accomplishments is required; also known as CV (curriculum vitae).

Rights Claims to certain treatment or to protection from certain treatment; expected to be honored by others, and enforced by standards or laws if necessary. Compare to *Duties*.

Rubber A historical term used in early 20th century Europe and North America for an unschooled massage practitioner who gave rubdowns to athletes; learned their skills on the job, or from other rubbers. See *Athlete masseur.*

Salary draw The money taken out of a business or practice monthly for the owner's personal use. See *First-year budget.*

Schedule C An IRS income tax form that reports small business income and expenses; attaches to *Form 1040.*

Scope of practice Refers to the legally allowed or professionally defined methods used by a certain profession; limits what a professional may or may not do; may include intention as well as techniques; massage falls within the scope of several health professions.

Self-awareness An aspect of emotional intelligence that involves recognizing a feeling as it happens and its accompanying emotion or impulse to act. See *Emotional intelligence.*

Self-care Refers to nurturing one's own well-being, while fulfilling career goals and being of service to clients; holistic self-care involves the whole person—body, mind, emotions, and spirit.

Self-disclosure Revealing personal information about the self; self-disclosure by a therapist can be a boundary crossing in the therapeutic relationship. See *Professional boundaries.*

Self-employment Operating a business as a sole proprietor or independent contractor; a person is his or her own employer; called being in private practice for a massage therapist. Contrast with *Employee.*

Self-employment tax (SE tax) Social Security and Medicare tax for self-employed individuals; applies to Social Security coverage for retirement, disability, survivor, and Medicare benefits; SE tax must be paid if net earnings from self-employment are $400 or more; SE tax is in addition to the regular income tax. See *Income tax.*

Self-reflection Aspect of critical thinking that takes into consideration the thinker's own prejudices and beliefs in determining the truth about something. See *Critical thinking.*

Service A value in which we hold our clients' well-being above our own desire for money, power, and worldly recognition; means that the primary motivation for being a massage therapist is to help people achieve their personal wellness goals.

Session planning The logical process of thinking through a specific massage session; includes collecting relevant information, assessing the situation and setting goals, choosing massage applications, performing the massage, and evaluating results. See *Goal-oriented planning.*

Sexual misconduct Refers to any sexualizing of the relationship between a massage therapist and a current client; can occur before, after, or during a massage session, and can be perpetrated by the massage therapist or by the client; forms of sexual misconduct range from those involving speech and body language to inappropriate touch to sexual contact to sexual assault. See *Intervention model.*

Simplified notes Forms of documentation that contain minimum information; used at venues like health fairs, trade shows, sports events, and outreach events where people receive a short, standard massage routine and will not be seen again by the practitioner. See *Documentation.*

Skilled touch Refers to abilities related to physical contact; four dimensions important to massage therapists include contact, qualities, communication, and palpation.

SOAP notes A standard form for documenting therapeutic sessions; SOAP is an acronym for subjective, objective, assessment, and plan. See *Documentation.*

Sobardoras Traditional Hispanic healers trained by apprenticeship to use massage in treating ailments; also use ritual, herbal remedies, and bone-setting manipulation techniques; part of the healing tradition of *curanderas.*

Social skills Methods of interacting with other people that promote harmony, understanding, and connection, while peacefully solving problems like disagreements, misunderstandings, and reconciliation after harm done; primary goal is building good relationships. Compare to *Communication skills.*

Sole proprietor A form of self-employment in which a person is the legally recognized business owner, the employer and employee combined. See *Self-employment.*

SOTAP A form of documentation for therapeutic sessions; variation of SOAP notes; acronym for subjective, objective, treatment, assessment, and plan; provides a separate T section for recording the massage and related techniques used in the session. Contrast with *SOAP notes* and *PSOAP.*

Spa Refers to a business that offers personal care services in an environment that focuses on overall well-being and renewal of mind, body, and spirit; emphasis on natural therapies and spa treatments using natural substances.

Specialty associations Organizations composed of practitioners of a particular style of massage or bodywork, or those who work in a particular setting. Contrast with *General membership organization.*

Specialty certification Refers to certification in a specific massage and bodywork system; involves some combination of education, skill development, internship, written and performance tests, ethical code, continuing education, and/or periodic renewal. See *Certification.*

Sports, fitness, and recreation settings Facilities whose main purpose is to provide opportunities for physical exercise and sports, but which also provide support services like massage.

Sports medicine center Refers to a rehabilitation facility specializing in athletic injuries and improvement of sports performance. See *Integrative medicine center.*

Standards of practice Documents describing the accepted and encouraged moral behavior of members of a profession; more detailed than a *code of ethics.*

Startup costs The initial expenses involved in setting up a business like a massage therapy practice. See *First-year budget.*

Subjective information Refers to what clients report to the therapist during goal-oriented planning; includes complaints and comments about their conditions and how they feel; written in S section of *SOAP notes.* Contrast with *Objective information.*

Substantiated claims Claims for a product or service that have a credible basis or evidence in their support; unsubstantiated claims for products or services are illegal according to consumer protection laws. See *Qualifying statements.*

Swedish massage A type of Western massage that combines massage techniques with joint movements and hydrotherapy; outgrowth of Ling's Swedish movement cure and Metzger's massage; first popularized in the early 20th century in salons; colleges of Swedish massage trained graduate masseurs and masseuses in the 1930s–40s. See *Western massage* and *Swedish masseuse.*

Swedish masseuse A historical term for a woman trained in Swedish massage and movements, reducing massage, nutrition, exercise, and hydrotherapy facilities; worked in salons in early to mid-20th century United States.

Telltack A historical term used in 19th and 20th century Middle East, Near East, Europe, and North America for a practitioner of a vigorous type of bodywork given at the Turkish baths or hammam.

Therapeutic relationship The fundamental relationship between a massage therapist and client in which each has a specific role to play; elements of a healthy therapeutic relationship include clarity about the nature of the relationship, understanding of individual roles within the relationship, and establishing clear boundaries related to roles. See *Professional boundaries.*

Time management A personal skill of scheduling daily and weekly activities to reflect personal priorities; involves identifying goals and priorities for a certain period of time and plotting a schedule accordingly; includes keeping to the schedule developed.

Tips Gratuities (i.e., given in gratitude) over and above the cost of a service; given directly to the person providing the service; given at the discretion of the person receiving the service; are taxable income reported to the IRS on income tax forms. See *Income tax.*

Trademarks Offer exclusive use of a name or symbol to identify unique goods and services; use the symbol ™ or ® for registered trademarks; distinguish a particular brand or company from others; handled by the U.S. Patent and Trademark Office in Washington, D.C.; may also be regulated on the state (United States) or provincial (Canada) level. Compare to *Copyright* and *Patent.*

Transcript A detailed record of a student's performance while in school, including specific subjects studied, grades, attendance, date of graduation, honors, school information, and other facts; an original transcript carrying the school seal is usually required for official purposes like obtaining a license to practice. Contrast with *Diploma.*

Transference A psychological phenomenon that occurs when a client transfers negative or positive feelings toward someone in their past into the therapeutic relationship; can lead to misunderstanding and problems in the therapeutic relationship. Contrast with *Countertransference.*

Treatment planning A form of goal-oriented planning in which the goal is alleviation of symptoms, or facilitation of healing of a pathological condition; used for medical, clinical,

and orthopedic massage applications; sometimes called a *plan of care*. See *Goal-oriented planning.*

Triptai A historical term used in ancient Greece for someone who specialized in rubbing; massage has been called the *anatriptic art; a*natriptic meant to "rub up" or toward the body's center.

Values Principles, traits, or qualities considered worthwhile or desirable; protected by ethical standards and codes of ethics. See *Ethics.*

Variable costs Fluctuating operating expenses that depend on the number of clients seen; examples: laundry and massage supplies. See *First-year budget*. Contrast with *Fixed costs.*

Verbal skills The ability to communicate by means of the spoken word; includes good articulation and voice quality; delivery of spoken word more important than content in some cases. See *Communication skills.*

Vision An element of a business plan that describes the broad scope of the proposed business; for a massage practice, it would include mission, size, format, location, and income goals.

Voice quality An aspect of verbal communication that includes the pitch, tone, volume, clarity, and richness of the sound of someone's speech; can affect a person's image or how they are perceived by others. See *Verbal skills* and *Communication skills.*

Wellness center Refers to a facility that offers fitness activities, rehabilitation programs, massage therapy, and classroom instruction in preventing disease and developing a healthy lifestyle; often connected to a hospital.

Wellness Massage Pyramid (WMP) A model for understanding the possible contributions of massage therapy to high-level wellness; pyramid levels from the base to the top are treatment, recovery, prevention, neutral zone, health maintenance, personal growth, and life enjoyment.

Wellness profession A profession or occupation with a scope of practice that spans the breadth of the wellness model, from treatment and recovery to personal growth and life enjoyment; focus is on attaining high-level wellness.

Western massage A form of soft tissue manipulation and related techniques developed in Europe and the United States over the past 200 years; technique categories commonly used to describe Western massage are effleurage, petrissage, tapotement, friction, vibration, touch without movement, and joint movements. See *Massage and Swedish massage.*

Work ethic An attitude that positions one's job as a high priority in life and that promotes applying oneself to high-quality performance; taking pride in one's work.

Written correspondence A form of communication that utilizes basic writing skills such as correct spelling, punctuation, grammar, sentence construction, and organization of thought; forms include memos, e-mail, and business letters.

Zoning ordinance A local law that specifies what type of housing or what kind of business can be in a certain location. Contrast with *Massage establishment license.*

Index

Page numbers in *italics* represent figures.

Pearson Education, Inc.

YOU SHOULD CAREFULLY READ THE TERMS AND CONDITIONS BEFORE USING THE CD-ROM PACKAGE. USING THIS CD-ROM PACKAGE INDICATES YOUR ACCEPTANCE OF THESE TERMS AND CONDITIONS.

Pearson Education, Inc. provides this program and licenses its use. You assume responsibility for the selection of the program to achieve your intended results, and for the installation, use, and results obtained from the program. This license extends only to use of the program in the United States or countries in which the program is marketed by authorized distributors.

LICENSE GRANT

You hereby accept a nonexclusive, nontransferable, permanent license to install and use the program ON A SINGLE COMPUTER at any given time. You may copy the program solely for backup or archival purposes in support of your use of the program on the single computer. You may not modify, translate, disassemble, decompile, or reverse engineer the program, in whole or in part.

TERM

The License is effective until terminated. Pearson Education, Inc. reserves the right to terminate this License automatically if any provision of the License is violated. You may terminate the License at any time. To terminate this License, you must return the program, including documentation, along with a written warranty stating that all copies in your possession have been returned or destroyed.

LIMITED WARRANTY

THE PROGRAM IS PROVIDED "AS IS" WITHOUT WARRANTY OF ANY KIND, EITHER EXPRESSED OR IMPLIED, INCLUDING, BUT NOT LIMITED TO, THE IMPLIED WARRANTIES OR MERCHANTABILITY AND FITNESS FOR A PARTICULAR PURPOSE. THE ENTIRE RISK AS TO THE QUALITY AND PERFORMANCE OF THE PROGRAM IS WITH YOU. SHOULD THE PROGRAM PROVE DEFECTIVE, YOU (AND NOT PRENTICE-HALL, INC. OR ANY AUTHORIZED DEALER) ASSUME THE ENTIRE COST OF ALL NECESSARY SERVICING, REPAIR, OR CORRECTION. NO ORAL OR WRITTEN INFORMATION OR ADVICE GIVEN BY PRENTICE-HALL, INC., ITS DEALERS, DISTRIBUTORS, OR AGENTS SHALL CREATE A WARRANTY OR INCREASE THE SCOPE OF THIS WARRANTY.

SOME STATES DO NOT ALLOW THE EXCLUSION OF IMPLIED WARRANTIES, SO THE ABOVE EXCLUSION MAY NOT APPLY TO YOU. THIS WARRANTY GIVES YOU SPECIFIC LEGAL RIGHTS AND YOU MAY ALSO HAVE OTHER LEGAL RIGHTS THAT VARY FROM STATE TO STATE.

Pearson Education, Inc. does not warrant that the functions contained in the program will meet your requirements or that the operation of the program will be uninterrupted or error-free.

However, Pearson Education, Inc. warrants the diskette(s) or CD-ROM(s) on which the program is furnished to be free from defects in material and workmanship under normal use for a period of ninety (90) days from the date of delivery to you as evidenced by a copy of your receipt.

The program should not be relied on as the sole basis to solve a problem whose incorrect solution could result in injury to person or property. If the program is employed in such a manner, it is at the user's own risk and Pearson Education, Inc. explicitly disclaims all liability for such misuse.

LIMITATION OF REMEDIES

Pearson Education, Inc.'s entire liability and your exclusive remedy shall be:

1. the replacement of any diskette(s) or CD-ROM(s) not meeting Pearson Education, Inc.'s "LIMITED WARRANTY" and that is returned to Pearson Education, or

2. if Pearson Education is unable to deliver a replacement diskette(s) or CD-ROM(s) that is free of defects in materials or workmanship, you may terminate this agreement by returning the program.

IN NO EVENT WILL PRENTICE-HALL, INC. BE LIABLE TO YOU FOR ANY DAMAGES, INCLUDING ANY LOST PROFITS, LOST SAVINGS, OR OTHER INCIDENTAL OR CONSEQUENTIAL DAMAGES ARISING OUT OF THE USE OR INABILITY TO USE SUCH PROGRAM EVEN IF PRENTICE-HALL, INC. OR AN AUTHORIZED DISTRIBUTOR HAS BEEN ADVISED OF THE POSSIBILITY OF SUCH DAMAGES, OR FOR ANY CLAIM BY ANY OTHER PARTY.

SOME STATES DO NOT ALLOW FOR THE LIMITATION OR EXCLUSION OF LIABILITY FOR INCIDENTAL OR CONSEQUENTIAL DAMAGES, SO THE ABOVE LIMITATION OR EXCLUSION MAY NOT APPLY TO YOU.

GENERAL

You may not sublicense, assign, or transfer the license of the program. Any attempt to sublicense, assign or transfer any of the rights, duties, or obligations hereunder is void.

This Agreement will be governed by the laws of the State of New York.

Should you have any questions concerning this Agreement, you may contact Pearson Education, Inc. by writing to:

Director of New Media
Higher Education Division
Pearson Education, Inc.
One Lake Street
Upper Saddle River, NJ 07458

Should you have any questions concerning technical support, you may contact:

Product Support Department: Monday–Friday 8:00 A.M. –8:00 P.M. and Sunday 5:00 P.M.-12:00 A.M. (All times listed are Eastern). 1-800-677-6337

You can also get support by filling out the web form located at http://247.prenhall.com

YOU ACKNOWLEDGE THAT YOU HAVE READ THIS AGREEMENT, UNDERSTAND IT, AND AGREE TO BE BOUND BY ITS TERMS AND CONDITIONS. YOU FURTHER AGREE THAT IT IS THE COMPLETE AND EXCLUSIVE STATEMENT OF THE AGREEMENT BETWEEN US THAT SUPERSEDES ANY PROPOSAL OR PRIOR AGREEMENT, ORAL OR WRITTEN, AND ANY OTHER COMMUNICATIONS BETWEEN US RELATING TO THE SUBJECT MATTER OF THIS AGREEMENT.